THE MAJOR SINS

CW00819313

Dar Al-Taqwa

Imam Shams ad-Din adh-Dhahabi

ISBN 978-1-870582-65-0

Translation: Aisha Bewley

Editors: Abdalhaqq Bewley and Muhammad Isa Waley

Cover desing by Mukhtar Sanders

Published by:
Dar Al Taqwa Ltd.
7A Melcombe Street
Baker Street
London NW1 6AE

Printed by:
IMAK OFFSET Printing Centre
T: 0090 212 656 49 97
F: 0099 212 656 29 29
www.imakofset.com.tr
isa@imakofset.com.tr

Contents

The author and *Kitab al-kaba'ir*   1

The Deadly Sins   3

1. Associating others with Allah   5
2. Murder   8
3. Sorcery   11
4. Neglect of the prayer   13
   Section: When a child should be ordered to pray   16
   Section: The punishment of the person who does
      the prayer like a pecking bird   19
   Section: Greater concern for attending the *'Isha'*
      and *Fajr* prayers   22
5. Refusing to pay *zakat*   23
6. Not fasting a day of Ramadan without a valid excuse   28
7. Not performing *hajj* when able to do so   29
8. Disrespect to parents   30
9. Shunning relatives   37
10. Fornication   40
11. Sodomy   45
   Section: The punishment of sodomites   47
   Section: anal intercourse with a woman is part
      of sodomy   48
12. Usury   50
13. Consuming the property of orphans and
      wronging them   53
14. Lying about Allah and His Messenger ﷺ   63
15. Fleeing from battle   59
16. A leader duping his followers and treating
      them unjustly   60
17. Pride   63
18. Perjury   65
19. Drinking alcohol   66
   Traditions from the Salaf about wine   70
   Section on hashish   70

20. Gambling 74
21. Slandering chaste women 77
22. Stealing from booty 79
23. Theft 82
24. Highway robbery 84
25. Deliberate false oaths 86
    Section: On swearing by other than Allah 87
26. Injustice 89
    Section: Being cautious about visiting the
        perpetrators of injustice 96
27. Tax Collecting 100
28. Consuming and receiving unlawful property 102
29. Suicide 106
30. Inveterate lying 108
31. Being corrupt in rendering judgement 111
32. Taking bribes for judgement 113
33. Women looking like men and men looking
        like women 114
34. Being a wittol 117
35. Marrying a woman to enable her to remarry
        her former husband 118
36. Not avoiding urine, something which the
        Christians are prone to 121
37. Showing-off 122
38. Teaching for the sake of this world and
        concealing knowledge 125
39. Treachery 128
40. Reminding people of one's charity 130
41. Denial of the Divine Decree 131
42. Eavesdropping on people and seeking out
        their secrets 136
43. Carrying tales 137
44. Cursing 140
    Section: On the permissibility of cursing those who
        disobey Allah 140
45. Perfidy and not fulfilling a promise 144
46. Believing soothsayers and astrologers 146
47. A wife disobeying her husband 148
48. Making images 154

49. Slapping, wailing, tearing garments, shaving the
        head, pulling out hair and lamenting loudly in
        a time of affliction   156
    Section on consoling   159
50. Transgression   166
51. Being overbearing towards the weak, slaves, girls,
        wives, and animals   168
52. Harming one's neighbours   174
53. Abusing and insulting other Muslims   176
    Section: Cautioning against inciting fights between
        believers and between animals of any kind   177
    Section: Encouraging reconciliation between people 177
54. Harming people and being overbearing
        towards them   180
55. Wearing waist-wrapper, robe, clothing and trousers
        long out of arrogance, pride and boastfulness   183
56. Men wearing silk and gold   185
57. Absconding by slaves   186
58. Slandering to other than Allah Almighty   187
59. Knowingly ascribing oneself falsely someone
        to other than one's real father   189
60. Argument, quarrelling and disputation   190
61. Denying spare water to others   193
62. Giving short weight and measure   194
63. Feeling secure from Allah's devising   196
64. Despairing of the mercy of Allah and losing hope   199
65. Abandoning the Group Prayer and praying alone
        without a valid excuse   200
66. Persisting in abandoning the Jumu'a and Group
        prayer without a valid excuse   201
67. Causing harm in bequests   205
68. Deceit and treachery   206
69. Spying on Muslims and pointing out their
        weak points   207
70. Insulting one of the Companions   208
Glossary   212
Index   217

iii

The author and *Kitab al-Kaba'ir*

The author's name is Shams ad-Din Muhammad ibn 'Uthman ibn Qaymaz at-Turmani al-Fariqi ad-Dimishqi ash-Shafi'i; he is commonly known as adh-Dhahabi.

His family originally came from Myafariqinayy, but he was born in Damascus in 673/1274. He studied with the shaykhs of Syria, Egypt and the Hijaz. He visited many cities for this purpose and was a recognised source in many fields of knowledge, especially with respect to the different recensions of the Qur'an and *hadith*. His memory was legendary. He is described as the imam of all others in respect of memory and also as the shaykh of analysis of narrators' character (*jarh wa ta'dil*). He was outstanding in every way and famous in all regions. Seekers of knowledge sought him out from every direction.

In an autobiographical note, adh-Dhahabi mentions thirteen hundred shaykhs from whom he took knowledge. He himself taught a large number of scholars, including a group of truly great scholars and famous writers. He held a number of teaching posts in Damascus and, when he went blind in 741 AH, he stopped writing altogether and, for the rest of his life he confined himself to teaching. He died on 3 Dhu al-Qa'da 748/1348. and was buried in the cemetery of al-Bab as-Saghir in Damascus.

Adh-Dhahabi left an ample legacy of knowledge which he recorded in the useful books he wrote, numbering about ninety in all and including works on *hadith*, history, biographies and other subjects. The largest of them is his great history *Ta'rikh al-Islam*. Other books include *Siyar an-nubula'*, *Mizan al-i'tidal*, *al-Mutashabih fi asma' ar-rijal*, and *Tajrid al-usul fi hadith ar-Rasul*. Many of these works are published and still in circulation.

Many writers, both old and modern, have discussed the books of adh-Dhahabi and have written a number of essays about him, both in Arabic other languages. All of them emphasise his knowledge and excellence and praise his scholarly legacy, which benefited the people of his time and those after them and succeeding generations down to our own time.

1

The present work *al-Kaba'ir* is one of the most important ones he wrote for ordinary readers. In it he deals with themes which are of great interest and benefit to them in both their *deen* and matters of this world, explaining matters which are less easy to understand in other books of knowledge written for specialist scholars and researchers.

In *al-Kaba'ir* adh-Dhahabi adopts the approach of a warning guide who seeks to correct people as regards their beliefs and lives and presents his material in easily understood language and in a clear attractive style. He avoids complexity, obscurity and artifices and his book is a useful source for speakers and preachers alike. By his words he awakens the heedless and bewildered, chides rebels and deviants, and guides those who desire to travel the path of Allah to the truth and to what is correct.

The Major Sins

In the Name of Allah the All-Merciful, Most Merciful

Praise be to Allah, the Lord of the worlds. There should be no aggression except against wrongdoers. Peace and blessings be on our master Muhammad, the Lord of the Messengers and Imam of the godfearing and on his family and all his Companions.

This is a book which contains a general discussion of the major wrong actions and forbidden things. Major wrong actions are those actions which Allah and His Messenger have forbidden in the Book, *Sunna* and through reports from the righteous Salaf. Allah has promised in His Mighty Book that avoiding major wrong actions and forbidden things will expiate minor bad actions, declaring:

"If you avoid the serious wrong actions you have been forbidden, We will erase your bad actions from you and admit you by a Gate of Honour." (4:31)

By this text Allah Almighty guarantees that anyone who avoids major wrong actions will enter the Garden.

Allah Almighty also says:

"Those who avoid major wrong actions and indecencies and who, when they are angered, then forgive." (42:37)

"To whoever avoids the major wrong actions and indecencies except for minor lapses, truly your Lord is immensely forgiving." (53:32)

The Messenger of Allah ﷺ said, "The five prayers, and *Jumu'a* to *Jumu'a*, and Ramadan to Ramadan, are expiation for everything between them if major wrong actions are avoided." (Muslim, at-Tirmidhi and Ibn Khuzayma)

It is therefore incumbent on us to investigate major wrong actions and learn what they are, so that we as Muslims may avoid them. We find that scholars disagree about how many of them there are. It is said that there are seven; so cite those who say as evidence the words of the Prophet ﷺ: "Avoid the seven deadly ones…" and he went on to mention associating others with Allah, sorcery, killing a soul which Allah has made sacrosanct except by legal right, consuming the property of orphans, practising usury, fleeing from the battlefield and slandering unaware chaste believing women. The *hadith* is agreed upon.

Ibn 'Abbas ؓ said, "There are more likely to be seventy than seven." By Allah, Ibn 'Abbas ؓ spoke the truth. The *hadith* does not include all major wrong actions. The fact is that if someone commits any wrong action for which there is a *hadd* punishment in this world – such as murder, fornication or theft – or any which have incurred a threat of Divine punishment, anger, or curse, indicated by a statement from our Prophet Muhammad ﷺ, it is considered a major wrong action.

It must be accepted that some major wrong actions are worse than others. Do you not see that the Prophet ﷺ counted *shirk* among the major wrong actions? – and we know that anyone who commits *shirk* will be in the Fire forever and will never be forgiven. Allah Almighty says:

"Allah does not forgive anything being associated with Him, but He forgives whomever He wills for anything else." (4:48)

1. Associating others with Allah

The worst of the major wrong actions is associating others with Allah Almighty, of which there are several categories. One of them is when a person treats something else as equal to Allah and worships something other than Him, be it a stone, a tree, the sun, the moon, a Prophet, shaykh, star, angel, or anything else. This is the greater *shirk* which Allah Almighty is alluding to when He says:

"Allah does not forgive anything being associated with Him, but He forgives whomever He wills for anything else." (4:48)

"Associating others with Him is a terrible wrong" (31:13)

"If anyone associates anything with Allah, Allah has forbidden him the Garden and his refuge will be the Fire." (5:72)

There are also many other *ayat*s which speak of it.

Anyone who associates others with Allah, and then dies while doing so, is absolutely one of the people of the Fire, just as anyone who believes in Allah and dies a believer is one of the people of the Garden, even if he is punished for a time in the Fire. It is reported in the *Sahih* that the Messenger of Allah ﷺ said three times, "Shall I inform you of the worst of the major wrong actions?" Those present answered, "Yes, Messenger of Allah." He said "Associating others with Allah and disobeying your parents." He was reclining and he sat up and then said, "False testimony, false testimony," and continued to repeat it until they said, "Would that he had been silent!" (al-Bukhari, Muslim and at-Tirmidhi) The Prophet ﷺ said, "Avoid the seven deadly ones," and among them he mentioned associating others with Allah. He ﷺ said, "If anyone changes his *deen*, kill him." (al-Bukhari, Ahmad, Ibn Hibban, an-Nasa'i and Abu Ya'la)

The second type of *shirk* is showing off one's good actions. As Allah Almighty says:

"Let him who hopes to meet his Lord act rightly and not associate anyone in the worship of his Lord." (18:110)

It means in this context that one should not act to show off to other people. The Prophet ﷺ said, "Beware of the lesser *shirk*!" The people asked, "Messenger of Allah, what is the lesser *shirk*?" He answered, "Showing off. Allah Almighty will say on the Day when He repays His slaves for their actions, 'Go to those to whom you used to show off your actions in this world, and see whether they have any reward for you.'" (Ahmad, al-Bayhaqi)

The Prophet ﷺ said that Allah says, "Whoever does an action in which he associates someone else with Me, it is for the one whom he associates and has nothing to do with Me." (Muslim) He ﷺ also said, "If anyone wants people to hear about him, Allah will let people know [the truth about] him. If anyone wants people to see him, Allah will show him up." (al-Bukhari and Muslim) Abu Hurayra ؓ said that the Prophet ﷺ said, "Many a fasting person only gains hunger and thirst from his fast, and many a person who prays at night is only deprived of sleep by his standing." (Ibn Majah) In other words, when prayer and fasting are not for the sake of Allah, they bring no reward.

It is also related that the Prophet ﷺ said, "The likeness of a person who acts merely to show off and for the sake of reputation is that of someone who fills his bag with pebbles and then enters the market to buy something. When he opens it in front of the buyer, there is nothing in the bag but pebbles and he strikes his face with it. The only benefit he gains from his bag is that people say, 'How full his bag is!' He is not given anything for it." That is how it is with someone who acts in order to be seen and for the sake of reputation. The only thing he gets from his actions is what other people say about him; he receives no reward in the Next World.

Allah Almighty says: *"We will advance on the actions they have done and make them scattered specks of dust."* (25:23) He means: We will nullify the reward for any actions they did other than for the sake of Allah Almighty and make them scattered dust. This is a reference to the specks of dust that can be seen in rays of sunlight.

'Adi ibn Hatim at-Ta'i ؓ related that the Messenger of Allah ﷺ said, "On the Day of Rising Allah will command groups of people to go to the Garden, and when they are close to it, smell its fragrance and look at its palaces and what Allah has prepared for those dwelling in it, they will be told to go away from it. They have no portion of it. So they will go back full of such regret and sorrow as none of the early or later ones have experienced. They will say, 'Our Lord, if You had admitted us to the Fire before showing us what You showed us of the reward You have prepared for Your friends, it would have been easier for us.' Allah Almighty will say, 'That is what I had intended for you. When you were alone you showed Me dreadful deeds, but when you were with other people you met them with humility, showing them actions which were the opposite of what You gave Me in your hearts. You feared people but did not fear Me. You respected people but did not respect Me. You refrained from things for people but did not refrain from them for Me. Today I will make you taste the pain of My punishment along with what I have denied you of My ample reward.'" (Ibn Abi Dunya. Its *isnad* is weak.)

A man asked the Messenger of Allah ﷺ, "Wherein lies salvation?" He ﷺ answered, "In not cheating Allah." The man asked, "How can someone cheat Allah?" He replied, "By doing an action which Allah and His Messenger have commanded while intending somrthing other than the pleasure of Allah by it. Beware of showing off. It is the lesser *shirk*. On the Day of Rising anyone who showed off will be summoned in front of mankind by four names: 'Show-off! Treacherous one! Impious one! Loser! Your actions are lost and your reward is annulled. You will have no reward from Us. Go and collect your reward from those for whom you acted, deceitful one!"

A wise man was asked, "Who is a sincere person?" He answered, "A sincere person is the one who conceals his good actions in the same way he conceals his evil actions." One man was asked, "What is the goal of sincerity?" He replied, "Not to care for people's praise."

Al-Fudayl ibn 'Iyad said, "To abandon an action for the sake of people is showing off and acting for the sake of people is *shirk*. Sincerity is that Allah protect you from both of these."

O Allah, protect us from both these things and pardon us!

2. Murder

Allah Almighty says:

"As for anyone who kills a believer deliberately, his repayment is Hellfire, to remain in it for ever. Allah is angry with him and has cursed him and has prepared for him an terrible punishment." (4:93)

"Those who do not call upon another god with Allah and do not kill anyone Allah has made inviolate, unless with the right to do so, and do not fornicate; anyone who does that will receive an evil punishment, and on the Day of Rising his punishment will be doubled, and he will be humiliated in it timelessly, forever, except for those who repent and believe and act rightly." (25:68-70)

"On account of that We decreed for the tribe of Israel that if anyone kills another person, unless it is in retaliation for someone else, or for causing corruption in the earth, it is as if they had murdered all mankind. And if someone saves another person's life, it is as if they had given life to all mankind." (5:32-35)

"When the baby girl buried alive is asked for what crime she was killed." (81:8-9)

The Prophet ﷺ said, "Avoid the seven deadly ones," and he mentioned taking a life which Allah has made inviolate without having the legal right do so. A man asked the Prophet ﷺ, "What is the worst sin in the sight of Allah Almighty?" He answered, "That you assign an equal to Allah when He created you." The man continued, "Then what?" He ﷺ replied, "That you kill your child out of the fear that he will eat with you." He asked, "Then what?" He ﷺ answered, "That you commit adultery with your neighbour's wife." (al-Bukhari, Muslim, at-Tirmidhi and an-Nasa'i) Allah revealed in confirmation of this: *"Those who do not call upon another god with Allah and do not kill anyone Allah has made inviolate, unless with the right to do so, and do not fornicate."* (25:68)

The Prophet ﷺ said, "When two Muslims meet with their swords, then the killer and the killed will both be in the Fire."

Someone asked, "Messenger of Allah, we understand that this is the case for the killer, but what about the one killed?" He answered, "It is because he wanted to kill his companion." (al-Bukhari, Muslim, Abu Dawud, an-Nasa'i, Ibn Majah and Ibn Hibban)

Imam Abu Sulayman al-Khattabi commented: "This applies when they do not have a legitimate reason for fighting and are only fighting out of enmity between them, or partisanship, or seeking enrichment, leadership or high position. If one is fighting rebels for a legitimate reason which demands that they be killed, or is defending himself or his family, this does not apply because he is commanded to fight to defend himself and has no desire to kill his companion. The *hadith* is not referring to people like this, but to other people who fight without a valid reason. Allah knows best."

The Messenger of Allah ﷺ said, "Do not revert to being unbelievers after my death, striking off one another's heads." (al-Bukhari and Muslim) The Messenger of Allah ﷺ said, "People will continue to find scope in their *deen* as long as they do not shed unlawful blood." (al-Bukhari and Muslim, at-Tirmidhi, an-Nasa'i and Ibn Majah) The Prophet ﷺ said, "The first thing to be judged between people on the Day of Rising will be the shedding of blood." (al-Bukhari and Muslim) In a *hadith* the Messenger of Allah ﷺ said, "Killing a believer is worse in the sight of Allah than the disappearance of this world." (an-Nasa'i and al-Bayhaqi) The Prophet ﷺ said, "The major wrong actions are: associating others with Allah, murder, and deliberate perjury." (al-Bukhari, Muslim and an-Nasa'i) The Prophet ﷺ said, "No person is unjustly killed without the responsibility for it falling on the elder son of Adam, for he was the first to make a *sunna* of murder." This is transmitted in both major *Sahih* collections.

The Prophet ﷺ said, "Anyone who kills someone covered by a treaty will not experience the fragrance of the Garden, even though its fragrance can be experienced at a distance of forty years." Al-Bukhari transmitted this. That is the case with someone who kills someone covered by a treaty, such as a Jew or Christian within the Land of Islam, what do you think will be the case if he kills a Muslim? The Prophet ﷺ said, "Whoever kills a person cov-

9

ered by treaty, who is under the protection of Allah and His Messenger, has broken the covenant of Allah and will not experience the fragrance of the Garden, even though its fragrance is sensed at a distance of fifty years." According to at-Tirmidhi this is a sound *hadith*.

The Prophet ﷺ said, "If anyone aids and abets the killing of a Muslim with even half a word he will meet Allah with the words 'Despairing of the mercy of Allah Almighty' written between his eyes." Imam Ahmad transmitted it. Mu'awiya ﷺ related that the Messenger of Allah ﷺ said, "Allah may forgive every sin except when a man dies an unbeliever or a man kills a believer deliberately." (an-Nasa'i and al-Hakim)

We ask Allah for protection.

3. Sorcery

We mention sorcery here because it necessarily involves unbelief. Allah Almighty says:

"But the shaytans disbelieved, teaching people sorcery." (2:102)

The sole aim of the accursed Shaytan in teaching people sorcery is to make them associate others with Allah. Allah Almighty says, referring to Harut and Marut:

"They taught no one without first saying to him, 'We are merely a trial, so do not disbelieve.' People learned from them how to separate a man and his wife, but they cannot harm anyone by it except with Allah's permission. They have learned what will harm them and will not benefit them. They know that any who deal in it will have no share in the Next World." (2:102)

Many people get involved in sorcery out of misguidance, thinking it only to be forbidden and not realising that it actually constitutes disbelief. They embark on studying natural magic (*simiya'*) and practising it, which is pure sorcery; they learn how to separate a man from his wife, which is sorcery; and how to cause a man to love or hate his wife and similar things through the use of unheard of words, most of which constitute *shirk* and misguidance.

The *hadd* punishment for a sorcerer is execution, because sorcery constitutes disbelief in Allah or something tantamount to disbelief. The Prophet ﷺ mentioned sorcery among the seven deadly wrong actions. 'Deadly' means that they can ruin people. So one should fear his Lord and not involve himself in something which will lose him this world and the Next. It is reported that the Prophet ﷺ said, "The punishment for sorcerers is to be executed by the sword." (at-Tirmidhi) We know, according to Jundub, that Bajala ibn 'Abda said, "A letter from 'Umar reached us a year before he died ordering us to kill every sorcerer and sorceress." (Abu Dawud) Wahb ibn Munabbih said, "I read in a book that Allah Almighty says: 'There is no god but Me. Anyone who practises sorcery or makes use of it, who is a soothsayer or has recourse

11

to soothsaying, or who reads omens or asks for them to be read, is nothing to do with Me."

'Ali ibn Abi Talib ﷺ said that the Messenger of Allah ﷺ said, "Three people will never enter the Garden: someone addicted to drink, someone who cuts off relatives, and someone who believes in sorcery." Imam Ahmad related this in his *Musnad*.

Ibn Mas'ud ﷺ said, "Incantations, amulets and witchcraft are *shirk*." Amulets are beads and things which the ignorant attach to themselves, their children and their animals claiming that they ward off the evil eye. This is an act belonging to the time of *Jahiliyya*. Anyone who believes in that has committed *shirk*. Witchcraft is what a woman uses to make her husband love her. That is an aspect of *shirk* since ignorant people believe it has an effect which goes against the decree of Allah Almighty.

Al-Khattabi said, "An incantation using the Qur'an or the Names of Allah is permitted because the Prophet ﷺ used one for al-Hasan and al-Husayn. He said, 'I seek refuge for you both with the perfect Words of Allah from every *shaytan*, avenging spirit, and critical eye.'"

Allah is the One who is asked for help and we rely on Him alone.

4. Neglect of the prayer

Allah Almighty says:

"An evil generation succeeded them, who neglected the prayer and followed their appetites. They will plunge into the Valley of Evil – except for those who repent and believe and act rightly." (19:59)

Ibn 'Abbas ﷺ said, "The meaning of 'neglected' here does not imply complete abandonment of the prayer but delaying it beyond its time." Sa'id ibn al-Musayyab, the Imam of the Tabi'un, said, "It means not praying *Zuhr* until the time of *'Asr*, not praying *'Asr* until the time of *Maghrib*, not praying *Maghrib* until the time of *'Isha'*, not praying *'Isha'* until the time of *Fajr*, and not praying *Fajr* until the sun has risen. If someone dies persisting in this state without repenting, Allah has promised him 'Ghayy', which is a deep valley in Hell whose food is disgusting."

Allah Almighty says in another *ayat*: *"Woe to those who pray and are forgetful of their prayer"* (107:4-5): in other words, who are negligent and careless about it. Sa'd ibn Abi Waqqas ﷺ said, "I asked the Messenger of Allah ﷺ about *'those who are forgetful of their prayer,'* and he said, 'It means delaying it" – in other words, delaying it beyond its time. (al-Bazzar) They are said to be 'praying' and yet they are negligent about the prayer and delay it beyond its time. Allah has promised such people *'Wayl'*, which means severe punishment. It is also said to be a valley in Hell. If the mountains of this world were placed in it, they would melt from the intensity of its heat. That will be the destination of those who are negligent about the prayer and delay it beyond its time – unless they repent to Allah Almighty and regret their negligence.

Allah Almighty says in another *ayat*:

"O you who believe, do not let your wealth or children divert you from the remembrance of Allah. Whoever does that is lost." (63:9)

Commentators say that what is meant by "remembrance of Allah" in this *ayat* is the five prayers. Anyone who is preoccupied by his wealth through buying and selling, or concern for his livelihood, or the welfare of his children, from the prayer at its time is one of the lost. That is corroborated by the words of the Prophet ﷺ: "The first action for which a person will be called to account on the Day of Rising will be the prayer. If it is in order, then he has been successful and won. If it is lacking, then he is ruined and lost." (al-Mundhiri)

Allah Almighty says reporting about the inhabitants of Hell:

"What caused you to enter Saqar?' They will say, 'We were not among those who prayed and we did not feed the poor. We plunged with those who plunged and denied the Day of Judgement until the Certain came to us. The intercession of the interceders did not help them." (74:42-48)

The Prophet ﷺ said, "The contract is determined by that which is between us and the prayer: whoever abandons it has disbelieved." (Ahmad, Abu Dawud, an-Nasa'i and at-Tirmidhi) And in another *hadith* the Prophet ﷺ said, "All that stands between a person and disbelief is abandoning the prayer." (Ahmad, Muslim, Abu Dawud, an-Nasa'i, at-Tirmidhi and Ibn Majah)

It is reported in *Sahih Bukhari* that the Messenger of Allah ﷺ said, "If anyone misses the *'Asr* prayer their actions fall away." In the *Sunan* we find that the Messenger of Allah ﷺ said, "If someone abandons the prayer deliberately he has stepped outside the covenant of Allah." (Ibn Majah and al-Bayhaqi)

The Prophet ﷺ said, "I have been commanded to fight people until they say, 'There is no god but Allah,' establish the prayer and pay the *zakat*. When they do that, their lives and property are protected from me, except when there is a legal right, and their reckoning is up to Allah." This is reported by the major *hadith* sources. The Prophet ﷺ says (about the prayers), "Whoever perseveres in them will have light, a proof and salvation on the Day of Rising. Whoever fails to persevere in them will have no light, proof or salvation on the Day of Rising. On the Day of Rising, he will be with Qarun, Haman and Ubayy ibn Khalaf." (Ahmad)

'Umar ibn al-Khattab ﷺ said, "Anyone who neglects the prayer has no portion of Islam." Al-Bayhaqi related that 'Umar ﷺ also said: "A man went to the Messenger of Allah ﷺ and asked, 'Messenger of Allah, which actions does Allah Almighty love the most in Islam?' He answered, 'The prayer at its time. Anyone who abandons the prayer has no *deen*. Prayer is the mainstay of the *deen*.'" When 'Umar ibn al-Khattab ﷺ was stabbed, someone said to him, "The prayer, *Amir al-Mu'minin*." He said, "Yes, there is no portion for anyone in Islam who abandons the prayer," and he prayed with his wound gushing blood.

'Abdullah ibn Shaqiq at-Tabi'i said, "The Companions of the Messenger of Allah ﷺ did not think that abandoning any action was tantamount to disbelief except in the case of the prayer." 'Ali ﷺ was asked about a woman who did not pray and said, "Anyone who does not pray is an unbeliever." (at-Tirmidhi and al-Hakim) Ibn Mas'ud ﷺ said, "A person who does not pray has no *deen*." Ibn 'Abbas ﷺ said, "Anyone who abandons the prayer deliberately will find Allah angry with him when he meets Him."

The Messenger of Allah ﷺ said, "If someone meets Allah having squandered the prayer, Allah will pay no attention to any good action he did after abandoning the prayer." Ibn Hazm said, "After *shirk*, there are no wrong actions greater than delaying the prayer beyond its time and killing a believer without right." Ibrahim an-Nakha'i said, "Anyone who abandons the prayer has disbelieved." Ayyub as-Sakhtiyani said the same. 'Awn ibn 'Abdullah said: "When a person is lowered into his grave, the first thing he will be asked about is the prayer. If his answer is satisfactory, then his other actions will be looked at, if not, then none of his other actions will be looked at."

The Prophet ﷺ said, "When someone prays the prayer at the beginning of the time, it rises to heaven accompanied by light until it reaches the Throne and asks forgiveness for the person who did it until the Day of Rising. It says, 'May Allah safeguard you as you safeguarded me.' When someone prays it outside its time, it rises to heaven accompanied by darkness. When it reaches heaven, it is rolled up like a tattered garment and thrown back in the face of the one who did it. It says, 'May Allah make you lost as you lost me.'" (at-Tabarani)

Abu Dawud related in his *Sunan* that 'Abdullah ibn 'Amr ibn al-'As ﷺ said that the Messenger of Allah ﷺ said, "Three will not have their prayer accepted: someone who leads a people by force, someone who enslaves a free person, and someone who comes to the prayer after its time has passed." It has come that the Prophet ﷺ said, "Anyone who combines two prayers without an excuse has come to a great door of wrong action." (al-Hakim)

We ask Allah for success and help. He is Generous, Magnanimous and the Most Merciful of the Merciful.

Section: when a child should be ordered to pray

Abu Dawud related that the Messenger of Allah ﷺ said, "Order your children to pray when they are seven, beat them to enforce it it when they are ten, and put them in separate beds." Imam Abu Sulayman al-Khattabi said, "This *hadith* indicates that the punishment should be extremely harsh if an adult abandons the prayer." One of the followers of Imam ash-Shafi'i uses it as proof of the obligation to put to death anyone who abandons the prayer after becoming adult. He says, "The fact that he deserves beating when he is not adult indicates that after puberty he deserves a more severe punishment than beating; and there is nothing more severe, after beating, than putting to death."

Scholars disagree concerning the ruling about people who abandon the prayer. According to Malik, ash-Shafi'i and Ahmad, a person who abandons the prayer should be put to death by beheading. There is disagreement about whether a person who abandons the prayer beyond its time without any excuse is an unbeliever or not. Ibrahim an-Nakha'i, Ayyub as-Sakhtiyani, 'Abdullah ibn al-Mubarak, Ahmad ibn Hanbal and Ishaq ibn Rahawayh say that he is an unbeliever. They find evidence in the words of the Prophet ﷺ, "The contract between us and them is the prayer. Whoever abandons it has disbelieved," and the words, "Abandoning the prayer is all that lies between a man and unbelief."

Section

We find in a *hadith*: "Whoever perseveres in the prescribed prayers, Allah Almighty will grant him five honours: He will release him from straitened circumstances, rescue him from the punishment of the grave, give him his book in his right hand, let him pass over the *Sirat* like lightning, and admit him to the Garden without reckoning. But whoever makes light of them, Allah will afflict him with fourteen punishments: five in this world, three at death, three in the grave, and three when he emerges from the grave. As for those in this world, the first is the removal of blessing from his life, the second is that the mark of the righteous is removed from his face, the third is that no action he does will have any reward from Allah, the fourth is that his supplications will not rise to heaven, and the fifth is that no supplications of the righteous will count for him. Those that will afflict him at death are firstly that he will die disgraced, secondly that he will die hungry, and thirdly that he will die thirsty. Even if he were to be given the all seas of this world to drink, that would not quench his thirst. As for those which will befall him in his grave, the first is that the grave will be made so narrow for him that his ribs are crushed, the second is that a fire will be kindled for him in the grave over whose embers he will be turned night and day, and the third is that a bald-headed poisonous snake with eyes of fire and fangs of iron will be given power over him. The length of each fang is the length of a day's journey. It will speak to his corpse and say, 'I am the bald-headed poisonous snake,' and its voice is like shattering thunder. It will say, 'My Lord commanded me to strike you for wasting the *Subh* prayer by delaying it until sunrise, to strike you for wasting the *Zuhr* prayer by delaying it until *'Asr*, to strike you for wasting the *'Asr* prayer by delaying it until *Maghrib*, to strike you for wasting the *Maghrib* prayer by delaying it until *'Isha*,' and to strike you for wasting the *'Isha'* prayer by delaying it until *Subh*.' Whenever he strikes him a blow, he sinks seventy cubits into the earth, and he will continue to be punished in this way until the Day of Rising. As for that which will afflict him

17

when he leaves his grave for the standing of the Resurrection, they are a harsh reckoning, an angry Lord and entrance into the Fire." One variant has: "He will come on the day of Rising with three phrases inscribed on his face. The first is: 'Neglecter of the right of Allah'; the second is: 'Singled out for the wrath of Allah'; and the third is: 'As you wasted the right of Allah in this world, despair today of the mercy of Allah.'"

The Messenger of Allah ﷺ said one day to his Companions ﷺ, "O Allah, do not leave among us any deprived wretch!" Then he asked, "Do you know who the deprived wretch is?" They asked, "Who is it, Messenger of Allah?" He said, "Someone who abandons the prayer." Ibn 'Abbas ﷺ related, "On the Day of Rising, a man will be brought and made to stand before Allah Almighty and He will command him to go to the Fire. He will ask, 'O Lord, why?' Allah Almighty will say, 'For delaying the prayer until after its time and making a false oath by Me.'"

It is related that the first faces to be blackened on the Day of Rising will be the faces of those who abandoned the prayer. There is a valley in Hell called *al-Mulham* which contains snakes. Every snake is like a camel's neck in thickness and a month's journey in length. They bite all those who abandoned the prayer and their venom will boil in their bodies for seventy years and then their flesh will rot.

A story is related about a woman of the tribe of Israel who went to Musa and said, "Messenger of Allah, I have committed a terrible sin and I have repented of it to Allah Almighty, so pray to Allah to forgive me my sin and relent towards me." Musa asked her, "What was your sin?" She answered, "Prophet of Allah, I committed adultery and bore a child and killed it." Musa ﷺ said to her, "Leave, strumpet, lest a fire from heaven descend and burn us for your misdeed!" She left with a broken heart. Jibril ﷺ descended and said, "Musa, the Almighty Lord says to you, 'Why did you reject the repentant woman, Musa? Have you not found worse than her?'" Musa asked, "Jibril, who could be worse than her?" He replied, "Someone who deliberately abandons the prayer."

There is another story from one of the Salaf, about a sister of his who died. He accidentally dropped a bag of money into her grave and did not become aware of it until he had left her grave.

Then he realised what had happened and returned to her grave and dug it up after the people had left. He found a fire burning her in her grave, put the earth back on top of her and returned to his mother weeping in sorrow. He said, "Mother, tell me about my sister and what she did." She said, "Why are you asking about her?" He said, "Mother, I saw a fire burning her in her grave." She wept and said, "My son, your sister neglected the prayer and delayed it beyond its time."

If that is the state of someone who just delays the prayer, what will it be like for someone who does not pray at all? We ask Allah Almighty to help us to keep to it at its prescribed times. He is Generous, Magnanimous.

Section: On the punishment of a person who performs the prayer like a pecking bird and does not properly complete the *ruku'* and prostration

It is related in the commentaries on the words of Allah Almighty: *"Woe to those who pray and are forgetful of their prayer,"* (107:4-5) that they refer to people who pray like a pecking bird and do not complete its *ruku'* and prostration.

The following is confirmed in the two *Sahih* collections from Abu Hurayra ☀: "A man entered the mosque while the Messenger of Allah ☀ was seated in it. The man prayed and then came and greeted the Prophet ☀, who returned his greeting and then said to him, 'Go back and pray. You have not prayed.' He went back and prayed as he had done the first time. Then he came and greeted the Prophet ☀, who returned his greeting and again said, 'Go back and pray. You have not prayed.' He went back and prayed as he had prayed. Then he went and greeted the Prophet ☀, and he returned his greeting and said, 'Go back and pray. You have not prayed.' The third time the man said, 'By the One who sent you with the Truth, Messenger of Allah, I cannot do any better than that, so teach me.' He ☀ said, 'When you stand for the prayer, say the *takbir* and then recite what is easy for you of the Qur'an. Then do *ruku'* until you are at rest in your *ruku'*. Then stand back up until you are completely upright. Then go into prostration until you are at rest in your prostration. Then sit back until you are at rest in the sitting position. Then go into prostration until you are at rest in your prostration. Do that throughout all of your prayer.'"

Imam Ahmad related from al-Badri that the Messenger of Allah ﷺ said, "A prayer in which a man does not make his spine straight in *ruku'* and *sujud* is not accepted." Abu Dawud and at-Tirmidhi related it. This is a text from the Prophet ﷺ invalidating the prayer of anyone whose back is not straight in *ruku'* and *sujud* in the obligatory prayer. It is also necessary to be at rest in each position which is when every limb has settled in its place.

It is confirmed that the Prophet ﷺ said, "The worst thief is someone who steals from his prayer." He was asked, "How can anyone steal from his prayer?" He said ﷺ, "By not properly completing his *ruku'*, *sujud* or recitation." Imam Ahmad related the *hadith* of Abu Hurayra ؓ in which the Messenger of Allah ﷺ said, "Allah does not look at a man whose spine is not straight between *ruku'* and prostration." The Prophet ﷺ said, "That is the prayer of the hypocrite who sits looking at the sun until it is between the horns of *shaytan*, and then stands up and pecks four times and only remembers Allah a little." (al-Bukhari and Muslim) Abu Musa ؓ said, "One day the Messenger of Allah ﷺ prayed with his Companions and then sat down. A man entered and rose to pray, and he began to bow and prostrate like a pecking bird. The Messenger of Allah ﷺ said, 'Do you realise that if this one died, he would die following something other than the religion of Muhammad ﷺ: pecking in his prayer as a crow pecks at blood?'" Abu Bakr ibn Khuzayma transmitted it in a sound *hadith*.

'Umar ibn al-Khattab ؓ related that the Messenger of Allah ﷺ said: "Everyone who prays has an angel to his right and an angel to his left. If he does the prayer properly, they take it up to Allah Almighty. If he does not, they strike his face." (ad-Daraqutni) Al-Bayhaqi related with an *isnad* from 'Ubada ibn as-Samit ؓ that the Messenger of Allah ﷺ said: "If someone performs *wudu'* properly and then stands for the prayer and properly completes the *ruku'*, prostration and recitation in it, the prayer says, 'May Allah preserve you as you preserved me!' Then it is taken up to heaven accompanied by an illumination and a light. The gates of heaven are opened for it, and it is taken to Allah Almighty and intercedes for its performer. If someone does not complete bowing, prostration or recitation in it, the prayer says, "May Allah neglect you as you neglected me!" Then it is taken up to heaven covered by darkness. The gates of heaven are closed to it and then it is rolled up like a tattered garment and is used to strike its performer in the face."

Salman al-Farisi ﷺ related that the Messenger of Allah ﷺ said, "The prayer is weighed and measured. Whoever gives it full measure is given full measure for it. Whoever stints – you know what Allah says about the stinters. Allah Almighty says: *'Woe to the stinters.'* (83:1) The stinters are those who give short measure or weight in goods or the prayer. Allah has promised them *Wayl*. It is a valley in Hell. Hell itself seeks refuge from its heat." We seek refuge from that.

Ibn 'Abbas ﷺ reported that the Messenger of Allah ﷺ said, 'When one of you prostrates he should put his forehead, nose and hands on the ground. Allah Almighty revealed that you should prostrate on seven limbs: the brow, the nose, both hands, the knees, and the tips of the toes. You should not prostrate on your hair or clothes. When someone prays and does not give every limb its due, that limb curses him until he finishes his prayer."

Al-Bukhari transmitted from Hudhayfa ibn al-Yaman ﷺ that he saw a man praying and not properly completing the bowing or prostration in the prayer. Hudhayfa told him, "You did not pray, and if you were to die praying this prayer you would die not conforming to the natural form of Muhammad ﷺ." One variant from Abu Dawud has that he asked, "For how long have you prayed the prayer like this?" He answered, "For forty years." He said, "You have not prayed at all for forty years. If you were to die you would die not conforming to the natural form of Muhammad ﷺ!"

Al-Hasan al-Basri used to say, "Son of Adam, what part of your *deen* can be said to be dear to you if your prayer is of no importance to you? It is the first thing which will be asked about on the Day of Rising, as is clear from the words of the Prophet ﷺ: 'The first of his actions which a slave of Allah will be called to account for on the Day of Rising is his prayer. If it is in order, he has been successful and has won. If it is not, then he has lost and is ruined.

If some of his obligatory prayers are lacking, then Allah Almighty will say, 'Look and see whether My slave has any voluntary prayers to make up for what is lacking of the obligatory;' and then all his other actions will be examined in the same way."

For this reason people should perform a lot of supererogatory prayers, so that they can make up for any shortfall in their obligatory ones.[1]

Section: Greater concern for attending the '*Isha*' and *Fajr* prayers

The Prophet ﷺ said, "There is no prayer heavier on the hypocrites than *Fajr* and '*Isha*'. If they only knew what is in them, they would come to them even if they had to crawl." (al-Bukhari and Muslim) Ibn 'Umar ﷺ said, "When a man failed to join us in the '*Isha*' and *Subh* prayers in the group, we used to consider him a hypocrite."

A narrative is recounted in which 'Ubaydullah ibn 'Umar al-Qawariri said: "I used to never miss the '*Isha*' prayer in a group. One night a guest arrived and I was busy with him and missed the '*Isha*' prayer in the group. I went out seeking to pray in the Basra mosque and found that all the people had already prayed and the mosques were shut. I returned to my house and said, 'There is a *hadith* which says that the prayer in a group is twenty-seven degrees better than the prayer alone.' So I prayed '*Isha*' twenty-seven times and then slept and dreamt that I was with some people on horses and I was also on a horse. We raced and I made my horse gallop but could not catch them up. I turned to one of them and he said to me, 'Do not exhaust your horse. You will never catch us up.' 'Why?' I asked. He said, 'Because we prayed '*Isha*' in a group and you prayed alone.' I awoke in sorrow because of that."

We ask Allah for help and success. He is Generous, Magnanimous.

---

1. To avoid repetition, the section on the punishment of the one who neglects the prayer (in a group) when able to perform it has been moved to No. 65, near the end of the book, which deals with it as a specific wrong action.

5. Refusing to pay *zakat*

Allah Almighty says:

"Those who are tight-fisted with the bounty Allah has given them should not suppose that that is better for them. No indeed, it is worse for them! What they were tight-fisted with will be hung around their necks on the Day of Rising." (3:180)

Allah Almighty also says:

"Woe to those who associate others with Him, those who do not pay zakat." (41:26)

He calls them idolators. Allah Almighty further says:

"As for those who hoard gold and silver and do not spend it in the Way of Allah, give them the news of a painful punishment on the Day it is heated up in the fire of Hell and their foreheads, sides and backs are branded with it: 'This is for what you hoarded for yourselves, so taste what you were hoarding.'" (9:34)

It is confirmed that the Messenger of Allah ﷺ said, "There is no one who has gold or silver and does not pay what is due on them without them being turned, on the Day of Rising, into slabs of fire and being heated in the Fire of Hell and their sides, foreheads and backs being branded with them. Every time they cool they will be heated again throughout a day whose length is fifty thousand years, until people's fates have been decided and they see their way open either to the Garden or to the Fire." He was asked, "Messenger of Allah, what about camels?" He ﷺ said, "There is no owner of camels who fails to fulfil what is due to them – and one of their rights is to be milked on the day they are watered – without, on the Day of Rising, being thrown on his face on account of them onto a very wide level plain. Not even one young camel will be missing and they will trample him with their hooves and bite him with their teeth. When the last of them have passed over him, then the first of them will return again to him throughout a day whose length is fifty thousand years until people's fates have been decided and he sees his way open either to the Garden or to the Fire." (al-Bukhari and Muslim) The Prophet 鐺 said, "The first three to enter the Fire will be a harsh ruler, someone with wealth who did not pay the right of Allah on his property, and a poor man who is boastful." (al-Mundhiri)

Ibn 'Abbas 鐺 said, "If someone has the wealth to allow him to complete *hajj* of the House of Allah Almighty and he does not make *hajj*, or the wealth on which *zakat* is obligatory and he does not pay *zakat*, he will ask to return when he dies." A man said to him, "Fear Allah, Ibn 'Abbas. It is only the unbelievers who ask to return." Ibn 'Abbas 鐺 said, "I will recite to you evidence for that in the Qur'an. Allah Almighty says: '*Give from what We have provided for you, before death comes to one of you and he says, "My Lord, if only You would give me a little more time so that I can give* sadaqa [i.e. pay *zakat*] *and be one of the righteous* [i.e. perform *hajj*].'" (63:10) He was asked, "When does *zakat* become obligatory?" He answered, "When a person's wealth reaches two hundred dirhams, then it is obligatory to pay *zakat* on it." He was asked, "What makes *hajj* obligatory?" He answered, "Provision and a mount."

Abu Hurayra 鐺 said that the Messenger of Allah 鐺 said, "If Allah gives someone wealth and he does not pay the *zakat* due on it, on the Day of Rising it will take on the likeness of a bald-headed poisonous snake with two black dots over its eyes which will encircle his neck, biting his jaws, and say, 'I am your wealth. I am your treasure.'" Then he recited this *ayat*: "*Those who are miserly with the bounty Allah has given them should not suppose that that is better for them. No indeed, it is worse for them! What they were miserly with will be hung around their necks on the Day of Rising*" (3:180). Al-Bukhari transmitted it.

Ibn Mas'ud 鐺 spoke about the words of Allah Almighty referring to those who refuse to pay *zakat*: "*On the Day it is heated up in the fire of Hell and their foreheads, sides and backs are branded with it*," (9:34) and said, "A dinar will not be put on top of a dinar or a dirham on top of a dirham. His skin will be expanded so that every dinar and dirham has its place." If it is asked why people's faces, sides and backs are singled out for branding, it is said that it is because when a miserly wealthy person sees a pauper, he scowls, averts his eyes and turns away. When he comes close to him, he turns his back. He is punished by being branded on these limbs so that the retaliation is made on the parts involved in the original action.

The Prophet ﷺ said, "Five for five." They asked, "Messenger of Allah, what is 'five for five'?" He answered, "A people do not break a contract without Allah giving their enemy power over them. They do not judge by other than what Allah has revealed without poverty spreading among them. Fornication does not appear among them without death spreading among them. They do not skimp in the weight and measure without being denied crops and experiencing famine. They do not deny *zakat* without rain being withheld from them."

Warning: Tell those who are distracted by this world that their delusions will vanish tomorrow and what they amassed will be of no use to them. What they were warned about will come about on the Day when their wealth will be heated up in Hellfire and their foreheads, sides and backs branded, so how can it be absent from their hearts and minds now? On the Day it is heated up in Hellfire and their foreheads, sides and backs are branded, their wealth will be taken to the place where the punishment is imposed and put into a crucible to be heated in order to increase its severity. It will be heated in the Fire of Hell and their foreheads, sides and backs will be branded with it.

When a poor person encounters them, he encounters harm. When he asks them for something, flames of anger fly from them like firebrands. They forgot the wisdom of their Creator regarding the wealth of this one and the poverty of that one. It is extraordinary how much grief they will encounter when they are in their graves. The Fire of Hell will be heated over them and their foreheads, sides and backs branded with it. Their heirs will inherit from them without difficulty. He will have thorns whereas his heirs will have fresh dates. If you could only see them in the depths of the Fire, being turned on a spit over the burning coals of their dinars and dirhams, trussed up because they were miserly with their wealth! If you could see them in Hellfire drinking boiling water and even those who are stoical crying out when their foreheads, sides and backs are branded. How often they were warned in this world and did not listen! How often they were told to fear the punishment of Allah and none of them were alarmed! How often they were told about refusing to pay *zakat* and were not moved!

Story: It is related that Muhammad ibn Yusuf al-Faryabi said: "I went out with a group of my companions to visit Abu Sinan. When we went into where he was and sat with him, he said, 'Let's go and visit a neighbour of ours whose brother has died and console him for his loss.' We rose with him and visited that man and found him weeping and grieving for his brother. We sat down to console him but he did not accept our comfort and consolation. We said, 'Do you not know that death is inevitable?' He said, 'Yes, but I weep for the morning and evening in which my brother is suffering punishment.' We asked him, 'Has Allah informed you of the Unseen?' He answered, 'No, but when I buried him and levelled the earth over him and the people left, I sat at his grave and there was a sound from his grave saying, "Oh! They have made me sit alone to undergo the punishment! I used to pray. I used to fast!"

'His words made me weep, and I removed the earth from him to see what was happening to him. His grave was filled with fire and there was a collar of fire around his neck. The compassion of brotherhood moved me to stretch my hands to remove the collar from his neck and my fingers and hand were burned.' He showed his hand to them and it was black and burned. He said, 'I put the earth back and left. How can I not weep for his state and grieve over him?' We asked, 'What did your brother use to do in this world?' He answered, 'He used to not pay *zakat* on his wealth.' We said, 'This is the confirmation of the words of Allah Almighty: *"Those who are miserly with the bounty Allah has given them should not suppose that that is better for them. No indeed, it is worse for them! What they were miserly with will be hung around their necks on the Day of Rising."* (3:180) Your brother has had his punishment hastened in his grave until the Day of Rising.'

"Then we left him and went to Abu Dharr 🙵, the Companion of the Messenger of Allah 🙵. We told him the story of the man and said to him, 'Jews and Christians die and we do not see that in their case.' He said, 'There is no doubt that they are in the Fire. Allah shows you the people of faith so that you may reflect. Allah Almighty says: *"Whoever sees clearly, does so to his own benefit. Whoever is blind, it is to his own detriment."* (6:104) Lord does not wrong His slaves.'"

We ask Allah for pardon and protection. He is Generous, Magnanimous.

6. Not fasting a day of Ramadan without a valid excuse

Allah Almighty says:

"You who believe, fasting is prescribed for you, as it was prescribed for those before you – so that perhaps you may be godfearing – for a specified number of days. But any of you who are ill or on a journey should fast a number of other days." (2:183-184)

It is confirmed in the two major *Sahih* collections that the Prophet ﷺ said, "Islam is based on five things: the testimony that there is no god but Allah and Muhammad is the Messenger of Allah, establishing the prayer, paying *zakat*, making *hajj* to the House [of Allah], and fasting Ramadan."

The Prophet ﷺ said, "If anyone breaks the fast one day of Ramadan without an excuse, even fasting all the time will not make up for it." (at-Tirmidhi, an-Nasa'i and Ibn Majah)

Ibn 'Abbas ﷺ said, "The supports of Islam and the pillars of the *deen* are three: testimony that there is no god but Allah; the prayer; and fasting Ramadan. Anyone who abandons any of them is an unbeliever."

We seek refuge with Allah from that.

7. Not performing *hajj* when able to do so

"Hajj to the House is a duty owed to Allah by all mankind – those who can do find a way to do it." (3:97)

The Prophet ﷺ said, "If someone possesses the provision and a mount which will convey him to the Sacred House of Allah but does not perform *hajj*, it does not matter if he dies a Jew or Christian. For Allah Almighty says, 'Hajj *to the House is a duty owed to Allah by all mankind – those who can do find a way to do it*' (3:97)." (at-Tirmidhi and al-Bayhaqi) 'Umar ibn al-Khattab ﷺ said, "I wanted to send men to these cities and examine everyone who has wealth but has not performed *hajj*, and impose the *jizya* on them. They are not Muslims."

Ibn 'Abbas ﷺ said, "Anyone who has not performed *hajj* and has not paid *zakat* on his property will ask to return when he dies." Someone said to him, "It is only the unbelievers who ask to return." He said, "That is proven in the Book of Allah Almighty: *'Give from what We have provided for you before death comes to one of you and he says, "Lord, if only You would give me a little more time so that I might give* sadaqa (i.e. pay zakat) *and be one of the righteous* (i.e. perform *hajj*.)" *Allah will not give anyone more time, once their time has come. Allah is aware of what you do.*' (63:10-11)." It was asked, "What makes *zakat* obligatory?" He answered, "Two hundred dirhams, or and their value in gold." It was asked, "What makes *hajj* obligatory?" He replied, "Provision and a mount." Sa'id ibn Jubayr said, "A wealthy neighbour of mine who did not perform *hajj* died and I did not pray over him."

8. Disrespect to parents

Allah Almighty says:

"Your Lord has decreed that you should worship none but Him, and that you should show kindness to parents, whether one or both of them reach old age with you. Do not say 'Ugh!' to them out of irritation and do not be harsh to them. (Meaning, 'Do not speak to them with annoyance when they are old. You must serve them as they served you since the one who acted first has superiority – how could there be equality? They bore that hoping for your life, so how could you harm them, hoping they will die?') *Speak to them with gentleness and generosity. Take them under your wing, out of mercy, with due humility, and say, 'Lord, show mercy to them as they did in looking after me when I was small.'"* (17:23-24)

Allah Almighty also says,

"Give thanks to Me and to your parents. To Me is your final return." (31:14)

Look, may Allah have mercy on you, at how He has combined thanks to them with thanks to Himself! Ibn 'Abbas ﷺ said, "Three *ayat*s are revealed connected to three things, none of which is accepted without the other. One is the words of Allah Almighty: *"Obey Allah and obey the Messenger."* (4:59) If someone obeys Allah but does not obey the Messenger, it is not accepted from him. The second is the words of the Almighty: *"Perform the prayer and pay the zakat."* (2:43) If someone prays but does not pay *zakat*, it is not accepted from him. The third is the words of Allah Almighty: *"Give thanks to Me and to your parents."* If someone thanks Allah, but does not thank his parents, it is not accepted from him. That is why the Prophet ﷺ said, 'The pleasure of Allah lies in pleasing one's parents and the anger of Allah lies in angering one's parents.'" (at-Tirmidhi)

Ibn 'Umar ﷺ said: "A man came to ask permission of the Prophet ﷺ to go on *jihad* with him. The Prophet ﷺ asked, 'Do you have parents?' 'Yes,' he answered. The Messenger of Allah said ﷺ,

'Then expend your effort on them.'" This is transmitted in the two *Sahih* collections. Look at how he ﷺ preferred the merit of being dutiful to one's parents and serving them to *jihad*.

We find in the two *Sahih* collections that the Messenger of Allah ﷺ said, "Shall I inform you of the greatest of wrong actions? Associating others with Allah, and disrespect to one's parents." Notice how he connected acting badly towards them and failure to be dutiful and kind to them with *shirk*. Also in the two *Sahih* collections the Messenger of Allah ﷺ said, "Someone who disrespects his parents, someone who reminds people of his charity to them, and a habitual drinker of wine will not enter the Garden."

The Prophet ﷺ also said, "If Allah knew of anything less than 'Ugh!', He would have forbidden it. No matter what someone who shows disrespect to his parents does, he will not enter the Garden. No matter what someone who is dutiful to them does, he will enter the Garden." (ad-Daylami) The Prophet ﷺ also said, "Allah curses anyone who disrespects his parents." The Prophet ﷺ further said, "Allah curses anyone who curses his father and Allah curses anyone who curses his mother." (Ibn Hibban) And the Prophet ﷺ said, "Allah defers all wrong actions for as long as He wishes until the Day of Rising except for disrespect to parents. Punishment is hastened for the one who does that." In other words, they receive punishment in this world before the Day of Rising. (al-Hakim)

Ka'b al-Ahbar ؓ said, "Allah hastens the death of a person when he shows disrespect to his parents in order to hasten the punishment for him. Allah increases the life of a person when he is dutiful to his parents in order to enable them to show more duty and kindness." Being dutiful towards them means spending on them when they need it. A man came to the Prophet ﷺ and said, "Messenger of Allah, my father says that he is in need of my property." The Prophet ﷺ said, "You and your property belong to your father." Ka'b al-Ahbar ؓ was asked about what disrespect to parents involves and said, "When a person's father or mother swears by him and he does not fulfil their oath; when he is commanded and he does not obey their command; when they ask him for something and he does not give it to them; and when they trust him and he betrays their trust."

31

Ibn 'Abbas ﷺ was asked about the people of the Ramparts (*al-A'raf*) and who they are and what the Ramparts are. He said, "The Ramparts is a mountain between the Garden and the Fire. It is called the Ramparts because it overlooks the Garden and Fire, and on it are trees, fruits, rivers and springs. As for the men who are on it, they are men who went out to *jihad* without the permission of their fathers and mothers and were killed in *jihad*. Being killed in the Way of Allah prevented them from entering the Fire and disobedience to their parents prevented them from entering the Garden, so they are on the Ramparts until Allah carries out His command on them."

The two *Sahih* Collections report that a man went to the Messenger of Allah ﷺ and asked, "Messenger of Allah, who is the person most entitled to my good company?" He answered, "Your mother." He asked, "Then who?" He said, "Your mother." He asked, "And then who?" He said, "Your mother." He said, "Then who?" He said, "Your father, and then the next closest kin and the next closest." He encouraged dutifulness to mothers three times and to fathers once. That is only because her concern and compassion is greater as well as what she endured in pregnancy, labour, birth, nursing and sleepless nights.

Ibn 'Umar ﷺ saw a man carrying his mother on his shoulders, taking her around the Ka'ba. He asked, "Ibn 'Umar, do you think that I have repaid her?" "No," he answered, "not for a single one of her labour pains, but you have done good. May Allah repay you with much for a little."

Abu Hurayra ﷺ said that the Messenger of Allah ﷺ said, "Allah has bound Himself not to admit four people to the Garden or let them taste its bliss: a habitual drinker, a consumer of usury, someone who consumes an orphan's property wrongly and someone who disrespects his parents, unless they repent." (al-Hakim)

The Prophet ﷺ said, "The Garden is under the feet of the mothers" (Ibn Majah and an-Nasa'i related the like.) A man went to Abu ad-Darda' ﷺ and said, "Abu ad-Darda, I have married a woman, but my mother is telling me to divorce her." Abu ad-Darda' said, "I heard the Messenger of Allah ﷺ say 'The parent is the middle gate to the Garden.' As you wish, you may forfeit that door or retain access to it.'" (Ibn Majah and at-Tirmidhi)

The Prophet ﷺ said, "Three supplications are answered without a doubt: that of the wronged, that of the traveller, and that of a parent against his child." (al-Mundhiri) The Prophet ﷺ said, "A maternal aunt is in the position of a mother," meaning in respect of dutifulness, generosity, ties and charity. (at-Tirmidhi)

Wahb ibn Munabbih said, "Allah Almighty revealed to Musa, 'Musa, respect your parents. Whoever respects their parents will have a long life and be given a child who respects him. Whoever disrespects his parents will have a short life and be given a child who disrespects him." Abu Bakr ibn Abi Maryam said, "I read in the Torah that whoever strikes his father should be killed." Wahb said, "I read in the Torah that stoning is prescribed for striking a father."

'Amr ibn Murra al-Juhani ﷺ said, "A man came to the Messenger of Allah ﷺ and said, 'Messenger of Allah, if I pray the five prayers, fast Ramadan, pay *zakat* and make *hajj* to the House, what do you think I will receive?" He answered, "Anyone who does that is with the Prophets, the true, the martyrs and the righteous – unless he disrespects his parents." (Ahmad and at-Tabarani)

The Prophet ﷺ said, "Allah curses anyone who disrespects his parents." It is related that the Messenger of Allah ﷺ said, "I saw in the Night Journey some people in the Fire suspended from stumps of fire. I asked, 'Jibril, who are these?' He said, 'Those who vilified their fathers and mothers in this world.'"

It is related that if someone insults his parents, an ember of fire descends into his grave. It is related that when someone who disrespected his parents is buried, the grave constricts him until it caves in his ribs. And the people with the most severe punishment on the Day of Rising will of be three kinds: those who associate others with Allah; those who fornicate; and those who disrespected their parents.

Warning. O you who withhold the most confirmed of rights, which is to be dutiful to your parents, through disobedience, and who forget what is obligatory for you and neglect what is in front of you, you owe your parents a debt. You claim to seek the Garden, yet it is under the feet of your mother. She bore you in her womb for nine months, as if she performed nine *hajj*s. She suffered in childbirth what melts the heart and she suckled you from her breasts with milk. She rushed from sleep for your sake and washed dirt from you with her right hand. She preferred you to herself with food and her lap became a cradle for you. She dealt with you with kindness and help. If an illness or complaint afflicted you, she was greatly upset, and her sadness and weeping lasted long. She spent her money on doctors to treat you. If she had been given a choice between your life and hers, she would have chosen the former. She did all this and yet you treat her badly time and time again.

She prayed for you to have success secretly and openly. But then when she needs you in old age, you consider her the least important of things. You are full and she is hungry. You are quenched and she is thirsty. Your wife and children treat her well but you treat her with neglect, her orders vex you even when they are slight. Her life seems long to you although it is short. This is despite the fact that your Lord has forbidden you to say "Ugh" and warned you that you risk being punished in this world through the disobedience of your own children and in the Next World by distance from the Lord of the worlds. He calls to you with rebuke and threat. *"That is on account of what you did. Allah does not wrong His slaves."* (3:182)

It is related that in the time of the Prophet ﷺ there was a young man called 'Alqama ؓ who strove a lot to obey Allah in prayer, fasting and *sadaqa*. When he became very ill, his wife sent for the Messenger of Allah ﷺ to say that her husband 'Alqama was in his death throes, saying, "I wanted to tell you of his condition, Messenger of Allah." The Prophet ﷺ sent 'Ammar, Suhayb and Bilal, saying, "Go to him and instruct him in the *shahada*." They went to see him and found him in the throes of death. They began to instruct him to say, "There is no god but Allah" but his tongue could not articulate it. They sent to the Messenger of Allah ﷺ to inform him that his tongue could not articulate the *shahada*. The Prophet ﷺ asked, "Are either of his parents alive?" It was said, "Messenger of Allah, his mother is very old." So the Messenger of Allah ﷺ sent to her, telling the messenger, "Ask her if she is able to travel to the Messenger of Allah ﷺ. Otherwise she should stay in her house until he comes to her."

The messenger went to her and told her what the Messenger of Allah ﷺ had said. She said, "My soul be ransom for his! I am duty bound to go to him." So she leaned on a staff and went to the Messenger of Allah ﷺ and greeted him, and he returned the greeting and said to her, "Mother of 'Alqama, tell me the truth. If you lie, revelation from Allah will come." What was the state of your son 'Alqama?" She said, "Messenger of Allah, he did much prayer, much fasting and gave much *sadaqa*." The Messenger of Allah ﷺ asked, "What is your state?" She answered, "Messenger of Allah, I am angry with him." "Why?" he asked. She said, "Messenger of Allah, he prefers his wife to me and disobeys me." The Messenger of Allah ﷺ said, "The anger of the mother of 'Alqama has veiled the tongue of 'Alqama from the *shahada*."

Then he said, "Bilal, go and bring me a lot of firewood." She said, "Messenger of Allah, what are you going to do?" He answered, "Burn him with fire in front of you." She said, "Messenger of Allah, my child! My heart cannot bear to see him burned with fire in front of me!" He said, "Mother of 'Alqama! The punishment of Allah is harsher and more enduring. If you were pleased with him Allah would forgive him, so be pleased with him. By the One who has my soul in His hand, 'Alqama will not be helped by his prayer, fasting or *sadaqa* as long as you are angry with him." She said, "Messenger of Allah, I testify to Allah Almighty and His angels and those Muslims who are present that I am pleased with my son 'Alqama." The Messenger of Allah ﷺ said, "Go to him, Bilal, and see if he is able to say, 'There is no god but Allah' or not. Perhaps the mother of 'Alqama has said something that is not in her heart, out of modesty before me."

He went and heard 'Alqama from inside the house saying, "There is no god but Allah." Bilal entered and said, "People! The anger of 'Alqama's mother veiled his tongue from the *shahada*, and her pleasure has released his tongue." Then 'Alqama died on that day and the Messenger of Allah ﷺ came and ordered that he be washed and shrouded, and then prayed over him and attended his burial. Then he stood on the edge of his grave and said, "Company of the Mujahirun and Ansar! Anyone who prefers his wife to his mother, on him is the curse of Allah, the angels and all mankind. Allah will not accept from him any compensation unless he repents to Allah Almighty and is good to her and seeks to please her. Allah is angry when she is angry. We ask Allah to give us success in His pleasure and to make us avoid His wrath. He is Generous, Magnanimous, Compassionate, Merciful."

9. Shunning relatives

Allah Almighty says:

"Have taqwa *of Allah in whose name you make demands on one another and also in respect of your kin,"* (4:1) meaning "Beware of cutting off ties with relatives."

"Is it not likely that if you did turn away you would cause corruption in the earth and sever your ties of kinship? Such are the people Allah has cursed, making them deaf and blinding their eyes." (47:22-23)

"Those who fulfil Allah's contract and do not break their agreement; those who join what Allah has commanded to be joined and are afraid of their Lord and fear an Evil Reckoning." (13:20-21)

He misguides many by it (the Qur'an) *and guides many by it. But He only misguides the deviators – those who break Allah's contract after it has been agreed, and sever what Allah has commanded to be joined, and cause corruption in the earth. It is they who are the lost."* (2:26-27)

The two *Sahih* collections report that the Messenger of Allah ﷺ said, "Anyone who severs ties of kinship will not enter the Garden." Anyone who severs his ties with weak relatives, shuns them, is arrogant towards them, and does not give to them out of goodness and charity if he is rich and they are poor, is included in this threat and will be forbidden to enter the Garden until he repents before Allah Almighty and is good to them. The Messenger of Allah ﷺ said, "Whoever has weak relatives and is not good to them but spends his *sadaqa* on others, Allah will not accept his *sadaqa* from him or look at him on the Day of Rising." (at-Tabarani) If he is poor, he should maintain ties with them by visiting them and asking how they are, going by the words of the Prophet ﷺ, "Maintain ties with your kin, even if only with a greeting."

The Prophet ﷺ said, "Whoever believes in Allah and the Last Day should maintain ties with his relatives." (al-Bukhari) The

Messenger of Allah ﷺ said, "He who maintains ties is not the one who treats his relatives the same as they treat him; he who maintains ties is the one who, when his kin cut him off, still maintains ties with them." The Prophet ﷺ said, "Allah Almighty says: 'I am the All-Merciful, and it is kinship (*rahm* from the same root as "Merciful"). Whoever maintains ties with kin, I maintain ties with him. Whoever cuts them off, I cut him off." (Abu Dawud and at-Tirmidhi) 'Ali ibn al-Husayn said to his son, "My son, do not keep the company of anyone who cuts off kin. I find him cursed in the Book of Allah in three places."

Abu Hurayra ﷺ related that he sat down to relate from the Messenger of Allah ﷺ and said: "I order anyone who severs ties with relatives to leave us." No one rose except a young man from the edge of the circle. He went to his paternal aunt, because he had been in conflict with her for some years, and made peace with her. His aunt asked him, "What has brought you, nephew?" He replied, "I was sitting with Abu Hurayra, the Companion of the Messenger of Allah ﷺ, and he said, 'I order anyone who severs ties with kin to leave us.'" His aunt said to him, "Go back to Abu Hurayra and ask him why." He went back to him and told him what had happened to him with my aunt and then asked, "Why should someone who severs ties not sit with you?" Abu Hurayra answered, "I heard the Messenger of Allah ﷺ say, 'Mercy does not descend on a group of people among whom are those who sever ties with their kin.'"

It is related that a wealthy man went on *hajj* to the Sacred House of Allah. When he reached Makka, he entrusted a thousand dinars to a man who was known for his trustworthiness and rectitude. He went to stand on 'Arafat and then returned to Makka, to find that the man had died in his absence. He asked the man's family about his property and learned that they had no knowledge of it. He went to the scholars of Makka and told them about his situation and his money. They told him, "In the middle of the night go to Zamzam and look into it and call, 'O So-and-so', using his name. If he was one of the people of the Garden, he will answer you the first time." So the man went and called into Zamzam; but no one answered.

He went back to the scholars and told them and they said, "We belong to Allah and to Him we return. We fear that your companion is one of the people of the Fire. Go to the land of Yemen where there is a well called Rahut. It is said that it is on the edge of Hell. Look into it at night and call out, 'So-and-so!' If he is one of the people of the Fire, he will answer you from it." So he went to Yemen and asked about the well. He was directed to it and went to it at night, looked into it and called out, "Where is my gold?" The answer came, "I buried it in such-and-such a place in my house, for I did not trust my son with it." He returned to the man's family and dug there and found it. He asked him, "What put you in the Fire when we thought good of you?" He answered, "I had a poor sister whom I shunned and was not compassionate to, so Allah punished me because of her and put me in this position."

That is confirmed by a sound *hadith* in which the Prophet ﷺ said, "Anyone who severs ties of kinship will not enter the Garden." This includes sisters, maternal or paternal aunts, nieces and other relatives. We ask Allah for success in obeying Him. He is Generous, Magnanimous.

10. Fornication

The Almighty says:

> "*Do not go near fornication. It is an indecent act, an evil way.*" (17:32)

> "*Those who do not call upon another god together with Allah, and do not take the life of anyone Allah has made inviolate, except with the right to do so, and do not fornicate; anyone who does that will receive an evil punishment and on the Day of Rising his punishment will be doubled and he will be humiliated in it timelessly, forever, except for those who repent.*" (25:67-70)

> "*A man and woman who commit fornication: flog both of them with a hundred lashes and do not let compassion for either of them possess you, where Allah's* deen *is concerned, if you believe in Allah and the Last Day. A number of the believers should witness their punishment.*" (24:2)

Scholars say that this is the punishment in this world for male and female fornicators if they are single and have not married. If they are married or have been married before, even once in their lives, they should be stoned to death. That is confirmed in the *Sunna* from the Prophet ﷺ. If they are not punished in this world and they die without repenting, they will be punished in the Fire with whips of fire.

It is confirmed that the Messenger of Allah ﷺ said, "A fornicator does not fornicate while he is a believer. A thief does not steal while he is a believer. A drinker does not drink wine while he is a believer. No plunderer plunders something of value which attracts people's eyes while he is a believer." (al-Bukhari and Muslim) The Prophet ﷺ said, "When someone commits fornication, faith leaves him and becomes like a shadow over his head. When he extricates himself, faith returns to him." (Abu Dawud, at-Tirmidhi and al-Bayhaqi) The Prophet ﷺ said, "If someone fornicates or drinks wine, Allah removes faith from him as a man removes a shirt over his head." (al-Hakim) We find in a *hadith* that the Messenger of Allah ﷺ said, "Allah will not speak to three kinds of people on the

Day of Rising, nor will be look at them or attest to their integrity and they will have a painful punishment: an old man who fornicates, a lying king, and a proud pauper." (Muslim and at-Tirmidhi)

Ibn Mas'ud ﷺ said, "I asked, 'Messenger of Allah, which sin is greatest in the sight of Allah Almighty?' He ﷺ replied, 'That you assign an equal to Allah although He created you.' I said, 'That is terrible. Then what?' He said, 'That you kill your child out of fear that he will eat with you.' I asked, 'Then what?' He said, 'That you commit fornication with your neighbour's wife.'" Allah Almighty revealed the confirmation of that: *"Those who do not call upon another god together with Allah and do not take the life of anyone Allah has made inviolate, except with the right to do so, and do not fornicate; anyone who does that will receive an evil punishment and on the Day of Rising his punishment will be doubled and he will be humiliated in it timelessly, forever, except for those who repent."* (25:67-69) (Muslim and an-Nasa'i) Notice how Allah links fornication with a neighbour's wife to associating something else with Him and killing a soul which He has made inviolate except by a legal right. This is a *hadith* which is transmitted in the two *Sahih* collections.

In *Sahih Bukhari* there is a *hadith* about a dream of the Prophet ﷺ in which Samura ibn Jundub ﷺ related that Jibril and Mika'il came to the Prophet ﷺ and said, "Come with us." He said, "We came to something like an oven, the upper part of which was narrow and the bottom wide. There was shouting and voices coming from it. We looked into it and there were naked men and women inside. Flames were flaring up at them from underneath them and when they reached them they shouted because of the intensity of the heat. I asked, 'Who are they, Jibril?' He answered, 'Those are male and female fornicators. This is their punishment until the Day of Rising.'" We ask Allah for safety and protection!

'Ata' said regarding the *tafsir* of the words of Allah Almighty about Hellfire, *"It has seven gates"* (15:44) that the worst of those gates with respect to regret, heat, grief and stench is for fornicators who committed fornication in full knowledge of what they were doing." Makhul ad-Dimishqi said, "The people of the Fire smell a foul smell and say, 'What is this most horrible stench we smell?' They are told, 'That is the smell of the genitals of fornicators.'" Ibn Zayd, one of the imams of *tafsir*, said that the people of the Fire will be harmed by the stink of the genitals of fornicators. One of the commandments which Allah wrote for Musa ﷺ is: "Thou shalt not steal or commit adultery, lest My Countenance become veiled to you."

It has come from the Prophet ﷺ that Iblis sent his armies to the earth and told them, "I will put a crown on the head of whichever of you misleads a Muslim, and the one who is most successful in tempting them will have the closest position to me." So one of them came to him and said, "I kept at so-and-so until he divorced his wife." He said, "You have not done anything. He will marry someone else." Then another came and said, "I kept at so-and-so until I put enmity between him and his brother." He said, "You have not done anything. He will reconcile with him." Then another came and said, "I kept at so-and-so until he committed fornication." Iblis said, "Yes, you have done well," and so he brought him close to him and put the crown on his head. We seek refuge with Allah from the evils of Shaytan and his armies.

Anas ﷺ related that the Messenger of Allah ﷺ said, "Faith is a garment with which Allah clothes whomever He wishes. When someone commits fornication, Allah removes the garment of faith from him. If he repents, He returns it to him." (al-Bayhaqi) It is reported that the Prophet ﷺ said, "Company of Muslims, fear fornication. It incorporates six features: three in this world and three in the Next World. The three in this world are removal of light from the face, an early death and enduring poverty. As for those in the Next World, they are the anger of Allah Almighty, a bad reckoning and being punished in the Fire." (Ibn al-Jawzi)

The Prophet ﷺ said, "If someone dies persisting in drinking wine, Allah will make him drink from the river of Ghawta, which is a river which flows in the Fire coming from the genitals of whores. Pus and suppuration flows from their vaginas in the Fire and then those who died persisting in drinking wine drink that." (Ahmad, Abu Ya'la and Ibn Hibban)

The Messenger of Allah ﷺ said, "There is no sin after *shirk* which is more terrible in the sight of Allah than a sperm which a man places in a vagina not lawful for him." He ﷺ also said, "There is a wadi in Hell with snakes in it and every snake is as thick as a camel's neck which bites the one who abandons the prayer. Its poison boils in his body for seventy years and then his flesh falls off. There is a wadi in Hell called the well of al-Hazan in which are snakes and scorpions. Each scorpion is like a camel with seventy stings and each sting has a poisonous barb. It stings the fornicator and its poison spreads in his body and he experiences bitter pain for a thousand years and then his flesh falls off and his genitals run with pus and suppuration." (Ahmad and at-Tabarani)

It is also related that if someone commits fornication with a married woman, half the punishment of this community will afflict him and her in the grave. On the Day of Rising, Allah will judge this to be among her husband's good deeds if he had no knowledge of it. If he knew and was silent, Allah will forbid the Garden to him because Allah Almighty has written over the gate of the Garden: "You are forbidden to the wittol." A wittol is a man who knows about the infidelity of his wife and is silent and not jealous.

It is also related that someone who puts a lustful hand on a woman who is not lawful for him will come on the Day of Rising with his hand chained to his neck. If he kisses her, his lips will be clipped in the Fire. If he commits fornication with her, his thigh will be made to speak and will speak against him on the Day of Rising, saying. "I committed the *haram*." Allah Almighty will look at him with the eye of wrath and the flesh of his face will fall off. If he is proud and says, "I did not do it," his tongue will testify against him and say, "I am that with which he said what was not lawful." His hands will say, "I am that with which he touched the unlawful." His eyes will say, "I am that with which he looked at the unlawful." His feet will say, "I am that with which he walked to the unlawful." His genitals will say, "I did it." The recording angels will say, "I heard." Another will say, "I wrote it." Allah Almighty will say, "I looked and veiled it." Then Allah Almighty will say, "My angels, take him and make him taste My punishment. My anger is severe on those who have little shame before Me." That is confirmed by the Book of Allah Almighty: "*On the Day when their tongues and hands and feet will testify against him about what they were doing.*" (24:24)

The worst fornication is that done with one's mother, sister, father's wife or female *mahram* relatives. Al-Hakim says that the report is sound: "Whoever has sex with a *mahram*, kill him." Al-Bara' said that the Messenger of Allah ﷺ sent his uncle to a man who had married his father's wife, in order to put him to death and take one-fifth of his property.

We ask Allah, the Generous by His bounty to forgive us our sins. He is Generous, Magnanimous.

11. Sodomy

In His Noble Book Allah Almighty recounts to us the story of the people of Lut in a number of places. One instance is the words of the Almighty:

"When Our command came, We turned their cities upside down and rained down on them stones of hard baked clay, piled on top of one another in layers, each one earmarked by your Lord. They are never far from the unbelievers." (11:82-83)

If other people act in the same way, then the same punishment will befall them.

The Prophet ﷺ said, "What I most fear for you is the action of the people of Lot. Whoever does their action is cursed. Allah has cursed anyone who commits the action of the people of Lut. Allah has cursed anyone who commits the action of the people of Lut. Allah has cursed anyone who commits the action of the people of Lut." (Ibn Majah and at-Tirmidhi) The Prophet ﷺ said, "If you find anyone committing the action of the people of Lut, put to death both the active and passive partner." (Abu Dawud, at-Tirmidhi and Ibn Majah) Ibn 'Abbas ؓ said, "Look for the highest building in the town and throw them from it and then follow that with stones, as was done to the people of Lut."

The Muslims agree that sodomy is one of the major wrong actions which Allah has forbidden. Allah says:

"Of all beings, do you lie with males, leaving the wives Allah has created for you? You are a people who have overstepped the limits."

In other words, "you have gone beyond what is lawful to the unlawful" (26:165-166). Allah Almighty says in another *ayat* reporting about his Prophet Lut ﷺ:

"We rescued him from the city which committed disgusting acts. They are evil people who were deviators." (21:74)

The name of the city was Sodom. Its people used to commit the vile actions which Allah Almighty mentioned in his Book. They used to commit sodomy with men, break wind in their gatherings and do other disliked things.

It is related that the Prophet ﷺ said, "Sex between women is fornication." (at-Tabarani) Abu Hurayra ؓ said that the Messenger of Allah ﷺ said, "Four are subject to the anger of Allah morning and evening." He was asked, "Who are they, Messenger of Allah?" He ﷺ replied, "Men who resemble women and women who resemble men, those who have sex with animals and men who go to men (i.e. commit sodomy)." (at-Tabarani)

It is related that when one man mounts another, the Throne of the All-Merciful trembles out of fear of the wrath of Allah Almighty and the heavens almost fall on the earth. The angels hold them back and recite *Surat al-Ikhlas* until the anger of Allah subsides. (as-Suyuti) The Prophet ﷺ also said, "Seven will be cursed by Allah Almighty and He will not look at them on the Day of Rising. He will say, 'Enter the Fire with those who enter it': one who does it and one to whom it is done (i.e. sodomy), one who commits bestiality, and the one who marries a woman and her daughter at the same time, one who masturbates – unless they repent."

It is related that the actions of the people of Sodom included backgammon, racing pigeons, dog fighting, ram fighting, cock fighting, entering baths without waist-wrappers; and giving short weight and measure. Woe to those who do that! It is reported that whoever plays with pigeons will not die until he tastes the pain of poverty. Ibn 'Abbas ؓ said, "If a sodomite dies without repenting, he will be turned into a pig in his grave." The Prophet ﷺ said, "Allah will not look at a man who comes to a man or woman by the anus." Abu Sa'id as-Sa'luki said, "There will be people in this community called sodomites. They are of three kinds: those who look, those who shake hands, and those who commit foul actions." (at-Tirmidhi, an-Nasa'i and Ibn Hibban)

Looking with lust at a woman or a beardless youth is a kind of fornication, for it is confirmed that the Prophet ﷺ said, "The fornication of the eye is by looking. The fornication of the tongue is by words. The fornication of the hand is by touching. The fornication of the foot is by walking. The fornication of the ear is by listening. The lower self desires and wants. The genitals confirm or deny that." (al-Bukhari and Muslim)" Because of that, the righteous have always strongly advised keeping away from beardless young men and have warned against looking at them, speaking to them and sitting with them. Al-Hasan ibn Dhakwan said, "Do not sit with the children of the wealthy. They have forms like those of virgins and they are a greater temptation than women."

One of the *Tabi'un* said, "I am less afraid of a beast of prey attacking a devout young man than I am of a beardless youth sitting with him." It used to be said: "A man should not spend the night in the same place as a beardless youth." One of the scholars forbade being alone with beardless youths in a house, shop or bath-house, drawing an analogy between them and women, because the Prophet ﷺ said, "A man is not alone with a woman without Shaytan being the third of them." (at-Tirmidhi)

There are beardless youths who are more beautiful than women and so the temptation is greater. Evil is possible in respect of them which is not possible in respect of women, and doubt is easy in respect of them which is not possible in respect of a woman. So it is more likely to be unlawful. The statements of the *Salaf* about avoiding them and being cautious about seeing them are too many to count, and they call them "foul" because they are impure legally.

Sufyan ath-Thawri entered the bath-house and a lad with a beautiful face also entered where he was. He said, "Get him away from me! Get him away! I see a shaytan with every woman and I see about ten shaytans with a lad with a handsome face." A man went to visit Imam Ahmad with a handsome lad and the Imam asked, "What is this one in relation to you?" He answered, "My nephew." He said, "Do not bring him to us again. Do not walk with him in the street, lest those who do not know you are related to him might think something bad about you." It is related that when the delegation of 'Abd al-Qays went to the Prophet ﷺ, a handsome beardless man was among them. The Prophet ﷺ made him sit behind him. He said, "The temptation of Dawud ﷺ was through the eye." It used to be said that the glance is the postman of fornication. We find in a *hadith*: "The glance is one of the poisoned arrows of Iblis. If someone abandons it for Allah, Allah will bequeath the sweetness of worship in his heart which he will experience until the Day of Rising."

Section: The punishment of sodomites

It is reported that Khalid ibn al-Walid ﷺ wrote to Abu Bakr as-Siddiq ﷺ that he found in a place a man who used to commit sodomy. Abu Bakr consulted the Companions ﷺ about his case. 'Ali ibn Abi Talib ﷺ said, "This is a sin which only one nation committed: the nation of Lut. Allah Almighty has informed us about what He did to them. I think that he should be burned." So Abu Bakr ﷺ wrote to him to burn him and Khalid ﷺ burnt him.

The Community agree that anyone who commits this act with his slave is considered a sodomite. It is related that in his travels 'Isa ibn Maryam ﷺ passed by a fire which was burning a man and took some water to put it out, upon which the fire turned into a boy and the man turned into fire. 'Isa ﷺ was amazed at that and said, "O Lord, return them to their former state so that I may ask them what happened to them." So Allah Almighty brought them to life and they appeared as a man and a boy. 'Isa ﷺ asked them, "What happened?" The man said, "Spirit of Allah, I was tempted by love for this boy and lust moved me to commit indecency with him. We both died and since then sometimes he becomes fire which burns me and sometimes I become fire which burns him. This is our punishment until the Day of Rising."

We seek refuge with Allah from the punishment of Allah and we ask for pardon, well-being and success in what He loves and is pleased with.

Section: anal intercourse with a woman is part of sodomy, which Allah and His Messenger have forbidden

Allah Almighty says: *"Your women are fertile fields for you, so come to your fertile fields however you like"* (2:223), in other words: "in whatever position you like, from the front or back, but in the same place." The reason for the revelation of the *ayat* was that the Jews in the time of the Prophet ﷺ used to say, "If a man has sexual intercourse with his wife from behind, any child will be born cross-eyed." The Companions of the Messenger of Allah ﷺ asked about that and Allah revealed this *ayat* to refute them. Muslim transmitted it. One variant has, "Avoid the anus and menstruation." The word used for the "same place" means the vagina, because it is the place of tillage, meaning the place of procreation The anus is the place of excretion. That is foul and dirty. Abu Hurayra ﷺ related that the Prophet ﷺ said, "Accursed is he who has sex with a menstruating woman or in a woman's anus." (Ahmad and Abu Dawud)

At-Tirmidhi related from Abu Hurayra ﷺ that the Prophet ﷺ said, "Anyone who has sex with a menstruating woman or a woman in the anus, or goes to a soothsayer, has disbelieved in what Allah revealed to Muhammad." Included in this strong threat is someone who goes to a soothsayer. meaning an astrologer or someone who claims to know about something which has been stolen and speaks about unseen matters. Many of the ignorant fall into these acts of disobedience owing to their lack of knowledge and failure to gain it. That is why Abu ad-Darda' ﷺ said, "Be a scholar, a teacher, a listener or a lover; be anything else and you will be destroyed" – that is, someone who does not know or teach or listen, and does not like people who do so is obliged to repent to Allah of all sins and errors.

We ask Allah for pardon from what was done in ignorance and for protection during the rest of our lives. O Allah, we ask You for pardon and protection in the *deen* and this world and the Next. You are the Most Merciful of the merciful.

12. Usury

Allah Almighty says:

"O you who believe, do not consume usury multiplied and then remultiplied. Fear Allah so that perhaps you may be successful." (3:130)

The Almighty says: *"Those who practise usury will not rise except as someone driven mad by Shaytan's touch"* – in other words, they will rise from their graves on the Day of Rising as someone who has been struck by Shaytan and thrown down by him – *"That is because they say, 'Trade is the same as usury.'"* (2:275) They say that usury is lawful, and so they make lawful what Allah has made unlawful.

When Allah resurrects people on the Day of Rising, they will emerge quickly except for those who have consumed usury. They will rise and fall down as someone thrown down tries to get up. Whenever they stand up, they fall down again. That is because they consumed usury in this world and so Allah made it grow in their bellies until it makes them top heavy on the Day of Rising. So whenever they want to get up, they fall over. They want to go quickly with the other people but are not able to do so. Qatada said, "Those who consumed usury will be raised on the Day of Rising insane. That is how usurers will be known by people at the Standing."

Abu Sa'id al-Khudri said that the Messenger of Allah said, "When I was taken on the Night Journey, I passed by some people whose bellies were sticking out in front of them. The belly of each of them was like a huge house. Their bellies extended, lining the path of the people of Pharaoh, who are presented to the Fire morning and evening. They are brought like defeated camels without hearing or understanding. When the people with those bellies become aware of them they try to stand up, but their bellies drag them down and they cannot get away so that the people of Pharaoh trample them; and this happens to them on the way there and the way back. That is their punishment in the *barzakh* (interspace) between this world and the Next." The Prophet continued, "I asked Jibril who they were and he said, 'Those are the people who consumed usury. They only rise as someone rises whom Shaytan has driven mad by his touch.'"

In one transmission we find: "When I was taken up, I heard thunder and lightning in the seventh heaven above my head. I saw men whose bellies stuck out in front of them like houses and there were snakes and scorpions in them which could be seen from the outside. I asked, 'Who are they, Jibril?' He answered, 'Those who consumed usury.'" (Ahmad)

It is related from 'Abd ar-Rahman ibn 'Abdullah ibn Mas'ud from his father ﷺ: "When fornication and usury appear in a town, Allah gives permission for its destruction." (Abu Ya'la) 'Umar ﷺ reported, "When people are stingy with dinars and dirhams and sell on credit and follow the tails of cattle and abandon jihad in the way of Allah, Allah will send down an affliction which will not be removed from them until they restore their *deen*." (Abu Dawud) The Prophet ﷺ said, "Usury does not appear in a people without madness making its appearance among them. Fornication does not appear in a people without death appearing among them. A people do not skimp with regard to weight and measure without Allah denying them rain." (Ibn Majah, al-Bazzar, al-Bayhaqi and al-Hakim)

It is related in a long *hadith* that those who consume usury will be punished from the time they die until the Day of Rising by being made to swim in the Red River, whose water is like blood, and being fed with stones, representing the forbidden property which they amassed in this world, which are extremely hard to swallow – stones of fire which they will be made to swallow just as they swallowed the unlawful wealth they amassed in this world. This punishment will take place in the *barzakh* before the Day of Rising in addition to the curse of Allah upon them.

In a sound *hadith* the Messenger of Allah ﷺ said, "It is incumbent on Allah not to admit to the Garden, nor to let taste its bliss, a habitual drinker, a consumer of usury, someone who consumes the wealth of orphans without a right, and someone who disrespects his parents – unless he repents."

It is related that those who consume usury will be resurrected as dogs and pigs because of the devices they employed to consume usury, in the same way that the people who violated the Sabbath were transformed for the way they trapped the fish which Allah had forbidden to be caught on the Sabbath. They dug holes into which the fish swam on the Sabbath and they would take them out the next day. When they did that, they were transformed by Allah into monkeys and pigs. That is how it will be with those who employ different types of devices to consume usury. Those devices are not hidden from Allah. Ayyub as-Sakhtiyani said, "They try to deceive Allah as they would a child. If they had been absolutely straightforward, it would have been better for them."

The Prophet ﷺ said, "Usury has seventy doors, the least of which is comparable to a man having sex with his mother. The worst kind of usury is a man attacking the honour of his Muslim brother." (at-Tabarani) Anas ؓ said, "The Messenger of Allah ﷺ addressed us and mentioned usury, making it clear how terrible it is. He said, "A dirham which a man gets from usury is worse than committing fornication thirty-six times in Islam." (Ibn Abi ad-Dunya and al-Bayhaqi) He ؓ also said that the Messenger of Allah ﷺ said, "Usury comprises seventy sins, the least of which is like a man having sex with his mother." (Ibn Majah) Abu Bakr as-Siddiq ؓ said, "The one who takes usury and the one who pays it will both be in the Fire:" i.e., "the one who takes it and the one who gives it are the same." We ask Allah for protection!

Ibn Mas'ud ؓ said, "If a man owes you a debt, and then gives you something, do not take it. It is usury." Al-Hasan said, "When you are owed a debt by a man, anything you eat from his house is ill-gotten." This is inferred from the words of the Prophet ﷺ: "Every loan which brings benefit is usury." Ibn Mas'ud ؓ also said, "If someone intercedes for a man and is then offered a gift, it is ill-gotten." That is confirmed by the words of the Prophet ﷺ: "If someone intercedes for a man who then gives him a gift and he accepts it, he has come to one of the great doors of usury." Abu Dawud transmitted it.

We ask Allah for pardon and protection in the *deen*, and in this world and the Next.

13. Consuming the property of orphans and wronging them

Allah Almighty says:

"People who consume the property of orphans wrongfully consume nothing in their bellies but fire. They will roast in a Searing Blaze." (4:10)

"And that you not go near the property of orphans before they reach maturity – except in a good way." (6:152)

Abu Sa'id al-Khudri ﷺ related that the Messenger of Allah ﷺ said, "In the Ascent during the Night Journey, I saw some men whose jaws were forced open; other men brought stones of fire which they threw into their mouths and which then emerged from their anuses. I asked, 'Jibril, who are those?' He said, 'Those who consume the property of orphans wrongly consume fire in their bellies.'" Muslim transmitted it. Abu Hurayra ﷺ related that the Messenger of Allah ﷺ said, "Allah Almighty will raise some people from their graves and fire will emerge from their bellies, burning their mouths with fire." Someone asked, "Who are those, Messenger of Allah?" He answered, "Do you not see that Allah says: '*People who consume the property of orphans wrongfully consume nothing in their bellies but fire*'?"

As-Suddi said, "Anyone who consumes the property of an orphan wrongly will be raised on the Day of Rising with flames of fire coming out of his mouth, ears, nose and eyes. Everyone who sees him will know that he consumed the wealth of an orphan." Scholars have said that if the guardian of an orphan is poor he may use his property correctly in order to maintain him in his best interests and to make his wealth grow. There is nothing wrong with that. But anything other than that is unlawful and forbidden. The Almighty says:

"Those who are wealthy should abstain from it altogether. Those who are poor should use it sensibly and correctly." (4:6)

There are four positions about using an orphan's wealth correctly. The first is that the guardian may take it as a loan, the second is that he may consume it according to need without extravagance, the third is that he may take what is appropriate for the work he does for the orphan, and the fourth is that he should only take it in real need. If he becomes wealthy, he should repay it, and if he does not become wealthy, what he has done is lawful. These positions were mentioned by Ibn al-Jawzi in his *tafsir*.

It is reported in al-Bukhari that the Messenger of Allah ﷺ said, "I and the guardian of an orphan will be in the Garden like this," and he indicated his index and middle fingers and the gap between them. Guardianship of an orphan entails managing his affairs and striving for his best interests in respect of food and clothing, and making his property increase if he has property. If he has no property, one should spend on him and clothe him seeking to please Allah Almighty.

The Messenger of Allah ﷺ said, "If someone lets a Muslim orphan eat and drink with him until Allah enriches him, Allah will make the Garden mandatory for him unless he commits a wrong action which is not forgiven." (at-Tirmidhi) The Prophet ﷺ said, "If someone strokes an orphan's head, and strokes it for the sake of Allah alone, he receives a good action for every hair over which his hand passes. If someone is good to a orphan boy or girl with him, he and I will be like these in the Garden." (Ahmad)

A man said to Abu ad-Darda' ﷺ, "Give me some advice." He said, "Show mercy to an orphan, bring him close to you and feed him from your own food. When a man came to the Messenger of Allah ﷺ to complain about the hardness of his heart, I heard the Messenger of Allah ﷺ say, 'If you want to soften your heart, then bring an orphan close to you, stroke his head and feed him from your own food. That will soften your heart and you will be able to do what you need.'" (at-Tabarani)

One thing related from one of the *Salaf* is that he said, "At the beginning I was addicted to things by which I disobeyed Allah and drinking wine. One day I got an orphan child and took him in, was good to him, fed him and clothed him and took him to the baths to remove his unkemptness. I honoured him as a man honours his child, and more. I went to sleep the night after that and dreamt that the Resurrection had taken place and I was summoned for the reckoning and was sent to the Fire for the acts of disobedience I had done. The *Zabaniyya* (angels of Hell) dragged me towards the Fire and I was humble and lowly before them. Suddenly there was that orphan, standing in front of me in the road. He said, 'Let him go, angels of my Lord! It is my right to intercede for him with my Lord. He was good to me and honoured me.' The angels said, 'We have not been commanded to do that.' Then a call came from Allah Almighty: 'Let him go. I have forgiven him for what he did, because of the intercession of the orphan and his kindness to him.' I awoke and turned to Allah Almighty. I exerted myself in showing mercy to orphans."

This is why Anas ibn Malik 🙵, the servant of the Messenger of Allah 🙵, said, "The best of houses is a house in which there is an orphan who is treated well, and the worst of houses is a house in which there is an orphan who is treated badly. The most beloved of people to Allah is the one who does something for an orphan or a widow." It is related that Allah Almighty revealed to Dawud 🙵, "Dawud, be like a merciful father to orphans and a kind husband to widows. Know that as you sow so shall you reap." It means that as you do, so shall it be done to you. So that must be the case if you die and leave an orphan child or widow. Dawud 🙵 said in his intimate conversation with his Lord, "My God, what is the recompense of someone who supports orphans and widows seeking to please You?" He answered, "His reward is that I will shade him in My shade on the Day when there is no shade but My shade."

Regarding the merit of being good to widows and orphans is a story about an 'Alawite (descendant of 'Ali), who was staying at Balkh in the land of the Persians. His wife was also an 'Alawite and they had some daughters. They lived in luxury and prosperity. Then the husband died and the woman and her daughters fell into poverty and need. She moved with her daughters to another town out of fear of abuse from her enemies. It happened that they left in a time of intense cold and, when they came to the new town, the woman left her daughters in a deserted mosque and went to try and find them some food. She passed by two groups: one group gathered around a Muslim who was the town's shaykh, and another around a Magian who was the town's tax collector.

She went first to the Muslim and explained her situation to him saying, "I am an 'Alawite woman and I have orphaned daughters whom I have left in a deserted mosque, and I want food for the night." He said to her, "Show me proof that you are a noble 'Alawite." She said, "I am a foreign woman in a land which does not know me." He turned away from her. So, brokenhearted, she left him and went to that Magian and explained her situation to him, telling him that she had orphaned daughters with her and was a foreign noble woman. She told him what had happened to her with the Muslim shaykh. He got up and sent for one of his wives, and they took her and her daughters to his house and gave them the best food and clothed them in the most splendid garments. They spent the night with him in luxury and honour.

In the middle of the night, that Muslim shaykh dreamt that it was the Day of Resurrection and the banner was set up at the head of the Prophet ﷺ. There were castles of emerald whose windows were pearls and rubies and which had domes of pearl and coral. He asked, "Messenger of Allah, who is this castle for?" He answered, "For a Muslim man who declares the unity of Allah." He said, "Messenger of Allah. I am a Muslim man who declares the unity of Allah." The Messenger of Allah ﷺ said, "Produce clear proof with you that you are a Muslim who declares the unity of Allah." He was bewildered.

The Prophet ﷺ said to him, "When the 'Alawite woman told her story to you, you said, 'Produce clear proof for me that you are an 'Alawite.' So produce for me clear proof that you are a Muslim." The man woke up in sorrow for having turned away the disappointed woman. Then he began to search in the town and ask about her until he was told that she was with the Magian. He went to him and said, "I would like to take the noble 'Alawite woman and her daughters off your hands." The man said, "Certainly not! I have the blessing of looking after them." He said, "I will give you a thousand dinars to hand them over to me." He said, "I will not do it." He said, "I must have them." He said, "I am more entitled to the thing you desire, and the castle you saw in your dream was created for me. Do you think your Islam makes you better than me? By Allah, I and my household did not sleep last night until we had become Muslim at the hand of the 'Alawite woman. I had the same dream as you. The Messenger of Allah ﷺ said to me, 'Are the 'Alawite woman and her daughters with you?' I answered, 'Yes, ' He said, 'The castle is for you and the people of your house. You and your household are among the people of the Garden. Allah created you a believer before time began.'" So the Muslim left in such a state of sorrow and grief as only Allah knows.

So look, may Allah have mercy on you, at the blessing which comes from being good to widows and orphans, and the honour it brings to a person in this world! This is why it is confirmed in the two *Sahih* collections that the Messenger of Allah ﷺ said, "The one who strives on behalf of widows and the poor is like someone who does *jihad* in the Way of Allah." The transmitter said, "I think he said, 'like someone who prays without flagging and fasts without breaking the fast.'" The one who strives on their behalf is the one who looks after their affairs and seeks their best interests seeking to please Allah Almighty.

May Allah benefit us by that by His favour and honour. He is Generous, Magnanimous, Compassionate, Forgiving, Merciful.

14. Lying about Allah Almighty and His Messenger 🌟

Allah Almighty says:

"On the Day of Rising you will see those who lied against Allah with their faces blackened." (39:60)

Al-Hasan said, "They are those who say, 'If we want to do something we will do it and if we do not want to we will not do it.'" Ibn al-Jawzi said in his *tafsir*: "A group of scholars believe that lying about Allah and his Messenger is disbelief which takes one out of Islam. There is no doubt whatsoever that lying about Allah and His Messenger by making what is lawful unlawful and the unlawful lawful is pure disbelief. The concern here is about lying in some way other than that."

The Prophet 🌟 said, "Whoever lies about me, a house will be built for him in Hellfire." (al-Bukhari and Muslim) The Prophet 🌟 also said, "Whoever deliberately lies about me, he will take his seat in the fire." The Prophet 🌟 further said, "Whoever relates a report allegedly from me thinking that it is a lie, he is one of the liars." (Muslim) The Prophet 🌟 said, "Lying about me is not like lying about someone else. Whoever lies about me deliberately, he will take a seat in the Fire." (Muslim) The Prophet 🌟 said, "Whoever says that I said anything that I did not say will take his seat in the Fire." The Prophet 🌟 said, "A believer may by nature be capable of anything except treachery and lying." (al-Bazzar and Abu Ya'la)

We ask Allah for success and protection. He is Generous, Magnanimous.

15. Fleeing from battle

This is when the enemy is not more than twice as many as the Muslims. An exception is made for withdrawing to rejoin the fight elsewhere or to support another group, even if far away. Allah Almighty says:

"Anyone who turns his back on them that day, except withdrawing to rejoin the fight or withdrawing to support another group, brings Allah's anger down on himself. His refuge is Hell. What an evil destination!" (8:16)

Abu Hurayra ؓ said that the Messenger of Allah ﷺ said, "Avoid the seven deadly sins." They asked, "What are they, Messenger of Allah?" He replied, "Associating others with Allah, sorcery, killing a soul which Allah has made unlawful except by a legal right, consuming usury, consuming the wealth of orphans, fleeing from battle, and slandering chaste, heedless, believing women." (Al-Bukhari and Muslim)

Ibn 'Abbas ؓ said, "When Allah revealed, *'If there are twenty of you who are steadfast, they will overcome two hundred'* (8:65), Allah prescribed for them that twenty should not flee from two hundred. Then it was revealed that *'Now Allah has made it lighter on you, knowing that there is weakness in you. If there are a hundred of you who are steadfast, they will overcome two hundred; and if there are a thousand of you, they will overcome two thousand with Allah's permission. Allah is with the steadfast.'* (8:66) So Allah prescribed that one hundred should not flee from two hundred. Al-Bukhari related it.

16. A leader duping his followers and treating them unjustly

Allah Almighty says:

"There are only grounds against those who wrong people and act as tyrants in this world without any right to do so. Such people will have a painful punishment." (42:42)

"Do not consider Allah to be unaware of what the wrongdoers perpetrate. He is merely deferring them to a Day on which their sight will be transfixed, rushing headlong – heads back, eyes vacant, hearts hollow." (14:42-43)

"Those who do wrong will soon know the kind of reversal they will receive!" (26:227)

"They would not restrain one another from the wrong things they did. How evil were the things they used to do!" (5:79)

The Messenger of Allah ﷺ said, "Whoever deceives us is not of us," (Muslim) And he ﷺ said, "Injustice will be darkness on the Day of Rising." (Al-Bukhari, Muslim and at-Tirmidhi) The Prophet ﷺ also said, "All of you are shepherds and each of you is responsible for his flock." (al-Bukhari and Muslim) The Messenger of Allah ﷺ further said, "Any shepherd who dupes his flock will be in the Fire." (at-Tabarani) The Prophet ﷺ said, "If someone is put in authority over people by Allah and does not deal with it faithfully, Allah will forbid him the Garden." (Al-Bukhari) And in another transmission: "If on the day he dies, he dies duping his flock, Allah will deny him the Garden."

The Prophet ﷺ said, "There is no governor who judges between people who will not be held on the Day of Rising, an angel taking hold of him by the back of the neck. If Allah says, 'Throw him down,' he will be thrown into Hell for forty years." Imam Ahmad related it. The Messenger of Allah ﷺ said, "Woe to amirs! Woe to captains! Woe to trustees! On the Day of Rising, some people will wish they had been hung by their hair from the Pleiades as a punishment and that they had not been given authority over anything." The Prophet ※ said, "A just judge will come on the Day of Rising and will wish that he had not judged between two people, even about a single date." (al-Bazzar) The Prophet ※ said, "There is no commander of ten who will not be brought on the Day of Rising with his hand chained to his neck. Either his justice will release him or his injustice will ruin him." (Ahmad and Ibn Hibban)

One of the supplications of the Messenger of Allah ※ was: "O Allah, if someone is put in authority over some part of this community and is kind to those under him, be kind to him. If he is harsh to them, be harsh to him." The Prophet ※ said, "Whoever undertakes some of the affairs of the Muslims and is veiled from their needs, want, and poverty, Allah will be veiled from his needs and want and poverty." (Muslim and an-Nasa'i) The Messenger of Allah ※ said, "There will be impious unjust rulers. Whoever believes their lies and assists them in their injustice is not from me and I am not from him. He will not come to my Basin [on the Last Day]." (Ahmad and at-Tirmidhi) The Messenger of Allah ※ said, "Two classes of my community will not obtain my intercession: unjust, corrupt rulers and people who are excessive in the *deen*. Witness will be borne against them and they will be excluded." (at-Tabarani)

We find in a *hadith* that the Prophet ※ said: "O people, command the right and forbid the wrong lest you call upon Allah and He does not answer you and ask forgiveness of Allah and He does not forgive you. When the rabbis of the Jews and the monks of the Christians stopped commanding the right and forbidding the wrong, Allah cursed them at the hands of the Prophets and then enveloped them in affliction." (al-Isfahani)

The Messenger of Allah ※ said, "If someone innovates something in this affair of ours which is not part of it, it is rejected" (al-Bukhari and Muslim) and: "Whoever innovates a matter or introduces an innovation, the curse of Allah, the angels and all people is on him, and Allah will not accept from him any recompense."

We also find in a *hadith*: "Whoever does not show mercy will not be shown mercy. Allah will not show mercy to someone who does not show mercy to other people." (al-Bukhari and Muslim)

The Prophet ﷺ said, "A just ruler will be shaded by Allah in His shade on the Day when there is no shade but His shade." (al-Bukhari and Muslim) He also said ﷺ, "The just will be on minbars of light: those who were fair in their rulings and to their family and in all their undertakings." (Muslim and an-Nasa'i)

When the Messenger of Allah ﷺ sent Mu'adh to Yemen, he said, "Beware of the best property, for there is no veil between the supplication of the wronged and Allah." Al-Bukhari related it. He ﷺ said, "There are three to whom Allah will not speak on the Day of Rising." He mentioned among them a lying king. (Muslim) He also said ﷺ, "You are eager for authority, but it will be a matter of regret on the Day of Rising." Al-Bukhari related it and also this: "By Allah, I will not appoint to this office anyone who asks for it or who is eager for it."

The Messenger of Allah ﷺ said, "Ka'b ibn 'Ujra, seek refuge with Allah from the command of fools: leaders who will come after me who do not follow my guidance and do not follow my *sunna*." (Ahmad) Abu Hurayra ﷺ reported that the Prophet ﷺ said, "If someone seeks to judge the Muslims and is placed in that position and then his justice overcomes his injustice, he will be in the Garden. If his injustice overcomes his justice, he will be in the Fire." (Abu Dawud)

'Umar ﷺ said to Abu Dharr ﷺ, "Relate to me a *hadith* which you heard from the Messenger of Allah." Abu Dharr ﷺ said, "I heard the Messenger of Allah ﷺ say: 'A ruler will brought to the Day of Rising and will be thrown onto the bridge over Hell. The bridge will shake so violently that all his joints will be dislocated. If he obeyed Allah in his work, he will pass over it. If he disobeyed Allah in his work, the Bridge will break under him and make him fall into Hell for fifty years.'" 'Amr ibn al-Muhajir that 'Umar ibn 'Abd al-'Aziz reported: "If you see me deviating from the truth, put your hand on mine and say, ''Umar, what are you doing?'"

17. Pride

This includes pride, boasting, conceitedness, haughtiness and vanity. Allah Almighty says:

> *"Musa said, 'I seek refuge in my Lord from every proud man who does not believe in the Day of Reckoning.'"* (40:27)

> *"He does not love people puffed up with pride."* (16:23)

The Messenger of Allah ﷺ said, "Once Allah made the earth swallow a man who was walking with an arrogant gait. He will sink in it until the Day of Rising" (al-Bukhari and an-Nasa'i). He ﷺ also said, "The tyrants and the arrogant will be gathered on the Day of Rising like grain on which people walk. Abasement will envelop them in every place." (an-Nasa'i and at-Tirmidhi)

One of the *Salaf* said, "The first sin by which Allah was disobeyed was pride." Allah Almighty says: '*We said to the angels, "Prostrate to Adam!" and they prostrated, with the exception of Iblis. He refused and was arrogant and was one of the unbelievers.*' (2:34) If someone arrogant towards God, his faith will not help him, as happened with Iblis."

The Prophet ﷺ said, "No one will enter the garden while there is atom of pride in his heart." Muslim related it. Allah Almighty says: *"Allah does not love anyone who is vain or boastful."* (31:18) The Messenger of Allah ﷺ said, "Allah Almighty says: 'Majesty is My waist-wrapper and pride is My cloak. If someone vies with Me for them, I will cast him into the Fire.'" Muslim related it.

The Prophet ﷺ said, "The Garden and the Fire argued. The Garden said, 'Why is it that only the weak and lowly will enter me? The Fire said, 'I was preferred for the tyrants and arrogant.'" Allah Almighty says: *"Do not avert your face from people out of haughtiness and do not strut about arrogantly in the earth. Allah does not love anyone who is vain or boastful."* (31:18)

Salama ibn al-Akwa' ﷺ said, "A man ate with the Messenger of Allah ﷺ using his left hand. The Prophet ﷺ said, 'Eat with your right hand.' The man replied, 'I cannot.' Then he said, 'You cannot? Only pride has stopped you.' After that he was never able to lift it to his mouth." Muslim related it. He ﷺ said, "Shall I inform you of who is in the Fire? It is every rough, strutting, arrogant person." (al-Bukhari and Muslim) Ibn 'Umar ؓ said, "I heard the Messenger of Allah ﷺ say, 'There is no man who is arrogant in his gait and arrogant in himself who will not meet Allah and find Him angry with him.'" (at-Tabarani) It is sound, corroborated by this *hadith* of Abu Hurayra ؓ: "The first three to enter the Fire will be an unjust ruler, a rich person who does not pay *zakat*, and a proud, poor person." (Ibn Khuzayma and Ibn Hibban) We find in *Sahih al-Bukhari* that the Messenger of Allah ﷺ said, "Allah will not look at three on the Day of Rising, will not declare them upright, and they will have a painful punishment: the one who wears his garment long (out of pride), the one who reminds people of his charity to them, and the one sells his goods by a false oath."

The worst kind of pride is that of someone who is arrogant towards people because of his knowledge and gloats over his own superiority. Such a person does not benefit at all from his knowledge. Someone who seeks knowledge of the Next World is rendered contrite by his knowledge; his heart is made humble and his lower self is abased. He lies in wait for his lower self and does not let up on it but calls it to account all the time and examines it. If he were to let it loose, it would refuse to follow the Straight Path and destroy him. If someone seeks knowledge out of pride and desire for leadership and exalts himself over other Muslims, thinking them to be foolish and belittling them, this is the worse kind of pride – and anyone who has an atom's weight of pride in his heart will not enter the Garden. There is no strength or power except by Allah, the High, the Immense.

18. Perjury

Allah Almighty says:

"Those who do not bear false witness." (25:72)

We find in a Tradition, "Perjury is equivalent to double *shirk* with Allah." Allah Almighty says: *"Have done with telling lies."* (22:30) Anther *hadith* states: "The feet of a false witness will not move on the Day of Rising until the Fire is made mandatory for him." (Ibn Majah and al-Hakim)

According to *al-Musannaf*: "Whoever commits perjury has committed several terrible sins. One of them is lying. The Almighty says: *'Allah does not guide any unbridled inveterate liar.'* (40:28)" We find in another *hadith*: "A believer can be naturally disposed to anything except treachery and lying." (Ibn Majah and al-Hakim) Another of his sins is that he wrongs the person against whom he testifies in order to take his wealth, honour and life. A third is that he wrongs the person against whom he testifies in order to acquire unlawful wealth. He takes it on oath, so the Fire becomes mandatory for Him. The Messenger of Allah ﷺ said, "If I judge that someone should have his brother's property, to which he in fact has no right, he should not take it. I have cut for him a piece of the Fire." (al-Bukhari and Muslim) A fourth sin is that he makes lawful what Allah Almighty has made unlawful and protected with respect to wealth, life and honour.

The Messenger of Allah ﷺ said, "Shall I tell you of the worst of serious wrong actions? Associating others with Allah, disrespect to parents, and perjury. And perjury.' He continued to repeat it until we almost said that we wished that he had been silent." Al-Bukhari related this.

We ask Allah almighty for safety and protection from every affliction.

19. Drinking alcohol

Allah Almighty says:

"You who believe, wine and gambling, stone altars and divining arrows are filth from the handiwork of Shaytan. Avoid them completely so that perhaps you will be successful. Shaytan wants to stir up enmity and hatred between you by means of wine and gambling, and to debar you from remembrance of Allah and from the prayer. Will you not give them up?" (5:90-91)

Allah Almighty forbids wine in this *ayat* and cautions against it.

The Prophet ﷺ said, "Avoid wine. It is the mother of foul things." (al-Hakim) Anyone who does not avoid it has disobeyed Allah and His Messenger and deserves punishment for disobeying Allah and His Messenger. Allah Almighty says:

"As for him who disobeys Allah and His Messenger and oversteps His limits, We will admit him into a Fire, to remain in it timelessly, for ever. He will have a humiliating punishment." (4:14)

Ibn 'Abbas ﷺ said, "When the prohibition of wine was revealed, some of the Companions went to one another and said, 'Wine has been forbidden and made equal to *shirk*.'" (at-Tabarani) 'Abdullah ibn 'Amr ﷺ believed that drinking wine was the greatest of the major wrong actions and it is, without a doubt, the mother of foul things. Those who drink are cursed in more than one *hadith*.

Ibn 'Umar ﷺ said that the Messenger of Allah ﷺ said, "Every intoxicant is wine and every sort of wine is forbidden. If someone drinks wine in this world and dies without having repented of it and is addicted to it, he will not drink it in the Next World." Muslim related it. *Khamr* (wine) means anything that overpowers the intellect whether it is moist or dry, eaten or drunk.

Imam Ahmad related in his *Musnad* in a *hadith* from Abu Hurayra ﷺ that the Messenger of Allah ﷺ said, "An habitual drinker of wine is like an idolator." He stated that when an habitual drinker dies without repenting, he will not enter the Garden.

An-Nasa'i related in a *hadith* from Ibn 'Umar ﷺ that the Messenger of Allah ﷺ said, "Anyone who disrespects his parents and habitually drinks wine will not enter the Garden." In one variant: "Allah has forbidden the Garden to three: an habitual drinker, someone who disrespects his parents, and a wittol, meaning someone who condones evil in his wife."

He also stated that Allah does not accept the good actions of a drunkard. Jabir ibn 'Abdullah ﷺ related that the Messenger of Allah ﷺ said, "Three who do not have their prayer accepted from them, and none of whose good actions rises to heaven: a runaway slave, until he returns to his owners and surrenders to them; a woman whose husband is angry with her, until he is pleased with her; and a drunkard until he becomes sober." (Ibn Khuzayma, Ibn Hibban, al-Bayhaqi and at-Tabarani)

Abu Sa'id al-Khudri ﷺ related that the Messenger of Allah ﷺ said, "Allah does not accept the prayer of anyone who drinks wine as long as any of it remains in his body." One transmission has: "If someone drinks wine, Allah does not accept anything from him. If someone becomes drunk on it, his prayer is not accepted for forty days. If he repents and then reverts, it is right for Allah to let him drink of the molten brass of Hellfire." The Messenger of Allah ﷺ said, "If someone drinks wine and does not get drunk, Allah turns away from him for forty nights. If someone drinks wine and gets drunk, Allah will not accept any compensation from him for forty nights. If he dies during this time, he dies as an idolator. It is right for Allah to let him drink from the ooze of poison." Someone asked, "Messenger of Allah, what is the ooze of poison?" He said. "The fluid, blood and pus of the people of the Fire."

The Prophet ﷺ said that anyone who drinks wine is not a believer when he drinks it. It is reported from Abu Hurayra ﷺ from the Prophet ﷺ that "A thief is not a believer when he steals. A fornicator is not a believer when he fornicates. Someone who drinks is not a believer when he drinks wine. Repentance can occur afterwards." Al-Bukhari transmitted it. We find in another *hadith*: "Whoever commits fornication or drinks wine, Allah removes Islam from him as a man removes a shirt from over his head." (al-Hakim) It is reported that "Anyone who drinks wine in

67

the evening becomes an idolator in the morning. Anyone who drinks it in the morning becomes an idolator in the evening."

The Prophet ﷺ said: "The scent of the Garden can be smelt from five hundred miles, but its fragrance will not be smelt by anyone who disrespects his parents, reminds people of his charity, habitually drinks wine or worships an idol." It is related by Imam Ahmad in the *hadith* from Abu Musa al-Ash'ari ﷺ that the Messenger of Allah ﷺ said, "A habitual wine drinker will not enter the Garden, nor will anyone who believes in sorcery or who cuts off kin. Whoever dies while drinking wine, Allah will let him drink from the river of *Ghuta*, which is fluid flowing from the genitals of whores, and the stink of their private parts nauseates the people of the Fire."

The Messenger of Allah ﷺ said, "Allah sent me as a mercy and guidance to the worlds. He sent me to do away with stringed instruments and wind instruments and the business of the *Jahiliyya*. My Lord Almighty has sworn by His might: 'None of My slaves takes a mouthful of wine without being given its like from the boiling water of Hell. None of My slaves leaves it out of fear of Me without My letting him drink in the fields of sanctity with the best companions.'" (Ahmad)

Abu Dawud related that the Messenger of Allah ﷺ said, "Wine itself is cursed, as are the one who drinks it, the one who serves it, the one who sells it and the one who buys it, the one who presses it or for whom it is pressed, the one who carries or accepts its delivery, and the one who consumes the money paid for it." Imam Ahmad related it from a *hadith* of Ibn 'Abbas ﷺ, who said: "I heard the Messenger of Allah ﷺ say, 'Jibril came to me and said, "Muhammad, Allah has cursed wine, whoever presses it or has it pressed, its seller and buyer, the one who drinks it, the one who consumes what is paid for it, its carrier and the one who asks for it to be carried, and the one who serves it or asks for it to be served."'"

There is a prohibition against visiting wine-drinkers when they are ill or greeting them. 'Abdullah ibn 'Amr ibn al-'As ﷺ said, "Do not visit wine drinkers when they are ill." Al-Bukhari relates that "Ibn 'Umar ﷺ said, 'Do not greet a wine drinker.'" The Prophet ﷺ said, "Do not sit with wine drinkers; do not visit those of them who are ill; and do not attend their funerals. A wine drinker will come on the Day of Rising with a black face, his tongue dangling down onto on his chest, and his spittle running down. Anyone who sees that will recognise that he was a wine drinker." (Ibn al-Jawzi)

One of the scholars said: "It is forbidden to visit them and greet them, because a wine drinker is deviant and cursed by Allah and His Messenger, as in the words of the Prophet ﷺ: 'Allah has cursed wine and the one who drinks it. If someone buys it and presses it, he is cursed twice. If he gives it to someone, he is cursed three times.' That is why it is forbidden to visit them and greet them unless they repent. If someone repents, Allah turns to him."

He stated ﷺ that it is not lawful to use wine for medicine. Umm Salama ؓ said, "A daughter of mine was ill and I made *nabidh* (a fermented drink) for her in a jug. The Messenger of Allah ﷺ came to me while it was boiling and asked, 'What is this, Umm Salama?' I mentioned that I was using it to treat a daughter of mine. The Messenger of Allah ﷺ said, 'Allah Almighty has not put the healing of my community in what He has made prohibited for it.'" (al-Bayhaqi) It is mentioned by Abu Nu'aym in *al-Hilya* from Abu Musa ؓ that he said, "The Prophet ﷺ was brought some *nabidh* in a jar which was bubbling and he said, 'Smash it against the wall. This is the drink of someone who does not believe in Allah and the Last Day.'"

The Messenger of Allah ﷺ said, "Anyone who has one *ayat* of the Book of Allah in his heart and pours wine on it will be brought on the Day of Rising and every letter of that *ayat* will take him by the forelock until he is made to stand before Allah – blessed is He and exalted – and argue with it. Whoever has the Qur'an argue with him is an opponent. Woe to anybody who has the Qur'an argue against him on the Day of Rising."

It is related that the Prophet ﷺ said, "There are no people who gather together to drink an intoxicant in this world without Allah gathering them together in the Fire. They will turn to one another blaming each other. One of them will say to the other, 'So-and-so, may Allah not repay you well. You are the one who brought me to this!' The other will say the same thing back."

Traditions from the Salaf about wine

Al-Fudayl ibn 'Iyad visited one of his students who was dying, and began to instruct him to say the *shahada*; but his tongue would not articulate it. So he repeated it to him but he said, "I do not say it. I am free of it." So al-Fudayl left him, weeping. Then after that he saw him in a dream being dragged to the Fire. He said to him, "Wretch! What stripped recognition from you?" He answered, "Master, I had an illness and I went to a doctor and he told me to drink a glass of wine every year. He told me that if I did not do it, my illness would continue. I used to drink it every year for medication." If that is the state of someone who drinks it for medication, what will be the state of someone who drinks it for any other reason? We ask Allah for pardon and protection from every affliction.

One of those who repented was asked about what brought it about and he said, "I used to disinter graves and I saw dead people in them turned away from the *qibla*. I asked their families about them and they said, 'They used to drink wine in this world, and they died without repenting.'" One of the righteous said, "A young son of mine died, and after I had buried him, I saw him in a dream and his hair was white. I said, 'My son, I buried you when you were young. What has made you white-haired?' He answered, 'Father, a man was buried beside me who used to drink wine in this world. Hell sighed when he came and there was no child who did not become white-haired from the intensity of its sigh.'" We seek refuge with Allah. We ask Allah for pardon and protection from anything which obliges punishment in the Next World.

Section. Hashish, which is made from the leaves of cannabis, is unlawful like wine, and anyone who consumes it should receive the same *hadd* punishment as someone who drinks wine. It is worse than wine since it destroys the intellect and constitution, making a man effeminate, a wittol or some other corrupt thing. Wine is more corrupting in another way because it leads to arguing and fighting. Both of them prevent remembrance of Allah and the prayer.

Some later scholars hesitate about the *hadd* punishment for hashish and believe that someone who uses it should receive a discretionary punishment which is less than the *hadd*. This is because they consider it to be something which alters the mind without giving pleasure, and because early scholars did not say anything about it. That is not the case. Rather people are intoxicated by consuming it and desire it like wine or even more, so that they cannot bear to be without it, and it stops them from remembering Allah and from the prayer when they use it often.

But when hashish is in a solid form and eaten and not drunk or smoked, scholars disagree about its impurity. There are three positions in the school of Imam Ahmad and others. It is said that it is impure like wine which is drunk; and that is the sound position. It is said that it is not impure because it is solid. It is said that there is a difference according to whether it is in a solid or liquid form. In any case, it is included in the category of intoxicants, which Allah and His Messenger have forbidden, both in word and meaning.

Abu Musa ﷺ said, "Messenger of Allah, give us a ruling about two drinks which we make in Yemen: *bit'*, which is made from fermented honey which becomes strong; and *mizr*, which is made from barley which is fermented until it becomes strong." The Messenger of Allah ﷺ said, "I have been given the final general statements;" and the Prophet ﷺ said, "Every intoxicant is forbidden." Muslim related it.

The Prophet ﷺ said, "When much of something intoxicates, a little of it is unlawful." The Prophet ﷺ did not distinguish between one type of intoxicant and another, as to whether it is eaten or drunk, since wine can be made into bread and hashish can be melted in water and drunk. Wine is eaten and drunk. Hashish is eaten and drunk. The scholars did not mention it because it was not a custom among the early generations. It came about when the Mongols came to the lands of Islam. By Allah, Iblis does not rejoice at anything as he does at hashish, because it is attractive to base souls and people consider it lawful and indulge in it.

Story. It is related from 'Abd al-Malik ibn Marwan that a young man came to him weeping in sorrow and said, "*Amir al-Mu'minin,*

I have committed a terrible sin. Can I repent?" The caliph asked, "What was your sin?" He replied, "My sin is terrible." He said, "What is it? Repent to Allah Almighty. He accepts the repentance of His slaves and pardons evil deeds." He said, "*Amir al-Mu'minin*, I used to rob graves and I saw extraordinary things in them." He asked, "What did you see?" He said, "*Amir al-Mu'minin*, one night I dug up a grave and I saw that its inhabitant had turned his face away from the *qibla*. I was afraid of him and wanted to leave. Then someone said in the grave, 'Why don't you ask why the corpse has turned his face away from the *qibla*?' So I asked, 'Why has he turned away?' I was answered, 'Because he made light of the prayer. This is the repayment of someone like him.'

"Then I dug up another grave and saw that the corpse had been turned into a pig and was bound with chains and fetters on his neck. I was afraid of him and wanted to leave, and a voice said, 'Why don't you ask what he did and why he is being punished?' So I asked, 'Why?' He said, 'He used to drink wine in this world and died without repenting.' The third time, *Amir al-Mu'minin*, I opened the grave and found the corpse driven into earth with pegs of fire and his tongue pinned to the back of his mouth. I was afraid and wanted to leave but there was a call, 'Why do you not ask about his state and why he is being punished?' I asked, 'What did he do?' He said, 'He did not avoid urine and he used to carry tales among people.' I opened a fourth grave, *Amir al-Mu'minin*, and found its inhabitant burning with fire and I was afraid of him and wanted to leave. Someone said, 'Why do you not ask about him and his state?' I asked, 'What is his state?' He said, 'He abandoned the prayer.'

I dug up a fifth, *Amir al-Mu'minin*, and found that it extended as far as the eye could see with a luminous light. The corpse was lying on a bed. His light shone and he was wearing beautiful garments. I was in awe of him and wanted to leave. It was said to me, 'Will you not ask about his state and why he is honoured in this way?' I said, 'Why is he honoured?' I was told, 'Because he was a devout young man who was brought up obeying and worshipping Allah Almighty." 'Abd al-Malik said at that, "This contains a lesson for the disobedient and good news for the obedient. It is

72

mandatory for anyone with these defects to quickly repent and obey Allah."

May Allah make us and you among the obedient and make us avoid the actions of the deviants. He is Generous, Magnanimous.

20. Gambling

Allah Almighty says:

"O you who believe, wine, gambling, stone altars and divining arrows are filth from the handiwork of Shaytan. Avoid them completely so that perhaps you may be successful. Shaytan wants to stir up enmity and hatred between you by means of wine and gambling and to debar you from remembrance of Allah and from the prayer. Will you not then give them up?" (5:90-91)

Gambling (*maysir*) is gambling of any type: backgammon, chess, dice, or something else. It is consuming the property of people under false pretences, which Allah forbids when He says: *"Do not devour one another's property by false means."* (2:188) It is encompassed by the words of the Prophet ﷺ, "Men who spend the property of Allah without due right will go to the Fire on the Day of Rising" (al-Bukhari). In *Sahih al-Bukhari* we also find that the Messenger ﷺ said, "If anyone says to his companion, 'Come on, I will make a bet with you,' he should give *sadaqa*." If merely saying the words obliges expiation or *sadaqa*, what do you think about actually doing it?

Section. Scholars disagree about backgammon and chess when there is no betting involved. They agree that it is forbidden to play backgammon since it is established sound proofs that the Messenger of Allah ﷺ said, "Whoever plays backgammon, it is as if he had dyed his hand with the flesh and blood of pigs." Muslim transmitted it. The Prophet ﷺ also said, "Anyone who plays backgammon has disobeyed Allah and His Messenger." (Malik, Abu Dawud, Ibn Majah) Ibn 'Umar ﷺ said, "Playing backgammon is gambling and is like greasing oneself with pig fat."

As for chess, most scholars believe that it is forbidden to play it, whether there is a bet or not. If betting is involved, it is gambling without a doubt. As for the statement that even if there is no betting, it is still a form of forbidden gambling according to most of the scholars, it is related in one transmission from ash-Shafi'i that it is permitted if it is done in privacy and does not distract anyone from an obligation or the prayer at its time. An-Nawawi was asked about playing chess and whether it was forbidden or permitted, and he answered, "It is forbidden according to most scholars." He was also asked whether it was permitted to play chess and whether anyone who played it sinned or not, and he answered, "If he delays a prayer beyond its time or he plays it to win money, it is forbidden. Otherwise it is disliked according to ash-Shafi'i and forbidden according to others." That is the position of an-Nawawi in his *Fatwas*.

The proof that it is forbidden in the view of the majority is found in the words of Allah Almighty: *"Forbidden for you are carrion, blood and pig meat ... by means of divining arrows."* (5:3) Sufyan and Waki' ibn al-Jarrah said, "Divining arrows includes chess." 'Ali ibn Abi Talib ؇ said, "Chess is the gambling of the Persians." He passed by some people playing it and said, "What are these images to which you devoting yourselves? It is better for one of you to hold a burning ember until it is extinguished than to touch them." Then he added, "By Allah, this is not what you were created for." He also said, "The one who plays chess is the most mendacious of people. One of them says, 'Checkmate' ["*Shah mat*: the King is dead"] when he is not."

Abu Musa al-Ash'ari ؇ said, "No one plays chess except someone in error." Ishaq ibn Rahawayh was asked, "Do you think that there is anything wrong with playing chess?" He answered, "It is totally bad." It was said to him, "The people of the frontiers play it for military training." He said, "It is impiety." Muhammad ibn Ka'b al-Qurazi was asked about playing chess and said, "The least that can be said about it is that those who play it will be presented [or gathered] on the Day of Rising with people of falsehood." Ibn 'Umar ؇ was asked about chess and said, "It is worse than backgammon." Imam Malik ibn Anas was asked about chess and said, "Chess is part of backgammon."

It has reached us that Ibn 'Abbas ؇ was made the guardian of an orphan's property and found a chess game among the things the orphan inherited from his father and burned it. If playing it had been lawful, it would not have been permitted to burn it since it was the property of an orphan. But since playing it is unlawful, he burned it and so it falls into the same category as wine. If wine is found in the property of an orphan, it has to be poured away. The same is true of chess. Ibrahim an-Nakha'i was asked, "What do you say about chess?" He answered, "It is cursed."

Abu Bakr al-Athram related in his collection from Wathila ibn al-Asqa' that the Messenger of Allah ﷺ said, "Allah looks at His creation three hundred and sixty times every day. A chess player does not benefit from that because he says, 'The king is dead.'" Abu Bakr al-Ajurri related with an *isnad* from Abu Hurayra ؓ that the Messenger of Allah ﷺ said: "When you pass by people playing with these arrows, backgammon and chess and other such distractions, do not greet them. When they gather and devote themselves to them, Shaytan comes to them with his armies and surrounds them. Whenever one of them averts his eye from it, Shaytan and his armies impel him to look back. They continue to play until they separate, like dogs which gather around a corpse, eat from it until their bellies are filled, and then separate. That is also because they lie and say, 'The king is dead ("*shah mat*" which becomes in English "checkmate").'" The Prophet ﷺ said, "The person with the worst punishment on the Day of Rising is someone who plays chess. Do you not see him say, 'I killed him' and 'By Allah, he is dead!'? By Allah, he lies against Allah."

Mujahid said, "When someone is dying, his companions with whom he used to sit present themselves to him. A man who used to play chess was dying and was told, 'Say: "There is no god but Allah,"' but he said, 'Mate!' and then died. So what he used to do in his playing when he was alive overpowered his tongue and instead of saying the *shahada*, he said, 'Checkmate.'"

There is no strength or power except by Allah the High, the Immense. This is like what is reported in another *hadith*: "Every man dies according to what he lives and is resurrected according to what he died." (Muslim)

We ask Allah the Gracious by His bounty to make us die as Muslims, not changing or altering or becoming misguided or swerving. He is Generous, Magnanimous.

21. Slandering chaste women

Allah Almighty says:

> "Those who accuse women who are chaste, but who are believers and not aware, are cursed in this world and the Next World, and they will have a great punishment on the Day when their tongues and hands and feet will testify against them about what they were doing." (24:23-24)

> "Those who make accusations against chaste women and then do not produce four witnesses: flog them with eighty lashes and never again accept them as witnesses. Such people are deviators." (24:4)

Allah Almighty tells us in the *ayat* that whoever accuses a chaste free woman who has been married of fornication and lewdness is cursed in this world and the Next and will have a painful punishment. In this world he receives the *hadd* punishment of eighty lashes and his testimony is not accepted, even if he has good character.

In the *Sahih* collection it is reported that the Messenger of Allah ﷺ said, "Avoid the seven deadly ones," and he mentioned among them slandering believing chaste women. Slander is to call a free chaste Muslim woman, to whom you are not related, an adulteress, whore or harlot, or call her husband, "husband of a whore," or her child, "child of a whore" or "child of an adulteress". When a man or a woman says that about a man or a woman, it is like someone calling a man an adulterer or accusing a free boy of engaging in pederasty. Such a person receives the *hadd* punishment of eighty lashes unless he brings a clear proof of that allegation.

The clear proof is as Allah says: four witnesses must attest to the truthfulness of a person's allegations about that woman or man. If there is no proof, then he is to be flogged if the man or woman he slandered so requests. That is also the case when someone slanders a slave or slave-girl by calling his slave an adulterer or his slave-girl an adulteress, whore, or harlot, since it is confirmed in the two *Sahih* collections that the Messenger of Allah ﷺ said, "If anyone accuses his slave of adultery, the *hadd* punishment will be carried out on him on the Day of Rising unless he is as he said."

Many ignorant people intemperately use these indecent words for which there is punishment in this world and the Next World. This is why it is confirmed in the two *Sahih* collections that the Messenger of Allah ﷺ said, "A man may say some words thoughtlessly because of which he will fall in the Fire deeper than the distance between the east and the west." Mu'adh ibn Jabal ﷺ asked, "Messenger of Allah, will we be punished for what we say?" He answered, "May your mother be bereft, Mu'adh! Are people thrown into the Fire on their faces for anything but the harvest of their tongues?" We find in a *hadith*: "Whoever believes in Allah and the Last Day should speak good words or be silent."

Allah – blessed and exalted is He - says in His Mighty Book: *"He does not utter a single word without a watcher by him, pen in hand!"* (50:18) 'Uqba ibn 'Amir ﷺ said, "Messenger of Allah, what brings salvation?" He ﷺ replied, "Control your tongue, keep to your house and weep over your errors. The furthest of people from Allah is someone who is hard-hearted." (Abu Dawud and at-Tirmidhi) The Prophet ﷺ also said, "The person Allah hates most is an indecent, coarse person."

May Allah protect us and you from the evil of our tongues by His grace and honour. He is Generous, Magnanimous.

22. Stealing from the booty

This includes stealing from the treasury and the *zakat*. Allah Almighty says:

"Allah does not love treacherous people." (8:58)

"No Prophet would ever be guilty of misappropriation. Those who misappropriate will arrive on the Day of Rising with what they misappropriated." (3:161)

According to *Sahih Muslim* Abu Hurayra ﷺ said, "The Messenger of Allah ﷺ stayed with us one day and he mentioned misappropriation and what a terrible thing it was. He said, 'Do not misappropriate. I would not like to see any of you coming on the Day of Rising with a camel groaning on his neck and saying, 'Messenger of Allah, help me!' I will say, 'I cannot do anything for you against Allah. I conveyed it to you.' I would not like to see any of you coming on the Day of Rising with a horse neighing on his neck and saying, 'Messenger of Allah, help me!' I will say, 'I cannot do anything for you against Allah. I conveyed it to you.' I would not like to see any of you coming on the Day of Rising with a sheep bleating on his neck and saying, 'Messenger of Allah, help me!' I will say, 'I cannot do anything for you against Allah. I conveyed it to you.' I would not like to see any of you coming on the Day of Rising with a soul on his neck shouting and saying, 'Messenger of Allah, help me!' I will say, 'I cannot do anything for you against Allah. I conveyed it to you.' I would not like to see any of you coming on the Day of Rising with garments fluttering on his neck and saying, 'Messenger of Allah, help me!' I will say, 'I cannot do anything for you against Allah. I conveyed it to you.' I would not like to see any of you coming on the Day of Rising with gold and silver on his neck, saying, 'Messenger of Allah, help me!' I will say, 'I cannot do anything for you against Allah. I conveyed it to you.'"

Anyone who takes any of these categories of booty before they are divided up among the fighters, or from the treasury without the permission of the ruler, or from the *zakat* which is collected for the poor, will come on the Day of Rising carrying it on his neck, as Allah Almighty said in the Qur'an: *"Those who misappropriate will arrive on the Day of Rising with what they have misappropriated."* (3:161) The Prophet ﷺ said, "Return even a needle and thread. Beware of misappropriation. It will be a disgrace for a person on the Day of Rising." The Prophet ﷺ stood on the minbar and praised Allah and said, "By Allah, none of you will take anything [without right] but that he will carry it on his back on the Day of Rising. I may recognise a man among you who will meet Allah carrying a camel grumbling, a cow mooing or a sheep bleating." Then he ﷺ raised his hand and said, "O Allah, have I conveyed it?"

Abu Hurayra ؓ said, "We went out with the Messenger of Allah ﷺ to Khaybar. When we conquered it we did not take any gold or silver. We took goods, food and clothing. Then we went to the wadi (Wadi al-Qura). The Messenger of Allah ﷺ had with him a slave (called Rifaʻa ibn Yazid, from the Banu ad-Dubayb) whom a man of the Banu Judham had given him. When we camped in the wadi, the slave of the Messenger of Allah ﷺ got up to remove his saddle and was killed by a random arrow. We said, 'Congratulations to him on martyrdom, Messenger of Allah.' The Messenger of Allah said, 'No, by the One who has my soul in His hand. The cloak which he took from the booty before it was divided up will turn into fire burning him.' The people were alarmed and a man brought a strap or two and said, 'I got this at Khaybar.' The Messenger of Allah ﷺ said, 'A strap or two of Fire.'" (al-Bukhari and Muslim)

'Abdullah ibn 'Amr ؓ said, "There was a man called Karkara who looked after the baggage of the Messenger of Allah ﷺ and he died. The Prophet ﷺ said, 'He is in the Fire.' They went to investigate, and found a cloak which he had misappropriated." (al-Bukhari)

Zayd ibn Khalid al-Juhani ؓ said that a man misappropriated something from the booty in the Khaybar expedition and the Prophet ﷺ refused to pray over him. He said, 'Your companion misappropriated something in the Way of Allah.' We searched his things and found in it some pearls worth two dirhams which had belonged to a Jew." (Malik, Ahmad and others) Imam Ahmad said,

"We do not know that the Prophet ﷺ refused to pray over anyone except misappropriators and suicides." It is related that the Prophet ﷺ stated, "Gifts to governors are a form of misappropriation." (Ahmad)

There are many *hadith*s on this subject. Some of them are found in the chapter on injustice. There are three types of injustice. One is consuming wealth under false pretences. The second is injustice to people by killing, beating, breaking and wounding them. The third is wronging people by abuse, curses, insults and slander. The Prophet ﷺ spoke at Mina and said, "Your lives, your property and your honour are sacred, like the sanctity of this day of yours in this month of yours in this land of yours." (al-Bukhari and Muslim) The Prophet ﷺ also said, "Allah does not accept a prayer without purity; nor does He accept *sadaqa* from misappropriated wealth." (Muslim)

We ask Allah for success in what He loves and is pleased with. He is Generous, Magnanimous.

23. Theft

Allah Almighty says:

"As for thieves, male or female, cut off their hands in reprisal for what they have done: an object lesson from Allah. Allah is Almighty, All-Wise." (5:38)

Ibn Shihab said, "The punishment of Allah for those who steal other people's property is amputation. Allah is Almighty in His retribution on theft, and All-Wise in imposing the obligation of cutting off the thief's hand."

Ibn 'Umar ﷺ said that the Prophet ﷺ cut off a hand for a shield worth three dirhams. 'A'isha ﷺ said, "The Messenger of Allah ﷺ cut off the hand of a thief for a quarter of a dinar or more." (al-Bukhari and Muslim) In one transmission, the Messenger of Allah ﷺ said, "The hand of a thief is not to be cut off for less than the price of a shield." 'A'isha ﷺ was asked "What is the price of a shield?" She answered, "A quarter of a dinar." (al-Bukhari and Muslim) In another transmission he ﷺ said, "Cut off the hand for a quarter of a dinar. Do not cut it off for less than that." A quarter of a dinar at that time was eqivalent to three dirhams, a dinar being worth twelve dirhams.

Abu Hurayra ﷺ narrated that the Messenger of Allah ﷺ said, "Allah cursed the thief who steals a helmet for which his hand is cut off and who steals a rope for which his hand is cut off." (al-Bukhari and Muslim) Al-A'mash said, "They considered that the helmet meant here was an iron helmet and they considered that the rope was one which was worth three dirhams."

'A'isha ﷺ reported: "A Makhzumi woman borrowed some goods and refused to return them, and the Prophet ﷺ commanded that her hand be cut off. Her family went to Usama ibn Zayd ﷺ and spoke to him about her and he spoke to the Prophet ﷺ, who said to him, 'Usama, do I see you interceding where one of the *hudud* of Allah is concerned?' The Prophet ﷺ rose to speak and said, 'Those before you were destroyed because when one of their nobles stole they would leave him alone, but when someone weak stole, thy would cut off his hand. By the One who has my soul in his hand, if Fatima the daughter of Muhammad were to steal, her hand would be cut off.' The hand of the Makhzumi woman was cut off."

'Abd ar-Rahman ibn Jarir said, "Fadala ibn 'Ubayd asked whether hanging the hand of a thief from his neck was part of the *Sunna*. He replied, 'A thief was brought to the Prophet ﷺ and he had his hand cut off and then commanded that it be hung from his neck.'" Scholars say that that a thief does not benefit from his repentance unless he returns what he stole. If he is bankrupt, then he must ask the owner of the property to absolve him. Allah knows best.

24. Highway robbery

Allah Almighty says:

"The reprisal against those who wage war against Allah and His Messenger, and go about the earth corrupting it, is that they should be killed or crucified, or have their opposite hands and feet cut off, or be banished from the land. That will be their degradation in this world and in the Next World they will have a terrible punishment." (5:33)

Al-Wahidi said, "Waging war against Allah and His Messenger means disobeying them. Anyone who disobeys you fights you. Corrupting the earth means by killing, theft and usurping wealth. To take up weapons against the believers is to wage war against Allah and His Messenger. That is the position of Malik, al-Awza'i and ash-Shafi'i."

As for His words, *"killed … banished from the land,"* al-Walibi said that Ibn 'Abbas ﷺ said that the word "or" used in this *ayat* indicates a choice. The meaning is that the ruler has permission to execute, crucify or banish. This is the position of al-Hasan, Sa'id ibn al-Musayyab and Mujahid. According to the transmission of 'Atiyya, however, the "or" does not indicate permission to choose but gives the order in the ruling for different crimes. If someone kills and robs, he is put to death and crucified. If he robs but does not kill, the punishment is amputation. If someone sheds blood but refrains from theft, he is to be put to death. If someone causes alarm on the road but does not kill, he is to be banished. This is the position of ash-Shafi'i.

Ash-Shafi'i also said, "Each of them receives a *hadd* punishment according to his actions. If someone is to be put to death and crucified, he is put to death before he is crucified because it is disliked to torture him. He is crucified for three days and then taken down. If someone is to be put to death but not crucified, he is put to death and returned to his family for burial. If anyone is sentenced to amputation without death, he has his right hand cut off and then cauterised. If he reverts and steals again, his left foot is cut off. If he reverts and steals again, his left hand is cut off, in accordance with what is related from the Prophet 🕮 about a thief: 'If he steals, cut off his hand. Then if he steals again, cut off his foot. Then if he steals again, cut off his other hand. If he steals again, cut off his other foot.' (Abu Dawud and an-Nasa'i) That is what Abu Bakr and 'Umar 🕮 did, and none of the Companions 🕮 disagreed with it. The reason why it is the left is that it is agreed that it should be the left foot after the hand. That is the meaning of His word 'opposite'."

Ibn 'Abbas 🕮 says about the words of the Almighty, "*or banishment from the land*": "It means that the ruler declares that he may be killed with impunity and says, 'If anyone meets him, he should kill him.' This concerns what he is able to do. If anyone is arrested, his banishment from the land is imprisonment or detention, because when he is imprisoned and cannot move in the land, he is banished from it."

We ask Allah for protection from every affliction and trial. He is Magnanimous, Generous.

25. Deliberate false oaths

Allah Almighty says:

"Those who sell Allah's covenant and their own oaths for a paltry price, such people have no portion in the Next World; and on the Day of Rising Allah will not speak to them or look at them or purify them. They will have a painful punishment." (3:77)

According to al-Wahidi this was revealed about two men who argued with the Prophet ﷺ about some property: the one against whom the claim was made wanted to swear an oath and so Allah revealed this *ayat*. The one against whom the claim was made withdrew and affirmed the right of the claimant.

'Abdullah [ibn Mas'ud] ﷺ reported that the Messenger of Allah ﷺ said, "Whoever swears an oath depriving someone of his property, and lies in his oath, will meet Allah and find Him angry with him." Al-Ash'ath ﷺ said, "By Allah, it was revealed about me. There was some land between me and a Jewish man, and he denied my claim to it, so I took him to the Prophet ﷺ who said, 'Do you have a clear proof?' I said, 'No.' He said to the Jew, 'Swear.' I said, 'Messenger of Allah, then he will swear and take away my property.' So Allah Almighty revealed, *'Those who sell Allah's covenant and their own oaths for a paltry price, such people have no portion in the Next World; and on the Day of Rising Allah will not speak to them, or look at them or purify them.'"* (al-Bukhari)

'Abdullah ibn Mas'ud ﷺ reported that he heard the Messenger of Allah ﷺ say, "Anyone who swears in order to take the property of a Muslim man without any right to it, will meet Allah while He is angry with him."

'Abdullah [ibn Mas'ud] ﷺ also said, "Then the Messenger of Allah ﷺ recited to us its confirmation in the Book of Allah: *'Those who sell Allah's covenant and their own oaths...'* (3:77) to the end of the *ayat*. This is transmitted in both *Sahih* collections. Abu Umama ﷺ said, "We were with the Messenger of Allah ﷺ when he said, 'Whoever usurps the right of a Muslim by means of his oath, Allah has made the Fire mandatory for him and forbidden him the

Garden." A man said, "Even if it be little, Messenger of Allah?" He answered, "Even if it be a stalk of '*araq.*" Muslim transmitted this in his *Sahih.* Hafs ibn Maysara said, "How severe this *hadith* is!" He said, "Is it not in the Book of Allah: *'Those who sell Allah's covenant and their own oaths for a paltry price...?'*"

Abu Dharr ﷺ reported that the Prophet ﷺ said, "There are three people whom Allah will not speak to or purify on the Day of Rising, and who will have a painful punishment" The Messenger of Allah ﷺ said this three times. Abu Dharr ﷺ said, "They are ruined and have lost, Messenger of Allah. Who are they?" He said, "Someone who wears his garment long (out of pride), someone who reminds people of his charity to them, and someone who sells his goods with a false oath." The Messenger of Allah ﷺ said, "The major wrong actions are: associating others with Allah, disrespecting parents, murder and a deliberate false oath." Al-Bukhari transmitted this in his *Sahih.*

Section on someone swearing by something other than Allah, such as the Prophet ﷺ, the Ka'ba, the angels, heaven, water, life, the spirit, the head, the life of the sultan, the blessing of the ruler and such like

Ibn 'Umar ﷺ narrated that the Prophet ﷺ said, "Allah has forbidden you to swear by your fathers! If someone swears, he should swear by Allah or remain silent." According to another transmission in the *Sahih:* "Someone who swears should only swear by Allah or be silent." 'Abd ar-Rahman ibn Samura ﷺ reported that the Messenger of Allah ﷺ said, "Do not swear by idols nor by your fathers." Muslim related it. Burayda ﷺ said that the Messenger of Allah ﷺ said, "Whoever swears by the trust is not one of us." Abu Dawud and others related it. Burayda also reported that the Messenger of Allah ﷺ said, "If someone swears using the words, 'Or I am free of Islam,' and is lying, that is how he is. If he is telling the truth, he will not return to Islam safe and sound."

Ibn 'Umar ﷺ related that he heard a man say, "By the Ka'ba!" He said, "Do not swear by anything other than Allah. I heard the Messenger of Allah ﷺ say, 'Anyone who swears other than by Allah has disbelieved and associated others with Him.'" At-Tirmidhi related it as did Ibn Hibban, who declared in his *Sahih* that it is sound, and al-Hakim.

The Prophet ﷺ said, "If someone makes an oath and says in his oath, 'By al-Lat and al-'Uzza,' he should say, 'There is no god but Allah.'" Some of the Companions ﷺ were accustomed to say this before Islam, and sometimes the tongue of one of them would get the better of him and he would swear by them, and therefore the Prophet ﷺ commanded that he say immediately, "There is no god but Allah" to expiate what his tongue had said. All success is by Allah.

26. Injustice

Injustice includes consuming other people's property, taking it without right, wronging people by striking them or insulting them, transgressing against them, and being overbearing to the weak.

Allah Almighty says:

> "*Do not consider Allah to be unaware of what the wrongdoers perpetrate. He is merely deferring them to a Day on which their sight will be transfixed, rushing headlong – heads back, eyes vacant, hearts hollow. Warn mankind of the Day when the punishment will reach them. Those who did wrong will say, 'Our Lord, reprieve us for a short time. We will respond to Your call and follow the Messengers.' But did you not swear to Me before that you would never meet your downfall, even though you inhabited the houses of those who had wronged themselves and it was made clear to you how We had dealt with them and We gave you many examples?*" (14:42-45)

> "*There are only grounds against those who do wrong.*" (42:42)

> "*Those who do wrong will soon know the kind of reversal they will receive.*" (26:227)

The Prophet ﷺ said, "Allah prolongs the life of the unjust but when He takes them, He will not let them escape. Then he recited, '*Such is the iron grip of your Lord when He seizes cities which do wrong. His grip is painful, violent*' (11:102)." (al-Bukhari and Muslim)

The Prophet ﷺ said, "Anyone who has done an injustice to his brother with respect to his honour or something else should seek to be absolved by him before the time when there will be neither *dinar* nor *dirham*, before some of his right actions will be taken from him by his brother, and if he does not have any good actions, some of the bad actions of his brother will be taken and cast on him." (al-Bukhari and at-Tirmidhi)

The Prophet ﷺ stated that his Lord – Blessed and Exalted is He – said, "My slaves, I have forbidden injustice to Myself and made it unlawful between you, so do not do wrong one another." (Muslim and at-Tirmidhi)

The Messenger of Allah ﷺ said, "Do you know who the true bankrupt is? They replied, "The bankrupt is someone who has neither money nor goods." He said, "The truly bankrupt person of my community is the one who performs the prayer, fasts and pays *zakat* but then insults this person, slanders that one, consumes the property of this person, sheds the blood of that one, and strikes this one. Some of them will be given some of his good deeds, and others will also be given some of his good deeds. If his good deeds are exhausted before this has finished, some of their sins will be taken and cast on him and then he will be thrown into the Fire." (Muslim and at-Tirmidhi)

All of these *hadith*s are in the *Sahih* collections. We have already quoted his advice to Mu'adh ﷺ when he sent him to Yemen: "Fear the supplication of the wronged. There is no veil between it and Allah." In some books Allah Almighty says, "My anger is severe against anyone who wrongs someone else who has no helper other than Me."

As someone recited:

Do not wrong others, for you have no real power.
    The end of injustice is regret.
Your eyes sleep but the wronged one is awake,
        praying against you,
        and the Eye of Allah never sleeps.

One of the Salaf said, "Do not wrong the weak lest you become one of the evil ones among the strong." Abu Hurayra ﷺ said, "The bustard dies in its nest fearing the injustice of the unjust." It is said that it is written in the Torah: "A caller shall calls from beyond the Bridge (*Sirat*): 'Company of transgressing tyrants! Company of affluent wretches! God swears by His might and majesty that no wrongdoer will cross this bridge today.'"

Jabir ﷺ said, "When the emigrants to Abyssinia returned to the Messenger of Allah ﷺ in the year of the Conquest, he asked, 'Will you tell me about the most extraordinary thing that you saw in the land of Abyssinia?' The youngest of them said, 'Messenger of Allah, one day while we were sitting, one of their old women passed by us carrying a jug of water on her head. One of their boys passed and put one of his hands between her shoulders and pushed her. The woman fell to her knees and the jug broke. When she got up, she turned to him and said, "You will know, treacherous one! When Allah sets up the Throne and gathers the first and the last, and hands and feet speak of what they earned, you will know the consequences of my business and your business with Him tomorrow."' The Messenger of Allah ﷺ said, 'She spoke the truth. How can Allah purify a people when the strong among them are not punished for what they do to the weak?'"

It is related that the Prophet ﷺ said, "There are five people with whom Allah is angry. If He wishes, He expresses His anger on them in this world, or He may order them to the Fire in the Next World: the ruler of a people who takes his right from his subjects but does not give them their rights from himself and does not avert injustice from them; a leader of a people who obey him but who does not treat the weak and strong equally and speaks from whim; a man who does not command his wife and children to obey Allah, and does not teach them their *deen*; a man who hires someone who does his work in full and who does not then give him his full wage; and a man who wrongs his wife in respect of her dowry."

'Abdullah ibn Salam ﷺ said, "When Allah Almighty created His creatures, they stood on their feet and raised their heads to the sky and said, 'Lord, who are You with?' He answered, 'With the wronged, until they are given their due.'" Wahb ibn Munabbih said, "A tyrant built a castle and fortified it. Then a poor old woman came and built a hut beside it where she could take refuge. The tyrant rode out one day and went around the castle, saw the hut and asked, 'Whose is this?' He was told, 'It belongs to a poor woman who lives in it.' He ordered that it be demolished. The old woman came and saw it destroyed and asked, 'Who destroyed it?' She was told, 'The king. He saw it and destroyed it.' So the old woman lifted her head to heaven and said, 'O Lord, since I was not present, where were You?' So Allah commanded Jibril to overturn the castle on top of those inside it, and he overturned it."

When Khalid ibn Yarmak and his son were imprisoned, he said, "Father, after all the power we had, we are now in chains in prison." He said, "My son, the supplication of the wronged was made at night and we neglected it, but Allah did not neglect it." Yazid ibn Hakim used to say, "I have never feared anyone at all except for a man I wronged. I know that he has no helper except Allah. He told me, 'Allah is enough for me. Allah is between you and me.'" Abu Umama ﷺ said, "The wrongdoer will be brought on the Day of Rising until he is on the bridge over Hell and he will meet the one he wronged, who will acquaint him with how he wronged him. Those who were wronged will keep at those who wronged them until they take the good deeds they have. If they do not find that they have any good deeds, the wrongdoers will take on their evil deeds in return for the wrongs they did until they go to the lowest rank in the Fire." (at-Tabarani)

'Abdullah ibn Unays ﷺ related that he heard the Messenger of Allah ﷺ say, "Allah's servants will be gathered on the Day of Rising barefoot, naked and uncircumcised. A caller will call to them with a voice which will be heard from afar, as it is heard close at hand: 'I am the King, the Judge. None of the people of the Garden shall enter the Garden nor any of the people of the Fire enter the Fire while he is guilty of an injustice, until I take retaliation from him, be it a slap or more. *Your Lord will not wrong anyone.*" (14:49)' We asked, 'Messenger of Allah, how will that be when we come barefoot and naked?' He replied, 'Repayment is brought about through good actions and evil actions. *Your Lord will not wrong anyone.*'" (Ahmad) It is reported that the Prophet ﷺ said, "Whoever strikes with a whip unjustly, retaliation will be taken from him on the Day of Rising." (al-Bazzar)

It is also mentioned is that Khusrau (the Persian emperor) adopted a teacher for his son to teach him and discipline him. When the child had reached the highest level of excellence and manners, the teacher summoned him one day and dealt him a severe blow without any reason. So the child harboured rancour towards the teacher until he became an adult. His father died, and he succeeded to the throne after him. He summoned the teacher and said to him, "What made you hit me on such-and-such a day with a painful blow without any reason?" The teacher answered, "Know, o King, that when you reached the highest level of excellence and manners, I knew that you would become king after your father. I wanted you to taste the pain of a blow and the pain of injustice so that you would never wrong anyone." He said, "May Allah repay you well." Then he had a reward brought for him and let him go.

One form of injustice is misappropriating the property of an orphan. The *hadith* of Mu'adh ibn Jabal ﷺ has already mentioned in which the Messenger of Allah ﷺ said to him, "Fear the supplication of the wronged. There is no veil between it and Allah." One variant states that the supplication of the wronged rises above the clouds, and the Lord Almighty says, "By My might and majesty, I will help you, even if it be after some time."

Section: One of the worst sins is to delay paying what one owes when one is able to pay it, because it is confirmed in the two *Sahih* collections that the Messenger of Allah ﷺ said, "The procrastination of the wealthy is injustice." One variant has: "The one who can pay commits an injustice which makes his honour and his punishment lawful." This means his creditor may complain about him publicly and he can be imprisoned.

Section. Another form of injustice is when a man wrongs a woman by failing to pay her due by way of dowry, maintenance and clothing. It is encompassed by the words of the Messenger of Allah ﷺ about the injustice which makes a man's honour and punishment lawful. Ibn Mas'ud ﷺ said: "The hand of a man or woman will be taken on the Day of Rising and there will be a call made in front of people: 'This is so-and-so son of so-and-so. Those who are owed anything by them should come and take what is due to them.'" He said, "A woman will be happy to receive her due from her father, brother or husband." Then he recited: *"That Day there will be no family ties between them and they will not be able to question one another."* (23:101) He added, "Allah will forgive whatever He wishes regarding what is due to Himself, but He will not forgive any of the rights due to other people. The person will be made to stand for people and then Allah Almighty will say to the people owed rights, 'Come and get your rights.'"

The Prophet ﷺ continued, "Allah Almighty will say to the angels, 'Take some of his righteous actions and give everyone who is seeking something what he is due.' If he is a friend of Allah and there is an atom's weight of his good deeds left, Allah will multiply it for him so that he enters the Garden through them. If he is a wretched slave, and nothing remains for him, the angels will say, 'Lord, his good actions have run out and there are still people with demands.' Allah will say 'Take some of their evil deeds and add them to his evil deeds.' Then he will be thrown into the Fire."

That is confirmed by the words of the Prophet ﷺ quoted above: "Do you know who the true bankrupt is?" He stated that the bankrupt person in his community is the one who comes on the Day of Rising having performed prayer, *zakat* and fasting, but has abused this one, struck that one, and taken the property of that one. Because of this some of his good actions will taken for this person and that person. If his good actions run out before he has settled what he owes, some of their sins will be taken and cast on him and then he will be thrown into the Fire.

Section. Another form of injustice is when someone hires a person to do some work but then does not give him his wages. It is confirmed in the *Sahih al-Bukhari* that the Messenger of Allah ﷺ said, "Allah Almighty says, 'I will be an adversary against three on the Day of Rising: a man who makes an agreement in My name and then breaks it; a man who sells a free man and consumes the proceeds; and a man who hires an employee and gets full work from him but fails to pay him his wages.'" The same applies when a person wrongs a Jew or Christian, short-changes someone, imposes work on someone beyond his capacity, or takes something from someone against their will. He is included in the words of Allah Almighty: "I will be an adversary against him on the Day of Rising." Another form of injustice is when someone swears about a debt he owes and lies. According to both *Sahih* collections the Messenger of Allah ﷺ said, "If anyone appropriates the right of a

Muslim by an oath, Allah has made the Fire mandatory for him and forbidden him the Garden." They said, "Even if it is something insignificant, Messenger of Allah?" He replied, "Even if it is only a stick of arak."

It is related that nothing will be more hateful to anyone on the Day of Rising than to see someone he recognises, fearing that he will seek him out because of an injustice he inflicted on him in this world; as the Prophet ﷺ said, "You will hand over to people their rights on the Day of Rising, so that even a hornless sheep will take revenge on a horned one." (Muslim) The Prophet ﷺ said, "Whoever has done an injustice to his brother in respect of his honour or anything else should seek to be absolved by him before the Day when there will be neither dinar nor dirham. If he has right actions, they will be taken from him to counterbalance the injustice he did; and if he does not have any good actions, some of the bad actions of his friend will be taken and he will be made to carry them. Then he will be cast into the Fire." (al-Bukhari and at-Tirmidhi)

'Abdullah ibn Abi ad-Dunya related from Abu Ayyub al-Ansari ﷺ that the Messenger of Allah ﷺ said, "The first to argue on the Day of Rising will be a man and his wife. By Allah, her tongue will not speak but her hand and foot will testify against her about the trouble she caused her husband in this world. A man's hand and foot will also testify against him as to whether he treated his wife well or badly. Then a man will be summoned with his servant for the same purpose. No ransom will be accepted from him, but the good actions of this wrongdoer will be given to the one he wronged. Then the tyrants will be brought in iron funnels and the order will come: 'Drive them to the Fire.'"

Qadi Shurayh used to say, "The wrongdoers will know who will fall short when they are awaiting their punishment and those they wronged are awaiting help and reward." It is related that if Allah desires good for His slave, Allah gives power over him to someone who will wrong him." Tawus al-Yamani visited [the Caliph] Hisham ibn 'Abd al-Malik and said to him, "Fear Allah on the Day of the Announcement!" Hisham asked, "What is the Day of the Announcement?" He replied that Allah Almighty says: *"Between them a herald will proclaim, 'The curse of Allah be on the wrongdoers.'"* (7:44) Hisham fainted. Tawus said, "If this is the effect of merely hearing a description, how will be when it is seen directly?"

O you who are content with the name of wrongdoer, how many wrongs do you have to your account? The prison is Hellfire and the judge is the Truth.

Section. Being cautious about visiting perpetrators of injustice, socialising with them and helping them

Allah Almighty says: *"Do not rely on those who do wrong, thus causing the Fire to afflict you."* (11:113) 'Rely' here means to be at ease with something and to incline to it with affection. Ibn 'Abbas ﷺ said, "Do not completely incline to them with love, gentle words and affection." As-Suddi and Ibn Zayd explained as meaning "Do not flatter wrongdoers." 'Ikrima said, "It means to obey them and love them." Abu al-'Aliyya stated that it means "Do not be pleased with what they do."

Allah Almighty says: *"Assemble those who did wrong together with their associates and what they worshipped."* (37:22) Ibn Mas'ud ﷺ reported that the Messenger of Allah ﷺ said, "There will be rulers who are attended by servants or courtiers who are perpetrators of injustice and lie. Anyone who goes to them to support them in their falsehoods and helps them in their injustice is not from me and I am not from him. Anyone who does not go to them, and does not help them in their wrongdoing, is from me and I am from him."

Ibn Mas'ud ﷺ also reported that the Prophet ﷺ said, "Anyone who helps a wrongdoer gives him power over himself." Sa'id ibn al-Musayyab said, "Do not fill your eyes with the helpers of injustice except with disapproval in your hearts, so that your righteous actions may not fall away." Makhul ad-Dimishqi said, "A caller will call on the day of Rising, 'Where are the perpetrators of injustice and their helpers?' Everyone who brought them ink, filled their inkwells, sharpened their pens, or did anything more than that will be present with them and they will be gathered together in a box of fire and thrown into Hellfire." A tailor went to Sufyan ath-Thawri and said, "I am a man who makes the Sultan's clothes.

Am I one of the helpers of the perpetrators of injustice?" Sufyan answered, "You yourself are one of the perpetrators of injustice. The helpers of the perpetrators of injustice are those who buy needles and thread from you."

It is related that the Prophet 變 said, "The first to enter the Fire on the Day of Rising will be the whippers who had whips with which they beat people on behalf of the perpetrators of injustice." Ibn 'Umar 變 said, "The helpers of the perpetrators of injustice and police are the dogs of the Fire on the Day of Rising."

It is related that Allah Almighty revealed to Musa: "The tribe of Israel should not recite any kind of remembrance of Me. I remember anyone who remembers Me and My remembrance of them is to place a curse upon them." In one version, "I remember any of them who remember Me with a curse." It is reported that the Prophet 變 said, "None of you should stand in a place where a wronged man is beaten. A curse will descend on those who attend that place unless they defend him."

It is related that the Messenger of Allah 變 said, "A man will go to his grave and be told, 'We are going to beat you with a hundred blows.' He will continue to plead with them until it becomes one blow which they will strike him with. Then his grave will be filled with fire. He will ask, 'Why did you hit me with this blow?' They answer, 'You prayed a prayer without being in a state of purity, and passed by a man being wronged and did not help him.'" If this is the state of someone who does not help one wronged person when he is able to, what will be the state of the wronger himself?

It is confirmed in the two *Sahih* collections that the Messenger of Allah 變 said, "Help your brother, whether he is inflicting wrong or is wronged." They said, "Messenger of Allah, we can help him if he is wronged but how we can help him if he is inflicting wrong?" He answered, "You can take hold of his hands to restrain him from doing wrong. That is helping him."

One the gnostics said, "I dreamt of a man who used to serve the perpetrators of injustice and tax collectors some time after his death, and he was in a bad state. I said to him, 'What is your situation?' He said, 'An evil one.' I asked, 'Where did you end up?' He replied, 'In the punishment of Allah.' I asked, 'What is the state of the perpetrators of injustice with Him?' He answered, 'The worst state. Have you not heard the words of Allah Almighty, *'Those who do wrong will soon know the kind of reversal they will receive.'* (26:227)?"

Someone reported: "I saw a man whose arm had been severed at the shoulder and who was crying out, 'Whoever sees me should not wrong anyone!' I went to him and asked him, 'My brother, what is your story?' He answered, 'My brother, my story is extraordinary. I was one of the helpers of the perpetrators of injustice and one day I saw a fisherman who had caught a large fish, which I wanted. I went to him and said, "Give me this fish." He said, "I will not give it to you. I will sell it and get food for my family." So I struck him and took it from him by force and went off with it. While I was walking carrying it, it bit my thumb and when I reached my house and put it down, it bit my thumb again. I felt such great pain that I could not sleep because of its severity and the distress it caused me. My hand swelled up. In the morning, I went to the doctor and I complained to him of the pain. He said, "This is the beginning of gangrene. I will cut your thumb off lest it spread and you lose your hand." So he cut off my thumb. Then it afflicted my hand and I could not sleep or be still owing to the intensity of the pain. I was told that my hand must be amputated, so it was amputated; but the pain then spread to my forearm. It was terrible and I could not be still. The only way to gain relief from the intensity of the pain was, I was told, to have my arm amputated at the elbow; so I did that. But the terrible pain spread to the upper arm and so I had to have my whole arm amputated at the shoulder.'

"'Someone asked me what had caused the pain and I mentioned the story of the fish to him. He told me, "If you had returned at the beginning of the affliction to the owner of the fish and given it back to him and placated him, you would not have lost a limb. Go now to him and ask his forgiveness before the pain reaches the rest of your body." I continued to seek him in the land until I found him and fell at his feet, greeting him and weeping. I said to him, "Sir, I ask you by Allah to pardon me!" He asked who I was and I said, "I am the one who took the fish from you by force," and I described to him what had happened and showed him my arm. He wept when he saw it and then said, "My brother,

I absolve you from what you did, since I see this affliction you have suffered." I said, "Sir, by Allah, did you pray against me when I took it?" "Yes," he replied. "I said, 'O Allah, this man has over-powered me by his strength to take unjustly what You provided me with, so show me Your power over him!'" I said, "Sir, Allah has shown you His power over me and I repent to Allah Almighty for my service to the perpetrators of injustice and I will never again stand at their door or be seen among their helpers as long as I live, Allah willing.""" All success is from Allah.

27. Tax Collecting

This is encompassed by the words of the Almighty:

"There are only grounds against those who wrong people and act as tyrants in the earth without right to do so. Such people will have a painful punishment." (42:42)

A tax-collector is one of the greatest helpers of the perpetrators of injustice. Indeed, he is one of them. He takes something he is not entitled to and gives it to someone who is not entitled to it. This is why the Prophet ﷺ said, "A tax-collector will not enter the Garden." Abu Dawud related it. That is because he has to take on himself the injustice people have suffered at his hands. Where will the tax collector be on the Day of Rising with respect to paying back to people what he took from them? It will be taken from his good actions if he has good actions. This is alluded to in the *hadith* of the Prophet ﷺ: "Do you know who the true bankrupt is?", which has already been mentioned.

We find in the *hadith* of the woman who purified herself through being stoned: "She repented in such a way that if even a tax-collector had repented in the same way, he would have been forgiven or it would have been accepted from him."

A tax-collector resembles a highway robber and is a thief. A tax-collector, his scribe, witness, and the one who takes from a soldier and an old man all share in the sin. They consume what is unlawful. It is sound that the Messenger of Allah ﷺ said, "No flesh nourished by the unlawful will enter the Garden, and the Fire is more entitled to it." The unlawful means anything which is ugly to mention and causes shame.

Al-Wahidi mentioned this subject in his explanation of the words of Allah Almighty: *"Bad and good are not the same."* (5:100) Jabir ﷺ reported that a man said, "Messenger of Allah, wine is my trade. I gathered wealth from its sale. Will that property benefit me if I use it to obey Allah Almighty?" The Messenger of Allah ﷺ said, "Even if you were to spend it on *hajj*, *jihad* or *sadaqa*, it would not turn into even the wing of a gnat in the sight of Allah. Allah only accepts the good. Allah Almighty has revealed the confirmation of that in His words: '*Bad things and good things are not the same even though the abundance of the bad things may seem attractive to you.*' (5:100)"

We ask Allah for pardon and protection.

28. Consuming and receiving unlawful property in any way

Allah Almighty says:

"Do not devour one another's property by false means." (2:188)

This means: "None of you may consume the property of another under any kind of false pretences." Ibn 'Abbas ؓ said that this means a man using a false oath to misappropriate the property of his brother. Consuming property under false pretences can take two forms. One is by way of injustice, such as through usurpation, treachery, or theft. The second is is by way of amusement and sport, such gambling, games and the like.

We find in *Sahih al-Bukhari* that the Messenger of Allah ﷺ said, "Men who spend the property of Allah without a legal right will go to the Fire on the Day of Rising," and in *Sahih Muslim*: "Then the Prophet ﷺ spoke about a man who goes on a long journey, is dishevelled and dusty, and stretches his hands to heaven saying, 'O Lord! O Lord!' when his food is unlawful, his drink is unlawful, his clothes are unlawful, and his sustenance is unlawful. How could such a man have his prayer answered?" Anas ؓ reported, "I said, 'Messenger of Allah, pray to Allah to grant me a supplication which is answered.' The Prophet ﷺ said, 'Anas, make your earning goodly and your supplication will be answered. A man may raise a morsel of the unlawful to his mouth and his supplication not be answered for forty years.'"

Al-Bayhaqi related with an *isnad* that the Messenger of Allah ﷺ said, "Allah has allotted your character traits to you, just as He has allotted provision to you. Allah gives this world to both those He loves and those He does not love; but He only gives the *deen* to those He loves, so if Allah gives someone the *deen*, He loves him. Whoever gains property unlawfully, whether they spend some of it from themselves, give part of it as *sadaqa*, or leave it behind when they die, it will not bring him any blessing, nor will it be accepted from him, it will only be fuel for the Fire. Allah does not erase evil by evil, but only erases evil by good."

Ibn 'Umar ﷺ reported that the Messenger of Allah ﷺ said, "This world is sweet and green. Whoever obtains lawful property and spends it properly, Allah will reward him and let him inherit the Garden. Whoever earns wealth in this world which is not lawful and spends it improperly, Allah will admit him to the Abode of Abasement. Many a person who spends what his lower self desires of the unlawful will go to the Fire on the Day of Rising." (al-Bayhaqi) It is reported that the Prophet ﷺ said, "If someone is not concerned about where he earns his wealth, Allah will not be concerned about whichever gate he enters the Fire by."

Abu Hurayra ﷺ said, "It is better for one of you to put dust into his mouth than to put something unlawful into his mouth." (Ahmad) It is related that Yusuf ibn Asbat said, "When a young man worships, Shaytan says to his helpers, 'Look at the source of his food.' If his food is from a bad source, he says, 'Let him become tired and strive. He has spared you himself. His efforts will not help him if he consumes the unlawful.'" That is supported by what is affirmed in the *Sahih* when the Prophet ﷺ said about a man whose food and drink are unlawful that an angel over Jerusalem calls every day and night, "Whoever consumes the unlawful, no recompense will be accepted from him." 'Abdullah ibn al-Mubarak said, "I prefer returning one dirham from a doubtful source to giving a hundred thousand in *sadaqa*." It is related that the Prophet ﷺ said, "If someone performs *hajj* using unlawful wealth and says 'At Your service,' the angel says, 'There is no "At Your service" for you. Your *hajj* is rejected.'" (at-Tabarani)

Imam Ahmad said, "If someone buys a garment for ten dirhams and even one of those dirhams is unlawful, Allah will not accept a prayer from him as long as wears it." Wahb ibn al-Ward said, "If you were to stand in a prayer like this column, it would not be of any benefit to you unless you checked to see whether what enters your stomach was lawful or unlawful." Ibn 'Abbas ﷺ said, "Allah does not accept the prayer of a man who has anything unlawful in his belly until he repents to Allah Almighty of eating it." Sufyan ath-Thawri said, "Someone who spends unlawful wealth in obeying Allah is like someone who purifies a garment with urine. A garment can only be purified with water. A wrong action can only be expiated with what is lawful."

'Umar ﷺ said, "We used to leave nine-tenths of what is lawful, for fear of falling into the unlawful." Ka'b ibn 'Ujra ﷺ reported that the Messenger of Allah ﷺ said, "A body nourished by the unlawful will not enter the Garden." Zayd ibn Arqam ﷺ said, "Abu Bakr had a slave who used to pay him a levy to buy his freedom. He used to come every day with his levy and Abu Bakr would ask him where he got it from. If he was pleased he would eat from it, otherwise he would leave it. He came to him one night with some food while Abu Bakr was fasting. He ate a morsel from it, forgetting to ask him about it. Then he said to him. 'Where did you get this from?' He answered, 'I used to act as a soothsayer for some people in the *Jahiliyya* although I was not good at soothsaying. I deceived them.' Abu Bakr said, 'Confound you! You have almost destroyed me!' Then he put his hand in his mouth and began to vomit but it did not come out.' He was told, 'It will only come up with water.' So he called for water and began to drink and vomit until he had got rid of everything in his stomach.' Someone said to him, 'May Allah have mercy to you! All of this for the sake of this morsel?' He said, 'If I had to die to remove it, I would do so. I heard the Messenger of Allah ﷺ say, "The Fire is entitled to any body which is nourished by the unlawful." I feared that some of my body would be nourished by this morsel.'"

The scholars hold that included under this heading are tax-collecting, treachery, counterfeiting, theft, falsity, usury, taking the property of an orphan, bearing false witness, borrowing something and then denying having done so, bribery, giving short measure and weight, selling something with a concealed fault, gambling, sorcery, astrology, making images, fornication, professional mourning, taking a wage without permission from the seller, and selling a free person as a slave and consuming the price.

Section: It is related that the Messenger of Allah ﷺ said, "On the Day of Rising some people will be brought who have a pile of good actions as huge as the mountain of Tihama – but when they bring them, Allah will make them scattered dust and then throw

104

those people into the Fire." It was said, "Messenger of Allah, how can that be?" He answered, "They used to pray, fast, pay *zakat*, and perform *hajj*; but when something unlawful was offered to them, they took it and so Allah made their actions come to nothing."

It is reported that one of the righteous was seen after his death in a dream and was asked, "What did Allah do with you?" He said, "Good, but I was held back from the Garden because of a needle which I borrowed and did not return."

We ask Allah Almighty for pardon and protection and success in doing what He loves and is pleased with. He is Generous, Magnanimous, Compassionate, Merciful.

29. Suicide

Allah Almighty says:

"Do not kill yourselves. Allah is Most Merciful to you. If any-one who does so out of enmity and wrongdoing, We will roast him in a Fire. That is an easy matter for Allah." (4:29-30)

Al-Wahidi said in his commentary on this *ayat* that *"Do not kill yourselves"* means "Do not kill one another, for you are the people of one *deen* and so you are like one soul." That is the position of Ibn 'Abbas and most others. Some people, however, believe that it prohibits suicide. The soundness of this is indicated by what Abu Mansur Muhammad ibn Muhammad al-Mansuri reported to us from 'Amr ibn al-'As. He said, "I had a wet dream during the expedition of Dhat as-Salasil, and was afraid that if I had a *ghusl* I would die, so I did *tayammum* and prayed *Subh* with my companions. I mentioned that to the Prophet and he said, ''Amr, did you pray with your companions when you were in *janaba*?' So I told him what had kept me from having a *ghusl*. I said that I had heard Allah's words: *'Do not kill yourselves. Allah is Most Merciful to you.'* The Messenger of Allah laughed and did not say anything." (Abu Dawud) This *hadith* indicates that 'Amr interpreted this *ayat* as being about killing oneself, not something else, and the Prophet did not contradict it.

Jundub ibn 'Abdullah reported that the Prophet said: "Among those before you was a man who had a wound and could not endure it. He took a knife and cut his arm with it and the blood flowed until he died. Allah Almighty said, 'My slave has hastened to Me by his own action and so I have denied him the Garden.'" (al-Bukhari and Muslim)

Abu Hurayra reported that the Messenger of Allah said, "If someone kills himself with a sharp implement, he will have it in his hand and be stabbing himself with it in the belly in the Fire of Hell forever. If someone kills himself with poison, he will have his poison in his hand and be swallowing it in the Fire of Hell forever. If someone throws himself from a mountain and kills himself he will be falling in the Fire of Hell forever." It is transmitted in the two *Sahih* collections.

Thabit ibn ad-Dahhak ﷺ related that the Messenger of Allah ﷺ said, "Cursing a believer is like killing him. Falsely accusing a believer of disbelief is like killing him. Anyone who kills himself with anything will be punished with it on the Day of Rising." A sound *hadith* reports about a man who was suffering from a wound and hastened his death by killing himself with the point of his sword. The Messenger of Allah ﷺ said, "He is one of the inhabitants of the Fire."

We ask Allah to inspire us with right guidance and to give us refuge from the evils of ourselves and the evils of our actions. He is Generous, Magnanimous, Forg9iving, Merciful.

30. Inveterate lying

Allah Almighty says:

"Call down the curse of Allah upon the liars." (3:61)

"Death to conjecturers" (51:10): in other words, liars.

Allah does not guide any unbridled inveterate liar." (40:28)

It is reported in the two *Sahih* collections from Ibn Mas'ud ﷺ that the Messenger of Allah ﷺ said, "Truthfulness leads to piety and piety leads to the Garden. A man may continue to tell the truth and attend to the truth until he is written with Allah as truthful. Lying leads to impiety and piety leads to the Fire. A man may continue to lie and attend to lying until he is written with Allah as a liar."

Also in the two *Sahih* collections is a report that the Prophet ﷺ said, "There are three signs of a hypocrite, even if he prays, fasts and claims that he is a Muslim: when he speaks, he lies; when he promises, he breaks his promise; and when he is trusted, he betrays his trust." The Prophet ﷺ said, "If anyone has four characteristics, he is a pure hypocrite, and if anyone has one of them, he has an aspect of hypocrisy until he gives it up: when he is trusted, he betrays his trust; when he speaks, he lies; when he makes an agreement, he breaks it; and when he quarrels, he speaks falsely." (al-Bukhari and Muslim)

Sahih al-Bukhari contains the *hadith* describing the vision of the Prophet ﷺ in the Night Journey, in which he said: "We came to a man who was lying on his back, and there was another man standing over him with an iron hook. He went to one side of his face and ripped open the side of his mouth until it reached the back of his neck and then his nostril to the back of his neck and his eye to the back of his neck. Then he moved to the other side and did the same thing as he had done to first side. When he finished that side, the first side had become whole again. Then he did the same thing all over again. He will continue to do that until the Day of Rising. I asked, 'Who is this?' They said, 'He would leave from his house and tell lies which spread everywhere.'"

The Prophet ﷺ said, "A believer may be naturally disposed to anything except treachery and lying." (Ahmad) One *hadith* has
"Beware of conjecture. Conjecture is the most lying kind of
speech." (al-Bukhari and Muslim) The Prophet ﷺ said, "Woe to
the one who tells lies to make people laugh! Woe to him. Woe to
him. Woe to him." (Ahmad)

Even worse are false oaths, as Allah Almighty reports about the
hypocrites when He says: *"They swear to falsehood and do so knowingly."* (58:14) In the *Sahih* it is reported that the Messenger of
Allah ﷺ said: "There are three whom Allah will not speak to on
the Day of Rising nor attest to their integrity and they will have a
painful punishment: a man with water to spare which he denies to
a traveller; a man who sells goods to a man and swears by Allah
that he paid a certain amount for it and the buyer believes him and
takes it when that is not true; and a man who gives a pledge to a
ruler only for worldly gain, and if he gives him something he is
loyal, but if he does not give him any of it he is not loyal."

The Prophet ﷺ said, "It is great treachery to say something to
your brother which he believes when you are lying." In another
hadith we find: "Whoever recounts a dream which he did not have
will have to tie a knot between two grains of barley, and will not
be able to do so." (al-Bukhari)

The Messenger of Allah ﷺ said, "The worst of lies is when a
man says his eyes have seen something which they have not seen."
It means that he says, "I dreamt such-and-such" when he did not
see anything. Ibn Mas'ud ﷺ said, "When someone continues to
lie, a black spot grows in his heart until all his heart becomes
black. Then he is written in the sight of Allah among the liars."
(Malik)

A Muslim should guard his tongue so that he speaks only beneficial words. There is safety in silence and nothing is equal to safety. We find in *Sahih al-Bukhari* from Abu Hurayra ﷺ that the
Messenger of Allah ﷺ said, "Whoever believes in Allah and the
Last Day should speak good or be silent." It is agreed that this
hadith is sound and is a text proving clearly that a human being
should only speak good words. Good words are those whose benefit is clear to the speaker.

Abu Musa ☺ reported, "I asked, 'Messenger of Allah, which of the Muslims is the best?' He said, 'The one from whose tongue and hand the Muslims are safe.'" We find in the *Muwatta'* of Imam Malik from the transmission of Bilal ibn al-Harith al-Muzani ☺ that the Messenger of Allah ☺ said: "A may man say what is pleasing to Allah and he does not suspect that it will have the result that it does, and Allah writes for him His good pleasure for it until the day when he meets Him. And a man may say what incurs the wrath of Allah and he does not suspect that it will have the result that it does, and Allah writes His wrath for him for it until the day when he meets Him."

There are many sound *hadith*s like those we have mentioned but what we have cited is sufficient. One man was asked, "How many faults exist in the son of Adam?" He said, "They are too many to count. I have counted eight thousand but I found that there is one good quality which, if you avail yourself of it, will conceal all of them. It is guarding the tongue."

May Allah make us avoid disobedience to Him and occupy us with that which pleases Him. He is Generous, Magnanimous.

Warning. O slave of Allah, there is nothing more precious for you than your life and yet you waste it. There is no enemy for you like shaytan and yet you obey him. There is nothing more harmful than consenting to what your lower self wants and yet you treat it like a friend. The best part of your life has passed and there remains only the white hair of dissolution. White hair is enough of a warning against dissolution. O heedless one! It is the best of qualities! Where is weeping out of fear of the Immense? Where is the time which was lost in playing games? How many silent tears there will be at the Rising for the wrong actions which the books of the scribe contain! Who will support me when I stand at the station of reckoning and I am asked, "What have you done with respect to every obligation?"

31. Being corrupt in rendering judgment

Allah Almighty says:

> "Those who do not judge by what Allah has sent down, such people are unbelievers." (5:44)

> "Those who do not judge by what Allah has sent down, such people are wrongdoers." (5:45)

> "Those who do not judge by what Allah has sent down, such people are deviators." (5:47)

Al-Hakam related from Talha ibn 'Ubaydullah ⁂ that the Prophet ⁂ said, "Allah does not accept the prayer of a ruler who judges by other than what Allah has sent down." The *Sahih* of al-Hakim also records from Burayda ⁂ that the Messenger of Allah ⁂ said: "There are three types of judges. One type will go to the Garden, and two types will be in the Fire. One type of judge recognises the truth and judges by it and so he will be in the Garden. One type of judge recognises the truth but is deliberately unjust and so he will be in the Fire. One type of judge judges without knowledge. He will also be in the Fire." They asked, "What is the wrong action of the one who is ignorant?" He replied, "His wrong action is that he should not have been a judge without having knowledge."

Abu Hurayra ⁂ reported that the Messenger of Allah ⁂ said, "Anyone who is appointed as a *qadi* has been slaughtered without a knife." (Abu Dawud and at-Tirmidhi) Al-Fudayl ibn 'Iyad said, "A *qadi* should spend one day in judgement and one day weeping for himself." Muhammad ibn Wasi' said, "The first to be summoned for reckoning on the Day of Rising will be judges." 'A'isha ⁂ said that she heard the Messenger of Allah ⁂ said, "A just *qadi* will be brought on the Day of Rising and experience such a harsh reckoning that he will wish that he had not judged between two people about a single date." (Ahmad and Ibn Hibban) Mu'adh ibn Jabal ⁂ said that the Messenger of Allah ⁂ said, "A *qadi* will slide down a slope in Hellfire further than Aden." 'Ali ibn Abi Talib ⁂ narrated that he heard the Messenger of Allah ⁂ say: "There is no ruler or *qadi* who will not be brought on the Day of Rising before he is made to stand before Allah Almighty on the *Sirat* and then his secrets will be unfurled and read out in front of people. If he is just, Allah will deliver him by his justice. If he was otherwise, that bridge will break completely and he will go between two of its supports (or stretch his limbs) for a certain distance and then the bridge will break, sending him into Hell."

Makhul said, "If I were given a choice being being a *qadi* and having my head chopped off, I would choose to have my head chopped off." Ayyub as-Sakhtiyani said, "I find that the people with the most knowledge are those who flee from it (becoming a *qadi*) the most." Ath-Thawri was told, "Shurayh has been asked to be *qadi*." He said, "What a man they have corrupted!" Malik ibn al-Mundhir summoned Muhammad ibn Wasi' to appoint him *qadi* of Basra and he refused. He repeated it and said, "You will sit as *qadi* or I will whip you!" He said, "If you do that, you are the ruler. It is better to be abased in this world than in the Next World!"

Wahb ibn Munabbih said, "When a judge intends injustice or acts unjustly, Allah will make decrease affect the people of his country, even in the markets, provisions, crops, milk and everything. When he intends good and justice, Allah will bring blessing to the people of his kingdom." One of the governors of Hims wrote to 'Umar ibn 'Abd al-Aziz, "The city of Hims is ruined and needs rebuilding." 'Umar wrote to him, "Fortify it with justice and clear its roads of injustice. Peace." He also said, "It is unlawful for a *qadi* to judge while he is angry. If a *qadi* lacks knowledge and has bad intention, bad character and lack of scrupulousness, his loss is complete and he must immediately resign and hasten to sincerity."

We ask Allah for pardon and protection and success in what He loves and what pleases Him. He is Generous, Magnanimous.

32. Taking bribes for judgement

Allah Almighty says: *"Do not devour one another's property by false means or offer it to the judges as a bribe, trying through crime to knowingly usurp a portion of other people's property."* (2:188) This means: "do not bribe or entice judges with your wealth in order to take a right belonging to someone else when you know that it is not lawful for you." Abu Hurayra ﷺ reported that the Messenger of Allah ﷺ said, "Allah curses both the briber and the one bribed for judgement." At-Tirmidhi transmitted it and considered it a *hasan hadith*. 'Abdullah ibn 'Amr ﷺ said, "The Messenger of Allah ﷺ cursed the briber and the one bribed."

Scholars have said that the curse attaches to the briber when he intends by it to harm a Muslim or to obtain by it something he is not entitled to. When he pays it in order to obtain his right or to defend himself from injustice, he is not subject to the curse. In the case of a judge, a bribe taken to avert injustice is unlawful for him. We find in another *hadith*: "The curse is on the go-between in any bribe." This follows the same rule as applies to a briber whose aim is good: the curse does not fall on him if that is the case, but otherwise it does.

Section. Abu Dawud related in his *Sunan* from Abu Umama al-Bahili ﷺ that the Messenger of Allah ﷺ said, "Whoever intercedes for a man who then gives him a gift for doing it, he has opened a great door among the doors of usury." Ibn Mas'ud ﷺ said, "It is unlawful for you to accept a gift given to you by someone for helping him to fulfil a need." Masruq related that he spoke to Ibn Ziyad about an injustice and he settled it. Then the one who had suffered the injustice gave him a servant, but he refused to accept the gift and returned it. He said, "I heard Ibn Mas'ud ﷺ say, 'If someone averts an injustice from a Muslim and then is given anything for doing so, be it little or much, it is unlawful.'" The man said, "Abu 'Abd ar-Rahman, we thought that what was unlawful was bribes in exchange for judgement." He said, "That constitutes disbelief."

We seek refuge with Allah from this enormity. We ask Allah for pardon and protection from every affliction and disliked thing.

Imam Abu 'Umar al-Awza'i, who lived in Beirut, said that a Christian came and told him, "A governor in Baalbek did me an injustice and I want you to write to him. Then he gave him a jar of honey." Al-Awza'i said, "If you wish, take back the jar and I will write to him. Or, if you wish, I will take the jar." So he wrote to the governor for him asking him to reduce some of the *kharaj* tax for the Christians. The Christian took the jar and letter and went to the governor and gave him the letter, and he reduced it by thirty dirhams through the intercession of the Imam. May Allah have mercy on him and gather us in his company.

33. Women looking like men and men looking like women

We find in the *Sahih* that the Messenger of Allah ﷺ said, "Allah has cursed women who imitate men and men who imitate women": in other words, those who resemble men in their dress and speech. Abu Hurayra ﷺ reported that the Messenger of Allah ﷺ said, "Allah curses a woman who wears men's clothes and a man who wears women's clothes."

When a woman dresses like a man, the curse of Allah and His Messenger attaches to her, and also to her husband if he allows her to do so and does not forbid it. For he is commanded to make her go straight in obedience to Allah and to forbid her to disobey Him. This is according to the words of Allah Almighty: "*Safeguard yourselves and your families from a Fire whose fuel is people and stones,*" (66:6), meaning: "Discipline them, teach them, command them to obey Allah and forbid them to disobey Allah, just as that is obligatory for you in respect of yourselves." The same is implied by the words of the Prophet ﷺ: "All of you are shepherds and each of you is responsible for his flock. A man is the shepherd of his family and will be responsible for them on the Day of Rising." (al-Bukhari and Muslim)

It is related that the Prophet ﷺ said, "Men are destroyed when they obey women." (Muslim) Al-Hasan said, "Today, if a man obeys his wife in what she desires, Allah Almighty will throw him into the fire." The Prophet ﷺ said, "Two types are people of the Fire: people with whips like the tails of cattle with which they beat people, and women who are naked despite being clothed, straying and tempting, their heads like the tilted humps of camels. They will not enter the Garden or experience its fragrance, although its fragrance can be experienced at such-and-such a distance." This was transmitted by Muslim.

Nafi' narrated that Ibn 'Umar ﷺ and 'Abdullah ibn 'Amr ﷺ were with az-Zubayr ibn 'Abd al-Muttalib ﷺ when a woman came driving some sheep and shouldering a bow. 'Abdullah ibn 'Umar ﷺ asked, "Are you a man or a woman?" She answered, "A woman." He turned to Ibn 'Amr ﷺ and said, "Allah Almighty has cursed on the tongue of His Prophet ﷺ women who resemble men and men who resemble women."

Among the actions for which a woman is also cursed are displaying adornments, gold and pearls from under the veil, wearing perfume when she goes out, and wearing attractive garments when she goes out. All of that is part of adornment which Allah hates and He hates those who do it in this world and the Next. Such actions have become predominant in most women. The Prophet ﷺ said about them, "I looked at Hell and saw that most of its inhabitants were women." He ﷺ also said, "I have not left behind me any trial more harmful to men than women."

We ask Allah to protect us from the trial they represent and to put them right by His favour and generosity.

34. Being a wittol (a man who condones his wife's infidelity)

Allah Almighty says:

"A man who has fornicated may only marry a woman who has fornicated or a woman of the idolators. A woman who has fornicated the may only marry a man who has fornicated or a man of the idolators. Doing such a thing is unlawful for believers." (24:3)

'Abdullah ibn 'Umar ﷺ related that the Messenger of Allah ﷺ said, "Three people will not enter the Garden: a person who disobeys his parents, a wittol, and a manly woman." An-Nasa'i relates that the Messenger of Allah ﷺ said, "Three will be forbidden the Garden by Allah: a habitual wine drinker, someone who disobeys his parents, and a wittol who accepts the licentious behaviour of his wife" – or in other words, condones it in his wife. We seek refuge with Allah from that.

One who thinks that his wife is involved in illicit behaviour but overlooks it because of his love for her or because he owes her a debt, or a heavy bride-price which he cannot pay, or because he has young children, is not as bad as one who simply ignores it, and there is no good in a man who has no jealousy.

We ask Allah for protection from every affliction and trial. He is Generous, Magnanimous.

35. Marrying a woman to enable her to remarry her former husband

There is a sound report from Ibn Mas'ud 🙵 that the Messenger of Allah 🙵 cursed men who married women to enable them to remarry their former husbands and husbands for whom it was done. At-Tirmidhi said, "(The unlawfulness of) that practice was agreed on by the people of knowledge, including 'Umar ibn al-Khattab, 'Uthman ibn 'Affan, and 'Abdullah ibn 'Umar 🙵. That was also the position of the *fuqaha'* among the Tabi'un. Imam Ahmad related it in his *Musnad*, and an-Nasa'i in his *Sunan* with a sound *isnad*. Ibn 'Abbas 🙵 related: "The Messenger of Allah 🙵 was asked about a marriage made for the purpose of allowing remarriage and said, 'No! Marriage is based on true desire for it. Marriage is not based on deception or mocking the Book of Allah Almighty. There must be consummation.'" Abu Ishaq al-Juzjani related it. 'Uqba ibn 'Amir 🙵 related that the Messenger of Allah 🙵 said, "Shall I tell you about the borrowed billy-goat?" They said, 'Yes, Messenger of Allah." He said, "It is a man who marries a woman in order to permit her first husband to remarry her. Allah curses this one and the one for whom it is done." Ibn Majah related this with a sound *isnad*.

Ibn 'Umar 🙵 related that a man asked him, "What do you say about a woman whom I married to make her lawful for her former husband if he has not commanded me to do so and does not know about it?" Ibn 'Umar 🙵 told him, "Marriage must be based on desire. If you like her, keep her. If you dislike her, separate from her. We considered this to be tantamount to fornication in the time of the Messenger of Allah 🙵."

As for the traditions from the Companions and the Tabi'un, al-Athram and Ibn al-Mundhir related that 'Umar ibn al-Khattab 🙵 said, "I would stone any man who married a woman so that she could remarry her former husband, and I would stone the one for whom it was done." 'Umar ibn al-Khattab 🙵 was asked about making a woman lawful for her husband and said, "That is fornication."

'Abdullah ibn Sharik al-'Amiri said that he heard that when Ibn 'Umar ﷺ was asked about a man who divorced his cousin and then regretted it and wanted to take her back and a man wanted to marry her to make her lawful for him, he said, "Both of them are fornicators, even if they remain for twenty years or the like of that, if he knows that he intended to make her lawful." Ibn 'Abbas ﷺ said that a man told him, "My cousin divorced his wife three times and then regretted it." He said, "Your cousin has disobeyed his Lord and regretted it. He has obeyed Shaytan, who will not give him a way out." He said, "What do you think about a man who makes her lawful for him?" He said, "If someone tries to trick Allah, He will trick him."

Ibrahim an-Nakha'i stated, "If the intention of one of the three, the first husband, the second husband or the woman, is to make remarriage lawful, then the second marriage is invalid and she is not lawful for her first husband." Al-Hasan al-Basri said, "If any of the three intends to make remarriage lawful, it is invalid." Sa'id ibn al-Musayyab, the imam of the Tabi'un, said about a man who married a woman in order to make her lawful for her first husband, "She is not lawful." Among those who also said that are Malik ibn Anas, al-Layth ibn Sa'd, Sufyan ath-Thawri and Imam Ahmad.

Isma'il ibn Sa'id said, "I asked Imam Ahmad about a man who married a woman thinking to make her lawful for her first husband while the woman did not know that." He replied, "He is someone trying to make a woman lawful for a husband who divorced her. If that is his intention, he is cursed." The position of the school of ash-Shafi'i is that if making remarriage lawful is stipulated in the contract, the contract is invalid, like a contract for temporary marriage. If the contract is made and it is not stipulated in the contract nor before it, then the contract is not invalid. If he marries her on the basis that when he has made her lawful, he will divorce her, there are two views about it, the sounder of which is that it is invalid. The argument for its invalidity is that it is a precondition whose validity prevents the continuance of marriage, and so it is like setting a time limit on the marriage. That is the soundest view according to ar-Rafi'i. The second argument is that it is an invalid precondition connected to the contract and so the marriage itself is not invalid, as is the case when someone marries with the stipulation that he will not marry another wife and will not travel with her. Allah knows best.

We ask Allah to grant us success in what pleasing to Him and to help us avoid acts of disobedience to Him. He is Generous, Magnanimous, Forgiving, Merciful.

Warning. By Allah, how excellent are people who leave this world before leaving it! They remove their hearts from it by aversion to the darkness of its form, and they choose the days of peace and obtain its fruits. They enjoy the words of their Master and submit to His command and surrender to Him. They accept His gifts with thankfulness and submit. They emigrate to obey Him with pleasure and contentment, and they hasten to Him from all people and prefer to obey Him with knowledge and perception. They are pleased and do not object, whatever may happen. They spend of themselves in what is an excellent business transaction. How excellent is their purchase! They serve Him and their hearts are open to His service. They knock on His door and the door is opened. They weep continually, and their eyelids are reddened by their tears. They stand before dawn like those who weep and mourn. You can recognise them by their mark. They show the effects of sincerity. They are redolent with the spread of His fragrant intimacy from the scent of their praise.

36. Not avoiding urine, something which the Christians are prone to

Allah Almighty said:

"Purify your clothes." (74:4)

Ibn 'Abbas ﷺ said, "The Prophet ﷺ passed by two graves and said, 'They are being punished, yet they are not being punished for anything great. One of them carried tales and the other did not keep himself free of urine:" in other words, he was not careful about it. It is transmitted in the two *Sahih* collections. The Messenger of Allah ﷺ said, "Keep yourself free from urine. Much of the punishment in the grave is due to it." Ad-Daraqutni related this.

If someone does not guard against urine on his body and clothing, his prayer is not accepted. Abu Nu'aym related in *al-Hilya* from Shaqi ibn Mati' al-Asbahi ﷺ that the Messenger of Allah ﷺ said, "There are things that increase the painful punishment of the people of the Fire in addition to what they are already suffering. They run between boiling water and the Blaze. They call out for destruction. They ask one another, 'Why do these things inflict pain upon us in addition what we are already suffering?' One man is put in a box of embers, another man drags his intestines, another man has pus and blood flowing out of his mouth, and yet another eats his own flesh. The person in the box is asked, 'Why are you making our suffering worse than it is already?' He says that he died with the wealth of people still on his neck. Then the one who is dragging his intestines will be asked, 'Why are you making our suffering worse than it is already?' He says that he was not concerned where urine splashed, and did not wash it off. Then the one whose mouth is running with pus and blood will be asked, 'Why are you making our suffering worse than it is already?' He says that he used to look at every ugly word and enjoy it." In one version, "He used to eat the flesh of people and carry tales."

We ask Allah for pardon and protection by His favour and generosity. He is the most Merciful of the merciful.

37. Showing off

Allah Almighty says about the hypocrites:

"They show off to people, only remembering Allah a little." (4:142)

"Woe to those who pray and are forgetful of their prayer, those who show off and deny help to others." (107:4-7)

"O you who believe, do not nullify your sadaqa *by demands of gratitude or insulting words, like him who spends his wealth, showing off to people."* (2:264)

"So let him who hopes to meet his Lord act rightly and not associate anyone in the worship of his Lord." (18:110)

This means that he should not show off his good actions.

Abu Hurayra ﷺ reported that the Messenger of Allah ﷺ said, "The first of mankind to be judged on the Day of Rising will be a man who was martyred. He will be brought and will be informed of the blessings he had and will acknowledge them. Allah will ask, 'What did you do with them?' He will say, 'I fought for You until I was martyred.' Allah will say, 'You lie. Rather you fought so it would be said, "A bold man!" and so it was said.' Then the command will be given and he will be dragged on his face until he is thrown into the Fire. There will also be a man to whom Allah gave much wealth and all sorts of property. He will be brought and informed of his blessings which he will acknowledge. Allah will ask, 'What did you do with them?' He will answer, 'There was no path in which You like spending to be done but that I spent in it for You.' He will say, 'You lie. Rather you did it so that it would be said, "He is generous," and so it was said.' Then the command will be given and he will be dragged on his face until he is thrown into the Fire. There will also be a man who studied knowledge and taught it and recited the Qur'an. He will be brought and informed of his blessings which he will acknowledge. Allah will ask, 'What did you do with them?' He will say, 'I studied knowledge and taught it and I recited the Qur'an for You.' He will say, 'You lie. Rather you studied so that it would be said, "A scholar!"

and you recited so that it would be said, "He is a reciter!" And so it was said.' Then the command will be given and he will be dragged on his face until he is thrown into the Fire." Muslim related it.

The Prophet 繫 said, "Whoever wants to be heard, Allah makes him heard. Whoever wants to be seen, Allah makes him seen." (al-Bukhari and Muslim) According to al-Khattabi it means: "Whoever does an action without sincerity, wanting people to see him and listen to him will be repaid for that so that he will be known for it and disgraced, and so what was inside him will appear on him. Allah knows best." The Prophet 繫 said, "Even a little of showing-off is *shirk*." (al-Hakim) The Prophet 繫 also said, "What I fear most for you is the lesser *shirk*." Someone asked, "What is it, Messenger of Allah?" He said, "Showing-off." (Ahmad)

Allah Almighty says about the Day when His slaves are repaid for their actions: "Go to those to whom you used to show off your actions and see if you find any reward with them." This is also said to be the subject of the words of the Almighty: *"What confronts them from Allah will be something they did not reckon with."* (39:47) They did actions which were seen as good actions in this world, but which will appear to them on the Day of Rising as evil deeds. One of the early righteous Muslims said when he read this *ayat*, "Woe to the people who show off! A show-off will be summoned on the Day of Rising with four names: 'O show-off, O treacherous, O impious, O loser. Go and take your reward from those for whom you acted. You shall have no reward from Us.'"

Al-Hasan said, "Anyone who shows off wants to override Allah's decree for him, and he is an evil man. He wants people to say that he is righteous, but then what will they say when he is in the position of those abased in the presence of his Lord? The hearts of believers must know that." Qatada said, "When someone shows off, Allah says, 'Look at My slave and how he mocks Me.'" It is related that 'Umar ibn al-Khattab 繫 looked at a man who was bowing his head [in the prayer and said], "O you who are bowing your neck, raise your head! Humility is not in the neck. Humility is in the heart." It is said that Abu Umama al-Bahili went to a man in the mosque who was prostrating and weeping and making supplication in his prostration. Abu Umama said to him, "You! You! This should be done your room!"

Muhammad ibn al-Mubarak as-Suri said, "Show your true demeanour in the night. That is better than showing it in the day, because one's demeanour in the day is towards creatures and one's demeanour at night is towards the Lord of the worlds." 'Ali ibn Abi Talib ﷺ said, "There are three signs of a show-off: he is lazy when he is alone; he is active when he is among people; and he does more when he is praised for it and less when he is criticised for it." Al-Fudayl ibn 'Iyad said, "Leaving action for the sake of people is showing off. Acting for the sake of people is *shirk*. Sincerity is that Allah protect you from both of these."

We ask Allah for help and sincerity in actions, words, movement and stillness. He is Generous, Magnanimous.

Warning. Slaves of Allah! Your days are few and the threats facing you are dire. Let the last report to the first and let the heedless awaken before the caravans depart. O you who have no doubt that you will travel but have no provision or mount! O you who dive into the gulf of passion, when will you reach the shore? Will you not awaken from total sleep, and attend with a heart which is not heedless and rise to pray at night, as does someone who is intelligent? Alas for the deceived, ignorant heedless one! Despite his mature age he is weighed down with wrong actions. He has squandered bravery and relied on the mount of passion. He is distracted from remembering his grave and yet still claims to be intelligent! By Allah, the heroes have preceded him to the highest station. He hopes for success despite his idleness. What a hope! What a hope! A hero does not win by idleness!

38. Teaching for worldly gain and concealing knowledge

Allah Almighty says:

"Only those of His slaves with knowledge have fear of Allah." (35:28)

This means "those with knowledge of Allah Almighty." Ibn 'Abbas ﷺ said, "He means those among His creation who fear Him since they possess knowledge of His power, might and force." Mujahid and ash-Sha'bi said, "The learned man is the one who fears Allah Almighty." Ar-Rabi' ibn Anas said, "Whoever does not fear Allah is not a man of knowledge."

Allah Almighty says:

"Those who hide the Clear Signs and Guidance We have sent down, after We have made it clear to people in the Book. Allah curses them, and the cursers curse them." (2:159)

This *ayat* was revealed about the scholars of the Jews. By "Clear Signs" He means stoning, *hudud* and other legal judgments, and by "Guidance" He means the coming of Muhammad ﷺ and his description. *"After We have made it clear to people* (meaning the tribe of Israel) *in the Book* (which is the Torah)." Those who concealed it are cursed. Ibn 'Abbas ﷺ said, "Everything except jinn and men curses them." Ibn Mas'ud ﷺ said, "Two Muslims do not curse one another without that curse reverting to the Jews and Christians who concealed the coming of Muhammad ﷺ and his description."

Allah Almighty says:

"When Allah made a covenant with those given the Book: 'You must make it clear to people and not conceal it.' But they toss it in disdain behind their backs and sell it for a paltry price. What an evil sale they make!" (3:187)

According to al-Wahidi: "This *ayat* was revealed about the Jews of Madina. Allah made a covenant with them in the Torah to explain about the coming of Muhammad ﷺ and his description and mission and not to conceal it. It is in the words of Allah Almighty: *"You must make it clear to people and not conceal it."* Al-Hasan said, "This is the covenant of Allah Almighty with the scholars of the Jews to make clear to people what is in their Book: in which the Prophet ﷺ is mentioned."

The Messenger of Allah ﷺ said, "Whoever learns knowledge whose purpose is to please Allah in order to obtain goods of this world will not experience the scent of the Garden." Abu Dawud related this. The Prophet ﷺ said, "Anyone who seeks knowledge in order to vie with scholars or argue with fools or to win people's hearts will go to the Fire." At-Tirmidhi transmitted this. The Prophet ﷺ said, "Anyone who is asked about a point of knowledge but conceals it will be bridled on the Day of Rising with a bridle of Fire." One supplication of the Messenger of Allah ﷺ was: "I seek refuge with You from knowledge which is not beneficial." The Prophet ﷺ said, "If someone learns knowledge and does not act by it, his knowledge only increases him in pride."

Abu Umama ؓ related that the Messenger of Allah ﷺ said, "An evil scholar will come on the Day of Rising and will be thrown into the Fire and will go round and round tethered by his intestines as a donkey goes round and round a mill. He will be asked, 'What has brought you to this? We were guided by you.' He says, 'I used to act differently from the way I instructed you to act.'" Hilal ibn al-'Ala' said, "Seeking knowledge is hard; preserving it is harder than seeking it; acting by it is harder than preserving it; and being safe from it is harder than acting by it."

We ask Allah for safety from every affliction and success in what He loves and is pleased with. He is Generous, Magnanimous.

Warning. Son of Adam, when will you remember the ends of matters? How long until you depart from these palaces? How long will you remain in what you built? Where are those before you in their houses and camps? Where is there anyone who will not die? All, by Allah, will depart, and will gather in their graves. They will rest in that roughest bed until the Trumpet is blown. When they rise for the Judgement and heaven is rolled up, the veil will be lifted, the curtains will be torn aside, and the true reality of actions will appear and be known to people's hearts. The *Sirat* will be set up – and how many feet will slip? Hooks will be set up on it to catch every deluded one. The faces of the godfearing will shine like full moons. The iniquitous will call woe and destruction. The Fire will be brought forth, led by reins, and it will be bubbling and seething. When people are thrown into it, they will hear it groaning as it boils. There is no happiness in this world for anyone who truly believes in the Resurrection. Happiness in this world is due only to ignorance or ingratitude.

39. Treachery

Allah Almighty says:

"O you who believe, do not betray Allah and the Messenger and do not knowingly betray your trusts." (8:27)

Al-Wahidi said, "This *ayat* was revealed about Abu Lubaba ﷺ when the Messenger of Allah ﷺ sent him to the Banu Qurayza while he was besieging them, and his family and children were among them. They said, 'Abu Lubaba, what do you think will happen to us if we submit to the judgement of Sa'd?' Abu Lubaba pointed to his throat, meaning 'Slaughter. Do not do it.' That was treachery on his part towards Allah and the Messenger. Abu Lubaba ﷺ said, 'My feet did not move from where I had been standing before I realised that I had betrayed Allah and His Messenger.'"

Ibn 'Abbas ﷺ said, "The "trusts" are the actions which Allah has imposed on His slaves," meaning the acts He has made obligatory for them. Al-Kalbi said, "As for treachery towards Allah and His Messenger, it means disobeying them. As for betraying the trust, everyone is entrusted with what Allah has made obligatory on him. If he wishes, he can betray it. If he wishes, he can carry it out. No one can see it except Allah Almighty."

Allah Almighty says: *"Allah does not guide the deviousness of traitors."* (12:52) In other words, He does not guide anyone who betrays His trust. Such people will be disgraced in the end by being deprived of guidance. The Prophet ﷺ said, "There are three signs of the hypocrite: when he speaks, he lies; when he promises, he breaks it; and when he is trusted, he betrays that trust." The Messenger of Allah ﷺ said, "Someone untrustworthy has no faith and someone who cannot keep a covenant has no *deen*."

Treason is always ugly, but some kinds of treachery are worse than others. Someone who betrays you by cheating you of a penny is not the same as someone who betrays you in respect of your family and your property and commits terrible things. The Messenger of Allah ﷺ said, "Return every trust to the one who entrusted you with it, and do not betray anyone who has betrayed you." We also find in *hadith*: "A believer may be naturally disposed to everything except treachery and lying." The Messenger of Allah ﷺ said, "Allah Almighty says, 'I am the third of two partners as long as neither of them betrays his friend.'"

Regarding this matter we are also told: "The first thing to be removed from people will be trustworthiness and the last to remain will be the prayer. Many a person who prays will gain no good from it." The Messenger of Allah ﷺ said, "Beware of treachery. It is an evil companion."

Ibn Mas'ud ﷺ said: "On the Day of Rising someone with a trust he betrayed will be brought and told, 'Deliver your trust.' He will say, 'Lord, how, when the world has gone?' The form of it on the day he accepted it will appear to him in the bottom of Hell, and he will be told, 'Go in and take it out.' He will descend into it and carry it on his shoulder, and it will be heavier than the mountains of this world, until he thinks that he is saved, and then it will fall and he will fall after it forever." Then he ﷺ said, "The prayer is a trust. *Wudu'* is a trust. *Ghusl* is a trust. The weight is a trust. The measure is a trust. The greatest trust is anything left for safekeeping."

O Allah, deal kindly with us and grant us Your pardon!

40. Reminding people of one's charity

Allah Almighty says: *"O you who believe, do not nullify your sadaqa by demands for gratitude or insulting words."* (2:264) According to al-Wahidi this refers to those who make people feel indebted for gifts they give. Al-Kalbi said that it is someone who considers his *sadaqa* a favour for Allah and injures its recipients. In the *Sahib* it is recorded that the Messenger of Allah ﷺ said: "There are three kinds of people whom Allah will not speak to or attest to their integrity on the Day of Rising and they will have a painful punishment: those who wear their garment long (out of pride); those who remind people of their charity towards them; and those who sell their goods with a false oath."

Another *hadith* says: "Three will not enter the Garden: someone who disrespects his parents, a habitual drinker and someone who makes people obligated through charity." An-Nasa'i related this. It is reported that the Prophet ﷺ said, "Beware of reminding people of your charity, which nullifies gratitude and erases the reward." Then the Messenger of Allah ﷺ recited the words of Allah Almighty: *"O you who believe, do not nullify your* sadaqa *by demands for gratitude or insulting words."* (2:264)

Ibn Sirin heard one man say to another, "I have been good to you and done such-and-such and such-and-such." Ibn Sirin told him, "Be silent. There is no good in charity when it is recounted."

41. Denial of the Divine Decree

Allah Almighty says:

"We have created all things in due measure." (54:49)

Ibn al-Jawzi said in his *tafsir* that there are two views about the reason for the revelation of this *ayat*. One of them is that the idolators of Makka went to the Messenger of Allah ﷺ to argue with him about the Decree and this *ayat* was revealed. Muslim alone transmitted this. The second view is that the bishops of Najran went to the Messenger of Allah ﷺ and said, "Muhammad, you claim that acts of disobedience happen by a decree but that is not how things are." The Prophet ﷺ said, "You are the opponents of Allah." So this *ayat* was revealed: *"The evildoers are indeed misguided and insane on the Day when they are dragged face-first into the Fire: 'Taste the scorching touch of Saqar!' We have created all things in due measure."* (54:47-49)

'Umar ibn al-Khattab ؓ related that the Messenger of Allah ﷺ said: "When Allah gathers the first and last on the Day of Rising, He will command a caller to give a call, which the first and the last will hear, saying: 'Where are the opponents of Allah?' The Qadariyya will stand and be ordered to go to the Fire. Allah will say, *'Taste the scorching touch of Saqar. We have created all things in due measure.'"* They are called the opponents of Allah because they argued that it is not possible for Him to decree disobedience for His slave and then to punish him for it.

Hisham ibn Hassan related that al-Hasan said, "By Allah, even if a Qadari fasts until he is like a thread and then prays until he is like a string, Allah will still drag him on his face into Saqar. Then he will be told: *'Taste the scorching touch of Saqar. We have created all things in due measure.'"* Muslim related in his *Sahih* from a *hadith* of Ibn 'Umar ؓ that the Messenger of Allah ﷺ said, "Every thing comes about by a decree, even powerlessness and cleverness." According to Ibn 'Abbas ؓ this means: "We created all things with a decree and measure written in the Preserved Tablet before they occur."

Allah Almighty says: *"Allah created both you and what you do."* (37:96) This can be understood in two ways. One is that 'what you do' is a verbal noun and so the meaning is: "Allah created both you and your actions." The second is that it means: "Allah created you and created the idols you make." This *ayat* shows that the actions of Allah's slaves are created, and Allah knows best. Allah Almighty says, *"He inspired it with depravity or* taqwa." (91:8) "Inspiring" is causing something to occur in the soul. Sa'id ibn Jubayr said, "He made it have its depravity or *taqwa*." Ibn Zayd said, "He put that into it by giving it success through its *taqwa* or ruin it through its depravity." Allah knows best.

The Messenger of Allah ﷺ said, "Allah is the one who is kind to some people and inspires them to good and admits them into His mercy. He tempts other people, ruins them, and rebukes them for their actions although they could not have done otherwise than fail in their test, He punishes them – and He is just. *'He will not be questioned about what He does, but they will be questioned.'* (21:23)"

Mu'adh ibn Jabal ؓ reported that the Messenger of Allah ﷺ said, "Allah has not sent any Prophet without there being Qadariyya and Murji'iyya in his nation. Allah has cursed the Qadariyya and Murji'iyya on the tongues of seventy Prophets." 'A'isha ؓ said that the Messenger of Allah ﷺ said, "The *Qadariyya* are the Magians of this Community." Ibn 'Umar ؓ narrated that the Messenger of Allah ﷺ said, "Every nation has Magians, and the Magians of this community are those who claim that there is no such thing as destiny and that actions are not predetermined." He continued, "When I meet them, I will tell them that I am quit of them and they are quit of me." Then he said, "By the One who has my soul in His hand, if one of them had had the equivalent of Uhud in gold and spent it in the way of Allah, it would not be accepted until he believes that both good and evil are decreed." Then he mentioned Jibril and his asking the Prophet ﷺ, "What is faith?" He answered, "It is that you believe in Allah and His angels and His Books and Messengers (and the Last Day), and that you believe in the decree, both good and bad."

His words, "that you believe in Allah" is affirmation that He – glory be to Him and exalted is He – exists and is characterised by the attributes of Majesty and Perfection, free of the attributes of imperfection; and that he is Single, Eternal, Creator of all creatures and disposes of them as He wishes, and He does as He wishes in His kingdom.

Faith in the angels means affirming that they are slaves of Allah.

"They are honoured slaves. They do not precede Him in speech, and they act on His command. He knows what is in front of them and what is behind them. They only intercede on behalf of those with whom He is pleased, and even they are apprehensive for fear of Him." (21:26-28)

Faith in the Messengers means affirming that they speak the truth in what they report from Allah; that Allah supported them with miracles which indicate their truthfulness; that they conveyed the Message from Allah Almighty and made clear to those responsible what Allah has commanded them to do; that they must be revered; and that no one should differentiate between any of them.

Faith in the Last Day is affirmation of the Day of Rising and what it involves: being brought back after death, the Resurrection, Gathering, the Reckoning, the Balance, the *Sirat*; the Garden and the Fire, which are the abode of the reward and punishment of those who do good and those who do evil; and other things transmitted on sound authority.

Faith in the Divine Decree is affirmation of what has already been mentioned. It is what is indicated by the words of the Almighty, *"Allah created both you and what you do"* (37:96) and *"We have created all things in due measure."* (54:49) An aspect of it is expressed in the words of the Prophet ﷺ in a *hadith* from Ibn 'Abbas ؓ: "Know that if a nation united to help you, it could only succeed in something which Allah has written for you. If they united to harm you they could only harm you with something which Allah has written for you. The pens (of the Divine Decree) have been lifted and the pages are dry."

The position of the *Salaf* and later imams is that anyone who definitely believes in these things without doubt or hesitation is truly a believer, whether that be through definitive proofs or out of simple faith. Allah knows best.

Section. Seventy of the *Tabi'un* and the imams of the Muslims, the *Salaf* and *fuqaha'* of the cities, agree that the *sunna* which the Messenger of Allah 變 died following is contentment with the Divine Decree and foreordination of Allah, submission to His command, steadfastness under His judgement, accepting what Allah has commanded and forbidden, sincere action for Allah, belief in the Divine Decree, both good and evil, abandoning doubt and debate and arguments in the *deen*, wiping over leather socks, accompanying any caliph, pious or impious, in *jihad*, and praying over those of the *qibla* (i.e. the Muslims) who have died.

Faith involves word, action and intention. It increases by obedience and decreases by disobedience. The Qur'an is the uncreated Words of Allah brought down by Jibril to His Prophet Muhammad 變. One should be steadfast under the banner of the ruler whether he be just or unjust. We do not rebel against our commanders with the sword, even if they are unjust, and we do not declare any of the people of the *qibla* to be unbelievers, even if they commit major wrong actions, unless they declare them to be lawful. We do not attest that any of the people of the Garden will have the Garden for any good which they have done unless the Prophet 變 testifies to that. We refrain from commenting on any conflict which occurred between the Companions of the Messenger of Allah 變. The best of creation after the Messenger of Allah 變 was Abu Bakr, then 'Umar, then 'Uthman, and then 'Ali, may Allah be pleased with all of them; and we ask for mercy for all the wives of the Prophet 變 and his children and Companions.

Point. There are certain statements which scholars say are tantamount to disbelief. One is mocking any of the Names of Allah, His command or Hs promise and threat. That constitutes disbelief. If someone were to say, "If Allah were to command me to do such-and-such, I would not do it," it constitutes disbelief. Or if they were to say, "If the *qibla* were in this direction, I would not pray towards it" that also constitutes disbelief. If someone is told, "You should not abandon the prayer or Allah will punish you," and he replies, "If He punishes me for it in view of my illness and hardship, He will wrong me," that also constitutes disbelief. If someone says, "Even if the Prophets and angels were to testify to that, I would not believe it," that constitutes disbelief.

Certain phrases are disliked and considered objectionable, such as: "You have no *deen*," "You have no faith," "You have no certainty," "You are impious," "You are a hypocrite," "You are a *zindiq*.," or "You are a deviant." Those and their like are all forbidden. It is feared for anyone who uses them that his faith will be stripped away and he will be forever in the Fire.

We ask Allah the Gracious by His kindness to make us die as Muslims following the Book and the *Sunna*. He is the Most Merciful of the merciful.

42. Eavesdropping on people and seeking out their secrets

Allah Almighty says:

"Do not spy." (49:12)

Yahya ibn Abi Kathir said, "Spying means prying into people's private affairs and listening secretly to what they say. According to some commentators spying means investigating the faults of the Muslims and their private affairs. The *ayat* means: "None of you should seek out the faults of your brother when Allah has veiled him." Ibn Mas'ud ﷺ was told by someone, "Al-Walid ibn 'Uqba's beard was dripping with wine." He said, "We are forbidden to spy. If anything visible appears to us, we will punish him for it."

The Messenger of Allah ﷺ said, "Whoever listens to what people are saying when they do not want him to will have molten iron poured into his ears on the Day of Rising." Al-Bukhari transmitted this. We seek refuge with Allah from it and ask Allah for success in what He likes and pleases Him. He is Generous, Magnanimous.

Warning. Slaves of Allah, death is close and exacting. Souls which have exhausted themselves in amassing goods are in hock. It is as if you were divested in the clutches of destruction. Slaves of Allah, all acts of disobedience are recorded and written and the selves are in hock for what they harvested and earned. They have what they earned and counted against them is what they earned. O you who are deluded by wishful thinking and false hopes and are engaged in ugly actions, not knowing who you are fighting! You who are like a body without a heart, are you content to miss what is truly good? O you whose life is rapidly disappearing, travelling at racehorse speed, you are white-haired! Have you not yet recognised the true marvels!

43. Carrying tales

This means carrying tales from one person to another in order to cause disharmony between them. It is unlawful by the consensus of the Muslims. There are legal proofs in the Book and the Sunna which demonstrate its unlawfulness. Allah Almighty says:

> *"Do not obey any vile swearer of oaths, any backbiting slander-monger."* (68:10-11)

It is reported in both *Sahih* collections that the Messenger of Allah ﷺ said, "A tale-bearer will not enter the Garden." According to one *hadith* the Messenger of Allah ﷺ passed by two graves and said, "They are being punished; and they are not being punished for anything that seems much, although it is in fact a great deal. One of them used not to free himself of his urine, and the other used to carry tales." Then he took a fresh branch, split it into two pieces, and stuck one half in each grave. He said, "Perhaps it will lighten the punishment for them as long as they have not dried up."

His words "they are not being punished for anything that seems much" mean that they did not think it much. Hence in one variant he said, "but it is in fact a great deal." Abu Hurayra ﷺ reported that the Messenger of Allah ﷺ said, "You will find that the worst people are the two-faced, who show one face to these and another face to those. Whoever has two tongues in this world, Allah will give him two tongues of fire on the Day of Rising." The meaning of "someone with two tongues" is that they say one thing to one person and another thing to a different person.

Imam Abu Hamid al-Ghazali said, "It is mostly applied to someone who carries the words someone has said about someone else to the person he talked about and says, 'So and so says such and such about you.' But tale-bearing is not confined to that. It is defined as disclosing anything that a person would dislike to be disclosed, whether through words, writing, gestures, allusion or any other way, and whether it involves a fault or something else. The real meaning of tale-bearing is to broadcast a secret and reveal anything that another person would not want to be disclosed. People should be silent about anything that they see of the states of people except when there is a benefit for the Muslims in reporting it or when it is done to avert a bad action."

He also said: "When someone tells another that a certain person has said anything about him, six things are incumbent upon the person addressed. Firstly, he should not believe him, because tale-bearers are by definition impious. Secondly, he should tell him not to do that and advise him that his action is wrong. Thirdly, he should dislike him for the sake of Allah Almighty. It is mandatory to dislike for the sake of Allah. Fourthly, he should not think anything evil about the person who was quoted, in accordance with the words of the Almighty: "*Avoid too much suspicion: some suspicion is a crime.*" (49:12) Fifthly, he must not carry out any kind of investigation to see if what he was told is true. The Almighty says: "*Do not spy.*" (49:12) Sixthly, he should be unhappy about the tale-bearing, which is forbidden, and so certainly must not pass it on to anyone else."

It is reported that a man mentioned to 'Umar ibn 'Abd al-'Aziz something about a man and 'Umar said, "If you wish, we will look into what you say. If you are speaking the truth, you are one of the people of this *ayat*, '*If a deviator brings you a report, scrutinize it.*' (49:6) If you are lying, then you are one of the people of this *ayat*, '*any backbiting slandermonger.*' (68:10) If you wish, we will pardon you.' He said, 'Pardon me, Amir al-Mu'minin! I will not do it again!'"

Al-Hasan al-Basri said, "If anyone tells you a story about someone else, know that he will also tell a story about you to someone else. There is a saying about this: 'Whoever transmits to you transmits from you, so beware.'" It is related that one of the righteous early Muslims visited a brother of his and mentioned to him something about one of his brothers which he disliked. He told him, "My brother, you have committed slander and made me commit three crimes: you have made me dislike my brother, you have distracted my heart by it, and you have made me suspect you." One of the righteous early Muslims used to say, "Whoever tells that your brother is abusing you is himself abusing you." A man went to 'Ali ibn al-Husayn and said, "So-and-so abused you and said such-and-such about you." He said, "Take me to him."

'Ali went with the man, who was thinking that he was going to defend himself. But when he reached him, 'Ali said, "My brother, if what you said about me is true, may Allah forgive me. If what you said about me is false, may Allah forgive you."

It is said about the words of Allah Almighty, "*The bearer of firewood*" (111:4), alluding to the wife of Abu Lahab, that she used to carry tales. Tales are called firewood because they are the cause of enmity, as firewood is used to kindle fire. It is said that the action of tale-bearers is worse than the action of Shaytan, because the action of Shaytan is by hidden whispering while the action of tale-bearing is face to face.

It is related that a man saw a boy being sold and was told that he had no fault other than tale-bearing. He thought that unimportant and bought him. After being with him some days, the boy said to the wife of his master, "My master wants to marry another wife as well as you or divorce you. He does not love you. If you want him to be kind to you and abandon what he has resolved to do, when he sleeps, you should take a razor, cut some hairs from his beard and give them to me." The woman's heart was filled with anxiety and she said to herself, "Yes, I will do that," and decided to do that the next time her husband was asleep.

Then the boy went to the husband and said, "My master, my mistress, your wife, has taken a lover other than you and has fallen in love with him and wants to be free of you. She has resolved to murder you tonight. If you do not believe me, then pretend to be asleep in the night and see if she comes to you with something in her hand, intending to cut your throat with it." His master believed him. In the night, the woman came with the razor to shave the hairs from under his beard. The man was pretending to sleep and said to himself, "By Allah, the slave was telling the truth."

When the woman lowered the razor towards his throat, he seized it from her and killed her with it. Her family came and saw that she had been murdered and so they killed him. In this way a destructive blood feud was brought about between the two families because of the malevolent mischief of that ill-fated lad. That is why Allah called tale-bearer a deviator in His words: "*If a deviator brings you a report, scrutinize it carefully, lest you attack people in ignorance and so come to greatly regret what you have done.*" (49:6)

139

44. Cursing

The Prophet ﷺ said, "Cursing a believer is like killing him." Al-Bukhari transmitted it. In *Sahih Muslim* we find that the Messenger of Allah ﷺ said, "Cursers will have no intercessors or witnesses on the Day of Rising." The Prophet ﷺ said, "A true person should not be a curser." The Messenger of Allah ﷺ said, "When anyone curses anything, the curse rises to heaven and the doors of heaven are locked against it. Then it descends to the earth and its doors are locked against it. Then it goes right and left and does not find any place to go and it returns to what was cursed if it deserved it. If not, it returns to the one who uttered it."

'Imran ibn Husayn ﷺ said, "While the Messenger of Allah ﷺ was on one of his journeys, a woman of the Ansar was riding a she-camel and she was annoyed and cursed it. The Messenger of Allah ﷺ heard that and said, 'Take what is on it and leave it. It is accursed.'" 'Umar ﷺ said, "I used to see it walking among people, and no one would stop it." Muslim transmitted this.

Section on the permissibility of cursing those who disobey Allah in a general way without naming specific individuals

Allah Almighty says:

"The curse of Allah is on the wrongdoers." (11:18)

"Then let us make earnest supplication and call down the curse of Allah upon those who lie." (3:61)

It is reliably reported that the Messenger of Allah ﷺ said, "Allah has cursed those who consume usury and those who pay it, those who witness it and those who record it." He said, "Allah has cursed the one who makes a woman lawful for remarriage and the one for whom it is done." He said, "Allah has cursed the woman who attaches false hair and the one who has it attached, the tattooer and the one tattoed, and the one who plucks hair between the eyebrows and the one who has it plucked."

140

The Messenger of Allah ﷺ cursed women who scream in affliction, women who shave off their hair in affliction, and women who tear their clothes in affliction. The Prophet ﷺ cursed those who make images. He cursed those who change property-line markers. And he said ﷺ, "Allah curses anyone who curses his parents and He curses anyone who insults own his mother." We find in the *Sunan* that he also said ﷺ, "Allah has cursed people who misguide a blind person from the right direction. Allah has cursed anyone who has sex with an animal. Allah has cursed anyone who commits the action of the people of Lut."

He cursed people who go to soothsayers. He cursed women who wail and those around them. He cursed anyone who leads a group of people when they dislike him. He cursed women who spend the night with their husband angry at them. He cursed a man who hears "Come to prayer, Come to success," and then does not respond. He cursed the one who slaughters in the name of other than Allah. He cursed thieves. He cursed anyone who reviles the Companions. He cursed effeminate men and masculine women. He cursed men who resemble women and women who resemble men. He cursed women who wears men's clothes and men who wears women's clothes. He cursed anyone who sows evil between a woman and her husband or a slave and his master. He cursed anyone who has sex with a menstruating woman or in a woman's anus.

He cursed anyone who points anything made from steel at his brother. He cursed anyone who refuses to pay *zakat*. He cursed anyone who lies about who his father is. He cursed anyone who brands an animal on its face. He cursed anyone who intercedes or is interceded for when one of the *hudud* of Allah is concerned after the case has reached the judge. He cursed any woman who leaves her house without her husband's permission. He cursed anyone who abandons commanding right and forbidding wrong when he is able to do so. He cursed the passive and active participants in sodomy. He cursed wine, those who drink, pour, ask for, sell, buy or carry it, and the one for whom it is carried, and those who use the proceeds of selling wine and those who direct people to it.

The Prophet ﷺ said, "Six are cursed by Allah and by every Prophet whose supplication is answered: anyone who denies the Decree of Allah, anyone who adds to the Book of Allah, anyone given power who exalts those Allah has abased and abases those Allah has exalted, anyone who makes lawful what Allah has made unlawful, anyone who makes it lawful to treat my family in a way Allah has forbidden, and anyone who abandons my *Sunna*."

He cursed anyone who commits adultery with his neighbour's wife. He cursed masturbators. He cursed anyone who marries both a mother and her daughter. He cursed anyone who gives bribes to gain a favourable judgement, the one bribed, and their go-between. He cursed anyone who conceals knowledge. He cursed people who hoard. He cursed anyone who disappoints a Muslim, as in other words does not help him. He cursed a ruler whpodoes not have mercy. He cursed men and women who refrain from marriage. He cursed anyone who travels in the wilderness alone.

We seek refuge with Allah from His curse and that of His Messenger!

Section. Know that cursing a protected Muslim is forbidden by consensus of the Muslims. It is permitted to curse people who possess bad qualities in general, for instance by saying: "Allah curses wrongdoers," "Allah curses unbelievers," "Allah curses the Jews and Christians," "Allah curses the impious," "Allah curses image-makers," and other such things. As for cursing a particular individual among those who are guilty of specific acts of disobedience, like a particular Jew or Christian, or someone unjust, or a fornicator, thief or usurer, the literal text of the *hadith*s above suggest that it is not forbidden. Al-Ghazali indicates that it is permitted in respect of people whom we know to have died as unbelievers, such as Abu Lahab, Abu Jahl, Pharoah, Haman and their like. He said, "The object of a curse is to distance someone from the mercy of Allah; but we do not how this or that impious person or unbeliever will end up."

He said, "As for those whom the Messenger of Allah ﷺ cursed himself, as when he said, 'O Allah, curse Ra'l, Dhakwan, 'Asiyya:

they disobeyed Allah and His Messenger,' those are tribes of desert Arabs and the Prophet ﷺ knew that they would die unbelievers." He said, "Praying for evil to befall a person is close to a curse, even against a wrongdoer, such as when a person says, "May Allah not mend his body," "May Allah not heal him," and other such things. Doing that is wrong. The same applies to cursing any animal or inanimate object. All that is wrong." Some scholars say that if one curses anyone who does not deserve to be cursed he should hasten to add, "if he deserves it".

Section. It is permitted for those who enjoin what is right and forbid what is wrong, and for every teacher, to say to someone he is addressing during the course of his work, "Woe to you!" or "How weak you are in understanding!" or "How lacking in self-reflection!" "O self-wronger!" or other such things if it is true; but there must be no expression in it which could be conveyed as clear slander, or injurious allusion, even if it is true. It is permitted provided its aim is simply discipline, or rebuke, or words to beneficially affect the hearer's self. Allah knows best.

O Allah, divest our hearts of connection to any but You! Make us to be among those You love and who love You. Forgive us, our parents and all Muslims!

45. Perfidy and breaking promises

Allah Almighty says:

"Fulfil your contracts. Contracts will be questioned about." (17:34)

Az-Zajjaj said, "All that Allah has commanded or forbidden is a contract. Allah Almighty also says: *"You who believe, fulfil your contracts."* (5:1) According to al-Wahidi Ibn 'Abbas ﷺ said about this, "The word 'contracts' here refers to what Allah has made lawful and unlawful, what He has imposed and explained in the Qur'an." Ad-Dahhak said, "The word 'contracts' refers to anything whose fulfilment Allah has imposed on this community as regards what is lawful and unlawful, obligatory prayers, shares of inheritance and contracts." According to Muqatal ibn Hayyan it means, "Fulfil the contracts which Allah has made with you in the Qur'an in respect of what He has ordered you to do and forbidden you to do, and the contracts which are between you and the idolators and between Muslims." Allah knows best.

The Prophet ﷺ said, "Whoever has four characteristics is a pure hypocrite, and whoever has one of them has an aspect of hypocrisy until he gives it up: whenever he is trusted, he betrays his trust; whenever he speaks, he lies; when he makes an agreement, he breaks it; when he quarrels, he speaks falsely." This is transmitted in both *Sahih* collections.

The Messenger of Allah ﷺ said, "Every traitor will have a banner on the Day of Rising which reads 'This one betrayed So-and-so.'" The Messenger of Allah ﷺ said, "Allah Almighty says, 'I will be the antagonist of three people on the Day of Rising: a man who makes a covenant in My name and then betrays it; a man who sells a free man and then consumes the money he gets for him; and a man who hires an employee and gets full work from him and then does not pay him his wages." Al-Bukhari transmitted this.

The Messenger of Allah ﷺ said, "Anyone who reneges on his duty of obedience will meet Allah on the Day of Rising with no evidence to defend him. Anyone who dies without having given the oath of allegiance will die the death of the *Jahiliyya*." Muslim transmitted this. The Messenger of Allah ﷺ said, "Whoever wants to be far from the Fire and enter the Garden should die believing in Allah and the Last Day and should treat people as he would like to be treated by them. Whoever gives allegiance to a leader should give him both his hand and his heart and should obey him if he can. If anyone contends with (that leader), he should be beheaded."

46. Believing soothsayers and astrologers

Allah Almighty says:

"Do not pursue what you have no knowledge of. Hearing, sight and hearts will all be questioned." (17:36)

According to al-Wahidi's commentaary on these words of the Almighty, al-Kalbi said, "Do not speak about something you have no knowledge of." Qatada said, "Do not say, 'I heard' if you did not hear, or 'I saw' if you did not see, or 'I know' if you do not know." According to al-Walibi, Ibn 'Abbas 🙵 said, "Allah will ask people about what they were charged to do. This impugns looking at what is not lawful, listening to what is forbidden and desiring what is not permitted. Allah knows best."

Allah Almighty says:

"He is the Knower of the Unseen and does not divulge His Unseen to anyone except a Messenger with whom He is well pleased." (72:26-27)

According to Ibn al-Jawzi: "The Knower of the Unseen is Allah Almighty alone with no partner in His kingdom, and He only informs any Messenger with whom He is pleased about unknown aspects of His Unseen because a proof of the truthfulness of the Messengers lies in their reporting about the Unseen." This is an indication that anyone who claims that the stars give knowledge of the Unseen is an unbeliever, and Allah knows best.

The Messenger of Allah 🙵 said, "Anyone who goes to a diviner or soothsayer and believes what he says has disbelieved in what was sent down to Muhammad." We find in the two *Sahih* collections that Zayd ibn Khalid 🙵 said: "The Messenger of Allah 🙵 led us in the *Subh* prayer after a rainy night. When he finished, he faced the people and said, 'Do you know what your Lord has said?' They said, 'Allah and His Messenger know best.' He said: 'This morning My slaves have become divided into believers and unbelievers. Those who say, "We had rain by the favour and mercy of Allah" believe in Me and not in the stars. Those who say

146

that it was because of a certain star, disbelieve in Me and believe in the star.'"

Scholars say that if a Muslim says, "We had rain through the rising of such-and-such a star," meaning that its rising was what brought the rain into existence, then he is an unbeliever or an apostate without doubt. If he means that it is a sign of the descent of rain and that rain descends at this sign but it descends by the action of Allah in His creation, he is not an unbeliever. Scholars disagree about whether it is disliked. The best view is that it is disliked because it is one of the expressions of disbelief.

The Messenger of Allah ﷺ said, "If someone goes to a diviner and believes what he says, his prayer will not be accepted for forty days." Muslim related it. 'A'isha ﷺ said, "Some people asked the Messenger of Allah ﷺ about soothsayers, and he said, 'It is nothing.' They asked, 'Messenger of Allah, did he not say such-and-such?' The Messenger of Allah ﷺ said, 'That true word was heard by a jinn who repeated it in the ear of his friend and mixed a hundred lies with it.'" This is transmitted in both *Sahih* collections.

'A'isha ﷺ reported: "I heard the Messenger of Allah ﷺ say, "The angels descend in the mists, which are the clouds, and mention that something has been decreed in heaven. A *shaytan* eavesdrops, hears it and then reveals it to the soothsayers, and they add a hundred lies of their own making to it.'" Al-Bukhari related this.

Qabisa ibn Abi al-Makhariq ﷺ related that he heard the Messenger of Allah ﷺ say, "Divining, birds and reading paths of flight are part of idol worship." Abu Dawud related it; and explained that reading paths involves holding birds to ascertain good or bad omens by their flight. If they fly to the right, it denotes good luck. If they fly to the left, it denotes bad luck." Ibn 'Abbas ﷺ related that the Messenger of Allah ﷺ said, "Anyone who plucks a branch of astrology has plucked a branch of sorcery. Whatever else of it he learns adds to it." 'Ali ibn Abi Talib ﷺ said, "A soothsayer is a sorcerer, and a sorcerer is an unbeliever." We ask Allah for protection in this world and the Next.

47. A wife disobeying her husband

Allah Almighty says:

"If there are women whose disobedience you fear, you may admonish them, refuse to sleep with them, and then beat them. But if they obey you, do not look for a way to punish them. Allah is All-High, Most Great." (4:34)

According to al-Wahidi: "The word 'disobedience' (*nushuz*) here refers to a wife's disobedience to her husband. It means putting herself above him in a disagreement." 'Ata' said, "It means trying to harm him, deny herself to him and to cease to obey him." The words 'admonish them' mean by the Book of Allah, and mean reminding them of what Allah has commanded them to do. Ibn 'Abbas ﷺ said that "refuse to sleep with them" means turning one's back on one's wife in bed and not speaking to her. Ash-Sha'bi and Mujahid said, "It means to shun her bed and not sleep with her." "Beat them" means with a blow that is not hard. Ibn 'Abbas ﷺ said that it means discipline such as a blow. A husband can deal with his wife's disobedience in the way Allah has allowed him which is mentioned in this *ayat*. Ibn 'Abbas ﷺ also said, "Do not look for reasons to punish them."

In the two *Sahih* collections we find that the Messenger of Allah ﷺ said, "If a man calls his wife to his bed and she does not come, the angels curse her until morning." One version has: "If he spends the night angry with her, the angels curse her until morning." The two *Sahih* collections also contain this *hadith*: "When a woman spends the night shunning the bed of her husband the One who is in heaven is angry with her until her husband is pleased with her." Jabir ﷺ related that the Prophet ﷺ said, "Three will not have their prayer accepted by Allah and no good action of theirs will rise to heaven: a runaway slave until he returns to his masters and surrenders himself to them, a woman whose husband is angry with her until he is pleased with her, and a drunkard until he is sober."

Al-Hasan said that it is related that someone heard the Prophet ﷺ say, "The first things a woman will be asked about on the Day of Rising are her prayer and her husband." Another *hadith* states: The Messenger of Allah ﷺ said, "It is not lawful for a woman who believes in Allah and the Last Day to fast when her husband is present without his permission, or to give permission for anyone to enter his house except with his permission." Al-Bukhari transmitted it. That applies only to voluntary fasting. She may not fast without his permission because of his right over her.

The Prophet ﷺ said, "If I had commanded anyone to prostrate to anyone, I would have commanded a woman to prostrate to her husband." At-Tirmidhi relates it. The aunt of Husayn ibn Mihsan said that when she mentioned her husband to the Prophet ﷺ he said, "See are where you are in relation to him. He is your Garden and your Fire." An-Nasa'i transmitted this. 'Abdullah ibn 'Amr reported that the Prophet ﷺ said, "Allah will not look at a woman who is not grateful to her husband in a situation when she could not manage without him." It is also reported that he ﷺ said, "When a woman leaves the house of her husband, the angels curse her until she returns or repents." The Prophet ﷺ also said, "If a woman dies while her husband is pleased with her, she will enter the Garden."

It is mandatory for a woman to seek to please her husband and avoid his anger, and not to refuse him when he wants her, according to the words of the Prophet ﷺ: "When a man calls his wife to his bed she should go to him, even if she is at the oven." Scholars have said, "Unless she has the excuse of menstruation or past-partum bleeding, for then it is not lawful for her to go to him, or for the man to ask that of her. He may not have sex with her until she has had a *ghusl*, in accordance with the words of Allah Almighty: *"Keep apart from women in menstruation and do not approach them until they have purified themselves"* (2:222): in other words, "do not have sex with them until they have purified themselves."

A woman should not dispose of her husband's property except with his permission, nor should she criticise his appearance. Al-Asma'i said, "A bedouin woman visited a beautiful woman who had an ugly husband and asked her, 'How could you be happy to be married to someone like this?' She said, 'Listen, you! Perhaps he was good with respect to what is between him and Allah His Creator and Allah made me his reward. Perhaps I was bad and He made him my punishment.'"

'A'isha ⚘ said, "Company of women, if you knew the right your husbands have over you, you would wipe the dust off your husband's feet with your cheeks." The Prophet ⚘ said, "Those of your women who are the people of the Garden are those who are loving and who, when their husbands are hurt or in pain, go to them and put their hands in theirs and say, 'I will not go to sleep until you feel better.'"

Section on the excellence of a woman who obeys her husband and the severity of the punishment of a disobedient wife

A woman who fears Allah Almighty should strive to obey Allah and obey her husband and seek to please him, as he is her Garden or her Fire according to the words of the Prophet ⚘: "Any woman who dies while her husband pleased with her will enter the Garden." In another *hadith* we find: "If a woman prays her five prayers, fasts the month (of Ramadan), and obeys her husband, she will enter the Garden by whichever gate of the Garden she wishes."

The Prophet ⚘ said, "I looked in the Fire and I saw that most of its inhabitants were women. That was because of their lack of obedience to Allah and His Messenger and their husbands and their great concern with self-adornment." Self-adornment means that, when she wants to go out, she puts on her most splendid garments, beautifies herself and goes out to attract people. Even if she is safe in herself, people are not safe from her. That is why the Prophet ⚘ said, "A woman is a private part. When she leaves her house, *Shaytan* looks at her." In another *hadith* we find: "A woman is a private part, so keep her in the house. When a woman goes out and her family ask her, 'Where are you going?' and she says, 'To visit an invalid or attend a funeral,' *Shaytan* keeps on at her until she leaves the house. A woman cannot seek the pleasure of Allah in any better way than by staying in her house, worshipping her Lord and obeying her husband."

'Ali ﷺ asked his wife Fatima ﷺ, "Fatima, what is best for a woman?" She answered, "That she not see men and they not see her." 'Ali ﷺ used to say, "Are you not ashamed? Are you not jealous? Some of you let their wives go out among men so that they look at the men and the men look at them." One day while 'A'isha ﷺ and Hafsa ﷺ were sitting with the Prophet ﷺ Ibn Umm Maktum ﷺ entered. He was blind. The Prophet ﷺ said, "Veil yourselves from him." They said, "Messenger of Allah, is he not blind so that he cannot see us or recognise us?" The Prophet ﷺ replied, "Are you blind so that you do not see him?" Mu'adh ibn Jabal ﷺ reported that the Messenger of Allah ﷺ said, "No woman harms her husband in this world without his wife among the houris saying, 'Do not harm him. May Allah fight you! Woe to the woman who disobeys her husband.'"

Section: While a woman is commanded to obey her husband and seek to please him, her husband is also commanded to treat her well and be kind to her, to put up with any bad character or other defect she may display, and to give her her due with respect to maintenance, clothing and good companionship, conforming to the words of Allah Almighty: *"Live together with them correctly and courteously"* (4:19), and by the words of the Prophet ﷺ: "You are instructed to be good to women. You have a right over your women and your women have a right over you. The right they are due is that you be good to them with respect to clothing and feeding them; and the right you are due from them is that they not allow anyone you dislike into their private quarters and not allow anyone you dislike into your homes at all."

The Prophet ﷺ said, "The best of you is the one who is best to his family;" and in one variant: "The best of you is the one who is kindest to his family." The Messenger of Allah ﷺ was very kind to women. The Prophet ﷺ said, "If a man is patient with the bad character of his wife, Allah will give him a reward like the one He gave to Ayyub ﷺ for bearing his affliction. If a woman is patient with the bad character of her husband, Allah will give the reward of the like the one He gave to Asiya, the daughter of Muzaham, the wife of Pharaoh."

151

It is related that a man went to 'Umar ﷺ to complain about his wife's character and stood at his door waiting for him to come out. He heard 'Umar's wife nagging him with her tongue, arguing with him, while Umar remained silent and did not answer her. So the man left saying, "If this is the state of 'Umar with all his severity and firmness, and he is the *Amir al-Mu'minin*, what about me?" 'Umar came out and saw him turning away from his door and called out to him saying, "What do you need, my man?" He answered, "*Amir al-Mu'minin*, I came to you to complain about my wife's bad character and her nagging me, and then I heard your wife doing the same, so I turned back and said, 'If this is the situation of the *Amir al-Mu'minin* with his wife, what can I say about mine?'" 'Umar said, "My brother, I put up with it for the rights I owe her: she cooks my food, bakes my bread, washes my clothes and nurses my children. She is not in fact required to do any of that. Through her my heart is stilled and protected from the *haram*. So I put up with that from her." The man said, "*Amir al-Mu'minin*, my wife is also like that." 'Umar said, "Put up with it, brother. It is but a short period of time."

It is related that a righteous man had a brother in Allah who was also a righteous man, and whom he used to visit once a year. He came to visit him and knocked at his door. The man's wife asked, "Who is it?" He answered, "Your husband's brother in Allah. I have come to visit him." She said, "He has gone to get firewood. May Allah not bring him back or keep him safe!" and she began to criticise him. While he was standing at the door, his brother came from the direction of the mountains with a bundle of firewood on the back of a lion which he was driving before him. He came and greeted his brother and welcomed him. He entered the house and put the firewood inside. He told the lion, "Go, may Allah bless you." Then he brought his brother in; and all the time his wife was criticising him but he did not reply to her. Then he ate something with his brother and then bade him farewell. The man left amazed at the patience of his brother with that woman.

The following year he went to visit his brother again, as was his custom, and knocked at the door. His wife asked, "Who is at the door?" He answered, "The brother in Allah of your husband, so-and-so." She said, "Welcome to you. Make yourself comfortable.

He will soon come, Allah willing, safe and sound." He was amazed at the softness of her words and manners. When his brother came carrying firewood on his own back, he was also amazed. He came and greeted him, entered the house and admitted him. The wife brought some food for them and began to pray for them in a gentle voice. When he was about to leave him, he said, "My brother, will you tell me about something if I ask you?" He said, "What is it, my brother?" He said. "Last year I came to you and heard the words of a woman with a coarse tongue and no manners, criticising you continually, and I saw you come from the mountains with firewood on the back of a lion which was subservient to you. This year I found a woman who spoke with kind words and without criticism; but I saw you come carrying the firewood on your back. Why is that?" He replied, "My brother, that ill-tempered wife of mine died. I was patient with her character and what she displayed, and endured the hardship, and so Allah subjected to me the lion you saw to carry the firewood for me because of my patience with her. When she died, I married this righteous woman and I have found tranquillity with her – and so I am cut off from the lion and have to carry firewood on my own back, because of the peace of mine I enjoy with this blessed obedient woman."

We ask Allah to provide us with patience in what He loves and pleases Him. He is Generous, Magnanimous.

48. Making images on clothes, walls, stones, coins and all things, whether it be in wax, paste, iron, copper, wool, or anything else

Allah Almighty says:

"As for those who abuse Allah and His Messenger, Allah's curse is on them in this world and the Next World. He has prepared a humiliating punishment for them." (33:57)

'Ikrima said, "This means those who make images." Ibn 'Umar ﷺ reported that the Messenger of Allah ﷺ said, "Those who make images will be punished on the Day of Rising. They will be told, 'Bring what you created to life.'" This is transmitted in both *Sahih* collections.

'A'isha ﷺ said, "The Messenger of Allah ﷺ came back from a journey and I had put up a curtain with images on it over an alcove of mine. When the Messenger of Allah ﷺ saw it his face changed colour and he said "A'isha, the people with the worst punishment from Allah on the Day of Rising will be those who make things like Allah's creation.'" 'A'isha ﷺ said, "So I cut it up and made two cushions from it." This is transmitted in both *Sahih* Collections.

Ibn 'Abbas ﷺ reported, "I heard the Messenger of Allah ﷺ say, 'Every image maker shall be in the Fire. Every image he made will be given a soul and he will be punished by it in the fire of Hell." This is transmitted in both *Sahih* collections. Ibn 'Abbas also reported that he heard the Messenger of Allah ﷺ say, "Anyone who makes an image in this world will be obliged to blow a spirit into it on the Day of Rising, and he will never be able to do that." The Prophet ﷺ said, "Allah Almighty says, 'Who does more wrong that someone who tries to create as I create? Let them cre-ate a grain or create an ant.'" This is transmitted in both *Sahih* Collections.

The Prophet ﷺ said, "A shape from the Fire will shoot up from it on the Day of Rising and say, 'I have been entrusted with three: all who called on another god with Allah, every stubborn tyrant and every image-maker." (at-Tirmidhi) The Messenger of Allah ﷺ

also said, "The angels do not enter a house in which there is a dog or an image." This is transmitted in the two *Sahih* collections. We find in the *Sunan* of Abu Dawud that 'Ali ibn Abi Talib ﷺ narrated that the Messenger of Allah ﷺ said, "The angels do not enter a house in which there is a dog, an image or anyone in *janaba*."

According to al-Khattabi, these words refer to angels who descend with mercy and blessing, rather than guardian angels, who do not leave whether someone is in *janaba* or not. He said that he does not mean someone who is *janaba* and delays *ghusl* to the time of the prayer, but rather someone who does not have a *ghusl* and with whom neglect of it becomes a habit.

'A'isha ﷺ said, "The Messenger of Allah ﷺ used to sleep while in *janaba* without having touched water." What he said about dogs applies when a dog is acquired other than for the purposes of farming, guarding or hunting. If someone needs a dog, there is no harm in them, Allah willing, in some cases, such as for guarding the house when necessary. As for images which are images of living things, whether they be in the form of statues or just drawn on a wall or ceiling, placed on a carpet, or woven into a cloth, the general position is that they should be avoided. All success is from Allah.

Destroying images is mandatory for anyone who is able to destroy them or remove them. Muslim related in his *Sahih* that Hayyan ibn Husayn said, "'Ali ibn Abi Talib ﷺ said to me, 'Shall I pass on to you something which the Messenger of Allah ﷺ passed on to me? Do not leave any image without destroying it, or any elevated grave without levelling it.'"

We ask Allah for success in doing what He has made obligatory and is pleased with. He is Generous, Magnanimous.

49. Slapping, wailing, tearing garments, shaving the head, pulling out hair and lamenting loudly in a time of affliction

We find in *Sahih al-Bukhari* that Abdullah ibn Mas'ud ﷺ reported that the Messenger of Allah ﷺ said, "Anyone who slaps his cheeks, rips his pockets and cries out in the way that people cried out in the time of the *Jahiliyya* is not one of us." And we find in the *Sahih* collections a *hadith* from Abu Musa al-Ash'ari ﷺ that the Messenger of Allah ﷺ "disowns a woman who wails, who shaves her hair or pulls it out [in grief], and a woman who tears her clothes in affliction." All of that is forbidden by the agreement of scholars. It is also forbidden to dishevel one's hair, slap one's cheeks, scratch one's face or wail loudly.

Umm 'Atiyya ﷺ said, "When we gave our oath of allegiance, the Messenger of Allah ﷺ imposed on us that we should not wail." Al-Bukhari related it. Abu Hurayra ﷺ reported that the Messenger of Allah ﷺ said, "There are two qualities which turn people into unbelievers: impugning people's lineage, and wailing over the dead." Muslim related it. Abu Sa'id al-Khudri ﷺ said that the Messenger of Allah ﷺ cursed a woman who wails and anyone who listens to her, as Abu Dawud relates. Abu Burda said, "Abu Musa al-Ash'ari ﷺ was ill and he fainted with his head in the lap of his wife. She started wailing and he could not stop her. When he recovered, he said, 'I disown whatever the Messenger of Allah ﷺ disowns. The Messenger of Allah ﷺ disowns women who wail, who shave their hair or pull it out [in grief], and women who tear their clothes in affliction.'"

According to both *Sahih* collections, the Messenger of Allah ﷺ said, "A dead person is punished in his grave for the wailing done over him." Abu Musa ﷺ said, "There is no one who dies and then those who are weeping over him stand and say, 'O master! O mountain!' and other such things, without two angels poking him and asking, 'Were you like that?'" At-Tirmidhi transmitted this.

The Prophet ﷺ said, "If a wailer does not repent before she dies, she will stand on the Day of Rising wearing trousers of tar and a shirt of scabies." Al-Hasan said, "Two sounds are cursed: flutes in blessing and wailing in affliction." The Messenger of Allah ﷺ said, "Those mourners will form two rows in the Fire and will bark at the people of the Fire as dogs bark." Al-Awza'i related that 'Umar ibn al-Khattab ﷺ heard the sound of wailing and went in with some others and started hitting those present until he reached the professional wailer and hit her so hard that her veil fell off. He said, "Hit her! She is a professional mourner with no inviolability! She is not weeping in sorrow for you but is shedding tears to take your dirhams. She harms the dead in their graves and the living in their houses because she debars patience when Allah commands it and commands despair when Allah debars it."

Know that this forbidden type of mourning involves raising the voice to a wail while recounting the good qualities of the dead person. In the opinion of scholars it is forbidden to raise the voice in excessive weeping. Weeping for the dead without lamenting or wailing is not forbidden. We find in *Sahih al-Bukhari* and *Sahih Muslim* from Ibn 'Umar ﷺ that the Messenger of Allah ﷺ visited Sa'd ibn 'Ubada accompanied by 'Abd ar-Rahman ibn 'Awf, Sa'd ibn Abi Waqqas, and 'Abdullah ibn Mas'ud ﷺ and the Messenger of Allah ﷺ wept. When the people saw the Messenger of Allah ﷺ weeping, they too wept. He said, "Listen! Allah does not punish for the tears of the eye or the sorrow of the heart; He punishes or shows mercy on account of this." He pointed to his tongue. We are informed by Usama ibn Zayd ﷺ that the Messenger of Allah ﷺ said that Sa'd ﷺ asked, "What is this, Messenger of Allah?" He answered, "This is mercy which Allah puts in the hearts of His slaves. Allah shows mercy to His slaves who are merciful."

It is related in *Sahih al-Bukhari* from Anas ﷺ that the Messenger of Allah ﷺ visited his son Ibrahim who was breathing his last, and the eyes of the Messenger of Allah ﷺ filled with tears. 'Abd ar-Rahman ibn 'Awf ﷺ said to him, "You, Messenger of Allah?" He said, "Ibn 'Awf, it is mercy." Then he said, "The eye weeps and the heart is sad. We only say what is pleasing to our Lord and I am sad at your leaving, Ibrahim."

As for the sound *hadith*s that a dead person is punished for the weeping of his family over him, they should not be taken literally in general, but interpreted. Scholars disagree about their interpretation. The most obvious position is, and Allah knows best, that it applies only when the dead person left instructions for that type of mourning. The followers of ash-Shafi'i said that it is permitted before and after death, but before it is more fitting because of the sound *hadith*. When death is inevitable, no one should weep. Ash-Shafi'i and his followers have a text that the dislike of weeping after death is precautionary, not prohibitive; and they interpreted the *hadith* "Do not weep" as expressing disapproval, and Allah knows best.

Section. Those who wail incur this punishment and curse because they encourage despair and discourage patience, while Allah and His Messenger instruct people to have patience and expectation of a reward and forbid despair and anger. Allah Almighty says:

> "*O you who believe, seek help in steadfastness and the prayer. Allah is with the steadfast. ...We will test you with something of fear, hunger, and loss of wealth and life and fruits. But give good news to the steadfast: those who, when disaster strikes them, say, 'We belong to Allah and to Him we return.'*" (2:153-156)

'A'isha ﷺ related that the Messenger of Allah ﷺ said, "There is no affliction which afflicts a believer but that by it Allah expiates something he has done – even a thorn which pricks him." Muslim related this. 'Alqama ibn Mirthadd ibn Sabit related from his father that the Messenger of Allah ﷺ said, "If someone suffers an affliction, he should remember in his affliction the loss of me, for it is the greatest of afflictions." The Messenger of Allah ﷺ said, "When anyone's child dies, Allah asks His angels, 'Have you taken the child of My slave?' They say, 'He praised You and said, "To Him we return."' Allah Almighty says, 'Build a house in the Garden for My slave, and call it the House of Praise.'" (at-Tirmidhi) The Messenger of Allah ﷺ said, "Allah Almighty says, 'When I take anyone from this world who is dear to a slave of Mine and he expects a reward, his recompense is the Garden.'" Al-Bukhari related this.

The Prophet ﷺ said, "One sign that a son of Adam is destined to be one one of the blessed in the Hereafter is contentment with what Allah has decreed. A sign that a son of Adam is destined to be one of the wretched in the Hereafter is his anger at what Allah has decreed." 'Umar ibn al-Khattab ﷺ said, "When the Angel of Death takes the soul of a believer, he stands at the door and there is an uproar among the people of the house. Some of them slap their faces, some tear their hair and cry out in lamentation. The Angel of Death says, 'What is the point of all this anguish and dismay? By Allah, I do not shorten the life of any of you or take any of your provision or wrong any of you at all. If you complain and are angry with me, by Allah, I am following orders. If it is for your dead, he has no choice. If it is against your Lord, then you are disbelievers in Him. I will return again and again until none of you are left.'" The Messenger of Allah ﷺ said, "By the One Who has my soul in His hand, if they were to see his situation and hear his words, they would ignore their dead and weep for themselves."

Section on consolation and condolence

'Abdullah ibn Mas'ud ﷺ said that the Prophet ﷺ said, "Whoever consoles anyone in affliction will have a similar reward." At-Tirmidhi related this. Abu Burda ﷺ related that the Prophet ﷺ told Fatima ﷺ, "Whoever consoles a bereaved person will be clothed in a robe of the Garden." At-Tirmidhi related this. 'Abdullah ibn 'Amr ibn al-'As ﷺ said that the Messenger of Allah ﷺ asked Fatima ﷺ, "What has brought you out of your house, Fatima?" She said, "I have come to the people of this house to wish mercy on their dead and to console them." 'Amr ibn Hazm ﷺ related from the Prophet ﷺ, "If any believer consoles his brother in an affliction, Allah will clothe him in robes of honour on the Day of Rising."

Know, may Allah have mercy on you, that offering condolences means encouraging people to have patience and saying things to console the friend of the deceased, alleviate his sorrow and lighten his affliction. It is recommended because it contains commanding what is right and forbidding what is wrong. It is part of what is alluded to by the words of Allah Almighty: "*Help each other to goodness and* taqwa." (5:2) This is the best evidence for expressing condolences.

159

Know that expressing condolences involves telling people to be steadfast, and it is recommended before and after burial. According to the followers of of ash-Shafi'i, it can be done from when someone dies until three days after his burial. According to our colleagues, it is disliked to offer condolences after more than three days, since consolation stills the heart of the afflicted; nornmally the heart is stilled after three days, and one should not renew their sorrow over the dead. That is what most of our colleagues say. Abu al-'Abbas, one of our colleagues, said, "There is no harm in consoling after three days. However you should go on doing it, even if the time is long." An-Nawawi said, "It is preferable not to do it after three days except in two situations: when either the consoler or the afflicted person is absent during the burial and then returns after three days. Condolence after burial is better than before it, because the family of the dead are usually preoccupied with preparing the dead before that time and also because loneliness occurs after burial, since the separation is felt more strongly."

The formulae of consolation are well-known. The best of them is what is related in the two *Sahih* collections, where Usama ibn Zayd ﷺ reported: "One of the daughters of the Prophet ﷺ sent to the Prophet to call him and inform him that her son was dying. The Prophet ﷺ told the messenger, 'Return to her and tell that to Allah belongs whatever He takes and whatever He gives. Everything thing has a term set by Him. Tell her to be steadfast in expectation of a reward.'" An-Nawawi said, "This *hadith* is one of the greatest of the rules of Islam and contains important things about the fundamentals, details and etiquettes of the *deen*, patience in all afflictions, cares and illnesses and other things."

The words of the Prophet ﷺ, "to Allah belongs whatever He takes" mean that the whole world is under the ownership of Allah and He does not take what is yours; He only takes back what He has lent you. His words, "and what He gives" mean that whatever He gives you is still under His ownership. It is His to do with as He pleases. Everything has a term set by Him, so do not be distressed. If He takes it, it means that the fixed term has ended and so it would not have been possible to delay it or advance it.

Knowing this, you should be patient and expect a reward for whatever befalls you. Allah knows best.

Mu'awiya ibn Ayas related from his father from the Prophet ﷺ
that he missed one of the Companions and asked about him. They
said, "Messenger of Allah, his son whom you have seen has died."
When the Prophet ﷺ met him, he asked about his son, and the
man told him that he had died. He offered him condolences for
his loss and then asked, "Which would you prefer: to enjoy your
life with him or to come tomorrow to one of the doors of the
Garden and find that he has beaten you to it and will open it for
you?" He answered, "Prophet of Allah, I would prefer him to have
beaten me to the Garden and to open it for me." He said, "You
have that." Someone asked, "Prophet of Allah, is this just for him
or for all Muslims?" He answered, "For all Muslims." (Ahmad)

Abu Musa ﷺ related that the Prophet ﷺ went to al-Baqi' and
went up to a woman who was weeping at a grave and said to her,
"Slave of Allah, fear Allah and be patient." She retorted, "Slave of
Allah, I am bereaved." He repeated, "Slave of Allah, fear Allah and
be patient." She said, "Slave of Allah, if you had suffered such a
loss, you would excuse me." He repeated, "Slave of Allah, fear
Allah and be patient." She said, "Slave of Allah, you heard me, so
now leave." So the Messenger of Allah ﷺ left her. One of the
Muslims saw her and went and asked her, "What did the man say
to you?" She told him what he had said and how she had replied to
him. He asked her, "Did you not recognise him?" "No, by Allah,"
she replied. He said, "You stupid woman! That was the Messenger
of Allah!" She ran quickly to catch him up and said, "Messenger of
Allah, I will be patient!" He replied, "Patience is at the first blow."
This means that patience is best shown when the affliction first
occurs. After that, solace occurs naturally.

We find this in *Sahih Muslim*: "The son of Abu Talha and
Umm Sulaym died. She said to her family, 'Do not tell Abu Talha
until I have told him myself.' When Abu Talha came she brought
him his meal, and he ate and drank. She then prepared for him
more than she used to prepare before, and he had sex with her.
When she saw that he was satisfied, she said, 'Abu Talha, what
would you think if some people lent something to the people of a
household and then asked for what they had lent to be returned?

Can they be refused?' He answered, 'No.' Umm Sulaym said, 'Then expect a reward for your son.' Abu Talha became angry and said, 'You left it until I had sullied myself to tell me about my son. By Allah, you shall not compel me be to be patient.' He went to the Messenger of Allah ﷺ and told him what had happened, and the Messenger of Allah ﷺ said, 'Allah will bless you in your night.'"

In a *hadith* we find: "No one is given a better and more all-embracing gift than patience." (al-Bukhari) A wise man wrote to a man who had suffered an affliction: "You have lost what you have been afflicted with, so do not lose the compensation: the reward for it." Another said, "An intelligent person does on the first day of affliction what an ignorant one does after five days." It is well-known that the passage of time assuages afflictions. That is why the Lawgiver commanded that the time for patience is at the first blow.

The news reached ash-Shafi'i that 'Abd al-Rahman ibn Mahdi had lost a son and was very distressed about it. Ash-Shafi'i sent to him the following message: "My brother, console yourself in the way you would console others, and consider ugly in your actions what you would consider ugly in the actions of others. Know that the sharpest afflictions are loss of happiness and deprival of a reward. What about when they are combined and added to them is committing a sin? Take your portion, my brother, when it is close by before you need to seek it when it is far away. May Allah inspire you with patience in afflictions, and reward us and you with the reward for it."

A man wrote to one of his brothers to console him for his son: "As long as he lives, a son is a source of sorrow and trial to his parents. If he dies before them, he is a blessing and a mercy. Do not grieve over the sorrow and trial you have lost, and do not waste the blessing and mercy Allah has given you in compensation."

Ibn 'Abbas ؓ said, "I heard the Messenger of Allah ﷺ say, 'If anyone of my community has two sons die before him, he will enter the Garden.'" Look, may Allah have mercy on you, at the blessing of offspring when they die young, male or female. Their parents benefit from them in the Next World if they are steadfast and expect a reward and say, "Praise be to Allah. We belong to

Allah and to Him we return." They will have what Allah Almighty promised in His words: *"Those who, when disaster strikes them, say, 'We belong to Allah and to Him we return.'"* (2:156) In other words, we are His property and He can do whatever He likes with us.

Thawban related that the Messenger of Allah ﷺ said, "No affliction befalls a person that is not due to one of two things: either a wrong action which Allah only forgives through that affliction, or a degree which Allah only made him attain by that affliction." Umm Salama ؇ related that she heard the Messenger of Allah ﷺ say, "Whoever says in affliction, 'We belong to Allah and to Him we return! O Allah, reward me for my affliction and give in exchange something better than it,' Allah will reward him and give him better than it instead." She said, "When Abu Salama died, I said, 'Who could be better than Abu Salama?' and then Allah gave me the Messenger of Allah ﷺ instead." Muslim related it.

Ash-Sha'bi reported that Shurayh said, "Whenever I suffer an affliction, I praise Allah for it four times. I praise Him for it not being worse. I praise Him for providing me with steadfastness in it. I praise Him for giving me success in saying, 'We return to Him' for which I hope for a reward. I praise Him for not making the affliction in my *deen.*"

As for someone who becomes angry in an affliction and loudly laments and slaps his cheeks, tears his shirt, dishevels his hair, or shaves, cuts or tears out his hair, Allah is angry with them and there is a curse upon them, whether it be a man or a woman. It is also related that they are like someone armed with a spear wanting to fight his Lord. It is related that Allah Almighty does not punish for the tears of the eyes or the sorrow of the heart, but for what the person suffering an affliction says with his tongue, i.e. lamentation and wailing. As has already been stated, a dead person is punished in his grave for the wailing done for him. When the wailer says, "O my support! O helper! O clothier!', the dead person will be tortured and will be asked, "Were you her support? Were you her helper? Were you her clothier?" So wailing is unlawful because it provokes sorrow and repels patience. It also entails not submitting to the Divine Decree or obeying the command of Allah Almighty.

163

Story. Salih al-Murri said, "One night before *Jumu'a* I was sitting in a graveyard and fell asleep. I dreamt that the graves opened up and the dead came out of them and sat in circles. Covered platters descended to them. Among them, however, there was a young man who was being punished with various torments. I went to him and asked, 'Lad, why are you being punished among these people?' He answered, 'Salih, by Allah, you must convey what I tell you and fulfil the trust and have mercy on my exclusion! Perhaps Allah Almighty will give me a way out at your hands. When I died, my mother gathered mourners and wailers to lament my loss every day, and I was punished for that. There was fire on my right and my left, behind me and in front of me, because of what my mother did. May Allah not repay her well from me!' Then he wept so much that I wept because of his weeping. Then he said, 'Salih, by Allah, you must go to her. She is in such-and-such a place. Tell her from me: "Mother, do not torment your son! You raised me and protected me from evils. Then when I died, you cast me into punishment! Mother, if only you could see the shackles on my neck and the fetters on my feet and the angels of punishment hitting me and berating me! If you could see my evil state, you would have mercy on me. If you do not stop your lamentation and wailing, Allah will judge between you and me on the Day when the heavens split from one another and creatures emerge for judgement."'"

Salih continued, "I woke up in alarm and remained where I was in a state of anxiety until dawn. In the morning, I entered the town with no thought other than that of reaching the house of the mother of the young lad. I asked for directions and went straight to it. The door was blackened and the sound of wailers and mourners could be heard from outside the house. I knocked on the door and an old woman came out to me and asked, 'What you want?' I replied, 'I want the mother of the lad who died.' She said, 'What do you want with her? She is busy with her grief.' I said, 'Send her to me. I have a message for her from her son.' She went and told her. The mother came out wearing black garments and her face was black, so much had she wept and slapped her face. She asked me, 'Who are you?' I replied, 'I am Salih al-Murri. Yesterday I was at the graveyard with your son. I saw him being punished and he said, "My mother! You raised me and protected me from harm, but then when I died you cast me into punishment. If you do not stop what you are doing, Allah will judge between you and me on the Day when the heavens split asunder.'" When she heard that, she fainted and fell to the ground. When she recovered, she wept copiously and said, 'My son is dear to me. If I had known that about his situation, I would not have done what I did. I repent to Allah Almighty of that.' Then she entered her house, drove off the mourners and put on other garments. She brought me a bag full of dirhams and said, 'Salih, give this as *sadaqa* for my son.'"

Salih continued, "I bade her farewell, prayed for her and went and gave *sadaqa* on behalf of her son with those dirhams. On the next Thursday night, I went to the graveyard, as was my custom, and fell asleep. I saw the inhabitants of the graves emerge from their graves and sit as was their custom, and platters came to them. That young man was laughing and happy and a platter was also brought to him and he took it. When he saw me he came to me and said, 'Salih, may Allah repay you well from me. Allah has removed the punishment from me because my mother stopped doing what she was doing, and what she gave as *sadaqa* on my behalf has come to me.' I said, 'What are these platters?' He answered, 'These are the gifts of the living to the dead resulting from the *sadaqa*, recitation and supplication they do on their behalf, which descend to them every Thursday night. They are told, "This is a gift from so-and-so to you." Return to my mother and greet her from me and tell her, "May Allah repay you well from me. What you gave as *sadaqa* for me has reached me, and you will soon join me, so get ready." I woke up later, and after some days, went to the house of the mother of the lad. There was a bier set up at the door. I asked, 'Who is this for?' They said, 'For the mother of the lad.' I attended her funeral prayer and she was buried beside her son in that cemetery. I prayed for both of them and left."

We ask Allah to make us die as Muslims and join us to the righteous, and to protect us from the Fire. He is Generous, Magnanimous, Compassionate, and Merciful.

50. Transgression

Allah Almighty says:

"There are only grounds against those who wrong people and act as tyrants in the earth without any right to do so. Such people will have a painful punishment." (42:42)

The Prophet ﷺ said, "Allah revealed to me that you should be humble, so no one should treat anyone unjustly and no one should boast over anyone else." Muslim transmitted it.

We find in a tradition, "If one mountain were to transgress against another, Allah would turn the transgressor into dust."

The Prophet ﷺ said, "There is no sin for which Allah is more likely to impose a punishment in this world as well as what awaits him in the Next World than transgression and cutting off ties with kin." (Ibn Majah and at-Tirmidhi)

Allah made the earth swallow Qarun when he transgressed against his people and Allah Almighty reported about him: *"Qarun was from the people of Musa, but he lorded it over them"* to His words, *"We caused the earth to swallow up both him and his house."* (28:76-81)

According to Ibn al-Jawzi, there are various statements about the transgression of Qarun. One is that he gave money to a prostitute to falsely accuse Musa ﷺ of having had sex with her. She did that and so Musa asked her to swear to what she had said and she told him what Qarun had made her do. That was his transgression. This is what Ibn 'Abbas said. The second is that he transgressed by disbelief in Allah Almighty. This is what ad-Dahhak said. The third is that it is by disbelief as Qatada said. The fourth is that he lowered his garment a span. That is what 'Ata' al-Khurasani said. According to al-Mawardi he used to serve Pharaoh and he wronged and transgressed against the tribe of Israel.

Concerning His words *"We caused the earth to swallow up both him and his house,"* when Qarun told the prostitute to slander Musa, Musa became angry and prayed against him and Allah revealed to him, "I have commanded the earth to obey you, so tell it. what to do." Musa said "Earth, take him!" It swallowed him until his bed disappeared. When Qarun saw that, he entreated Musa for mercy but he said, "Earth, take him!" It took him until his feet disappeared. He continue to say, "Earth, take him!" until he disappeared. So Allah revealed to him, "Musa, by My might and majesty, if he had asked Me for succour, I would have given it to him!" Ibn 'Abbas said, "The earth swallowed him down to the lowest earth."

Muqatil said, "When Qarun was destroyed, the tribe of Israel said, 'Musa destroyed him in order to take his wealth and house,' and so Allah swallowed up his house and wealth after three days."

"There was no group to come to his aid against Allah:" that is, defend him from Allah. *"He was not someone who is helped:"* that is, protected from what happened to him. Allah knows best.

O Allah, when You turn towards someone, You give safety, When You turn aside, You give safety. When You give success, you inspire; and when You disappoint, You suspect.

O Allah, remove the darkness of our sins by the light of knowledge of You and Your guidance; and make us among those to whom You turn, that we may turn from what is other than You. Forgive us and our children and all the Muslims! Amen.

51. Being overbearing towards the weak, slaves, girls, wives, and animals

Allah Almighty commands us to be good to them in His words:

"Worship Allah and do not associate anything with Him. Be good to your parents and relatives and to orphans and the destitute, and to neighbours who are related to you and neighbours who are not related to you, and to companions and travellers and your slaves. Allah does not love anyone vain or boastful." (4:36)

Ibn Mas'ud ﷺ said, "A bedouin came to the Prophet ﷺ and said, 'O Prophet of Allah, advise me.' He answered, 'Do not associate anything with Allah, even if you are cut up and burned. Do not fail to perform the prayer at its time. It is the protection of Allah. Do not drink wine: it is the key to every evil.'" (al-Mundhiri)

Being good to your parents means showing them kindness and gentleness and not answering them harshly or glaring at them or raising your voice to them. Your humility towards them should be that of a slave before his master. Being good to relatives involves maintaining ties with them and being kind to them. Where orphans are concerned you should be gentle to them and stroke their heads. With respect to the poor you should spend on them and address them in a good manner. Neighbours who are related to you are those with whom you have kinship. You owe them both the rights of kinship and the rights of the neighbour as well as the rights of Islam. Neighbours who are not related to you are those with whom you have no kinship.

'A'isha ﷺ reported that the Prophet ﷺ said, "Jibril continued to advise me to treat neighbours well until I thought that he would ask me to make them my heirs." Anas ibn Malik ﷺ reported that the Messenger of Allah ﷺ said, "A neighbour will hang on to his neighbour on the Day of Rising and say, 'Lord, You gave prosperity to this brother of mine and deprived me. I spent the night starving and this one spent the night satisfied. Ask him why he locked his door against me and denied me the prosperity You gave to him.'"

Regarding the companions referred to in the *ayat*, Ibn 'Abbas ﷺ and Mujahid said that it means companions on a journey who are owed the rights of companionship and rights of a neighbour. The travellers referred to are those who are needy and must be given hospitality until they reach their destination. Ibn 'Abbas ﷺ said, "It means a traveller to whom you give shelter and food until he leaves you." Slaves should be well provided for and their mistakes forgiven. *"Allah does not love anyone vain or boastful."* Ibn 'Abbas ﷺ said that someone vain is someone who considers himself innately superior and does not fulfil the rights of Allah, and someone boastful is someone who vaunts himself over other people by reason of the honour and blessings Allah has given him.

Abu Hurayra ﷺ reported that the Messenger of Allah ﷺ said, "While a young man from those before you was walking in a robe in a state of arrogance and boastfulness the earth swallowed him up. He will continue to sink into it until the Last Hour arrives." Usama reported that he heard Ibn 'Umar ﷺ say, "I heard the Messenger of Allah ﷺ say, 'Whoever drags his garment out of arrogance, Allah will not look at him on the Day of Rising.'"

In his final illness when the Messenger of Allah ﷺ was on the point of leaving this world, he commanded people to safeguard the prayer and to be good to slaves. He said, "Allah! Allah! The prayer and those you own!" In a *hadith* we find: "Good ownership is good fortune and bad ownership is misfortune." The Messenger of Allah ﷺ said, "Bad owners will not enter the Garden."

Abu Mas'ud ﷺ said, "I was hitting a slave with a whip when I heard a voice behind me: 'Know, Abu Mas'ud, that Allah has more power than you over this slave.' I said, 'Messenger of Allah, I will never strike a slave again after this.' (In one transmission, "The whip fell from my hand out of awe of the Messenger of Allah ﷺ." In another: "I said, 'He is freed for the sake of Allah.' He said, 'If you had not done that, the Fire would have scorched you on the Day of Rising.'" Muslim related it.from

Muslim also related in a *hadith* from Ibn 'Umar ﷺ that the Messenger of Allah ﷺ said, "If someone flogs a slave for a punishable crime he did not commit or slaps him, his expiation is to free him." Part of a *hadith* narrated by Hakim ibn Hizam ﷺ is that the Messenger of Allah ﷺ said, "Allah will punish those who torture people in this world." In another *hadith*: "Whoever strikes someone with a whip wrongfully, retaliation will be taken from him on the Day of Rising." (at-Tabarani) The Messenger of Allah ﷺ was asked, "How many times should we pardon a servant?" He answered, "Seventy times a day." (Abu Dawud and at-Tirmidhi)

One day the Prophet ﷺ had a toothstick in his hand and he summoned a servant of his who was slow in coming. He said, "Were it not for retaliation, I would hit you with this toothstick!" (Ahmad) Abu Hurayra ﷺ had a black slave-girl and he raised a whip to her one day and said, "Were it not for retaliation, I would render you unconscious. But as it is I will sell you to the One who will give me your full price. Go. You are free for the sake of Allah."

A woman came to the Prophet ﷺ and said, "Messenger of Allah, I called my slave girl a whore." He asked, "Have you seen her act in that way?" "No," She answered. He said, "Then she will seek retaliation from you on the Day of Rising." So she went back to her slavegirl and gave her a whip and told her, "Whip me." The slavegirl refused and so she set her free. Then she went back to the Prophet ﷺ and told him that she had freed her. He said, "Perhaps." (al-Hakim) In other words, "Perhaps your freeing her will expiate your slander of her."

It is reported in both *Sahih* collections that the Messenger of Allah ﷺ said, "Whoever slanders a slave who is innocent of what he said will be flogged on the Day of Rising with a *hadd* punishment of flogging unless he is as he says."

We read in a *hadith*: "A slave is owed his food and clothing, and should not be made to do what he is unable to do." (Muslim) The Prophet ﷺ instructed the Muslims when he left this world: "Allah! Allah! The prayer and what you own. Feed them from what you eat and clothe them from what you wear. Do not impose work on them which they cannot do. If you burden them, then help them. Do not torture Allah's creatures. He let you own them. If He had wished, they could have owned you." (at-Tabarani)

A group visited Salman al-Farisi when he was the governor of al-Mada'in. They found him kneading dough and asked him, "Why do you not let your slave-girl do this?" He replied, "We sent her on a task and did not want to add another task to it."

Section. One of the worst things that can be done to a slave or slavegirl is to separate them from their children or from those they love since it is reported that the Prophet ﷺ said, "If someone parts a mother and her child, Allah will part him from those he loves on the Day of Rising." (at-Tirmidhi)

'Ali ؓ said, "The Messenger of Allah ﷺ gave me two boys who were brothers and I sold one of them. The Messenger of Allah ﷺ said, 'Take him back! Take him back!'" Another bad thing is to let a slave or slave-girl or animal suffer from hunger. The Messenger of Allah ﷺ said, "It is enough sin for a man to deny his food to those he owns." (Muslim)

It is wrong to hit an animal or to cause it pain or to tie it up in such a way that it cannot stand up by itself or to make it carry a load beyond its capacity. It is reported that animals will be brought while people are standing on the Day of Rising and they will take their retaliation. So if a man has struck an animal unnecessarily or made it go hungry or thirsty or made it bear more than it was able to, then it will take retaliation from him on the Day of Rising according to how he wronged it or made it go hungry. The evidence for that is what is confirmed in both *Sahih* collections from Abu Hurayra ؓ who said, "The Messenger of Allah ﷺ said, 'A woman was punished on account of a cat which she tied it up until it died of hunger. She did not feed it or water it when she imprisoned it, nor did she let it eat from the vermin of the earth.'" The Prophet ﷺ saw a woman hanging in the Fire with a cat clawing her in the face and breast and torturing her because she tortured it in this world by imprisonment and hunger.

This applies to all sorts of animals. And the same applies if someone tries to make an animal do more than it is able to: it will take retaliation from him on the Day of Rising, according to what is established in the two *Sahih* collections by the words of the Messenger of Allah ﷺ: "While a man was driving a cow he mounted it and hit it. It said, 'I was not created for this. I was created for tillage.'" That was a cow which Allah made speak in this world to defend itself so that it would not be harmed or used in a manner other than that for which it was created. If someone imposes on an animal what it is not capable of or hits it without right, it will take appropriate retaliation from him on the Day of Rising.

Ibn 'Umar ؓ passed by some boys of Quraysh who were using a bird as a target. They gave its owner every arrow that missed. When they saw Ibn 'Umar, they bolted. He said, "Who did this? Allah has cursed the one who does this!" The Messenger of Allah ﷺ cursed anyone who made a target of a living creature. If it is something whose killing is authorised by the *Shari'a*, such as snakes, scorpions, mice and dogs, it should be killed immediately and not tortured, as evidenced by the words of the Prophet ﷺ: "When you kill, kill well. When you slaughter, slaughter well. Let each of you sharpen his blade and put the animal to be slaughtered at ease." Similarly an animal should not be burned since it is confirmed in sound *hadith* that the Messenger of Allah ﷺ said, "I commanded you in the past to burn so-and-so and so-and-so with fire. Only Allah punishes with fire. If you find them, then kill them both."

Ibn Mas'ud ؓ said, "We were with the Messenger of Allah ﷺ on a journey and he went to respond to a call of nature. We saw a sparrow with two chicks. We took her chicks and the sparrow came and began to flutter. The Prophet ﷺ came back and said, 'Who has distressed this one with her offspring? Leave her with her children.' The Messenger of Allah ﷺ also saw an anthill which we had burned and said, 'Who burned it?' We replied, 'We did.' The Prophet ﷺ said, 'No one should punish with fire except its Lord.'" (Abu Dawud) That is a prohibition of killing and torturing by the use of fire, even lice, fleas and other such creatures.

Section. It is disliked to kill animals for sport, since it is related that the Prophet ﷺ said, "If someone kills a sparrow for sport, on the Day of Rising, it will cry out to Allah: 'Lord, ask this one why he killed me in vain and did not kill me for any purpose!'" It is also disliked to hunt birds (even for food) when they are nesting since that is related in traditions. It is disliked to slaughter an animal in front of its mother, in accordance with what Ibrahim ibn Adham related: "A man slaughtered a calf in front of its mother and Allah withered his hand."

Section on the excellence of freeing slaves. Abu Hurayra ؓ reported that the Prophet ﷺ said, "If someone frees a believing slave, Allah will free forever one of his limbs by one of his limbs from the Fire until he frees his genitals by his genitals." Al-Bukhari transmitted this. Abu Umama 🙵 reported that the Prophet 🙵 said, "If a Muslim frees a Muslim man, he has ransomed himself from the Fire. Every limb of his expiates one of his limbs. If Muslim man frees two Muslim women, they are his redemption from the Fire: every two limbs of theirs expiates one of his limbs. If a Muslim woman frees a Muslim woman, she will be her redemption from the Fire and every limb or hers expiates one her limbs." At-Tirmidhi related this and described it as sound.

O Allah, make us among Your successful party and righteous slaves.

52. Harming one's neighbours

It is confirmed in both *Sahih* collections that the Messenger of Allah ﷺ said, "By Allah, he does not believe. By Allah, he does not believe!" He was asked, "Who, Messenger of Allah?" He said, "He whose neighbour is not safe from his treachery." In one variant, "He whose neighbour is not safe from his evil will not enter the Garden."

The Messenger of Allah ﷺ was asked about the greatest sin in the sight of Allah, and he mentioned three things: appointing an equal to Allah when He created you, killing your child out of fear that he will eat with you, and committing adultery with your neighbour's wife." A *hadith* states: "Anyone who believes in Allah and the Last Day should not harm his neighbour."

There are three kinds of neighbours: Muslim neighbours who are kin, who are owed the rights of a neighbour, the rights of Islam and the rights of kinship; Muslim neighbours who are owed the rights of a neighbour and the rights of Islam; and unbelieving neighbours who are owed the rights of a neighbour. Ibn 'Umar ﷺ had a Jewish neighbour, and whenever he slaughtered a sheep he said, "Take some of it to our Jewish neighbour." It is related that a poor neighbour will be hung on his rich neighbour on the Day of Rising and will say, "Lord, ask him why he denied me charity and closed his door to me."

A neighbour should endure the annoyance caused by his neighbour. It is part of being good to him. A man went to the Prophet ﷺ and said, "Messenger of Allah, direct me to an action which, if I do it, I will enter the Garden." He said, "Do good." He asked, "Messenger of Allah, how will I know if I am doing good?" He said, "Ask your neighbours. If they say that you are doing good, then you are doing good. If they say that you are doing bad, then you are doing bad." Al-Bayhaqi mentioned this. From Abu Hurayra ﷺ it is related that the Prophet ﷺ said, "Anyone who closes his door to his neighbour out of fear for his family and wealth is not a believer. Anyone whose neighbour is not safe from his evil is not a believer."

It is said: "It is less harmful for a man to fornicate with ten women than to commit adultery with his neighbour's wife. It is less harmful for a man to steal from ten houses than to steal from his neighbour's house." According to the *Sunan* of Abu Dawud, Abu Hurayra ﷺ said: "A man went to the Prophet ﷺ to complain about his neighbour, and he told him, 'Go and be patient.' He came to him two or three times and then he said, 'Go and put your belongings into the street.' The man did so. People began to pass by him and ask him what was wrong and he told them about his situation with his neighbour. They began to curse his neighbour and say, 'May Allah do such-and-such to him.' His neighbour went to him and said, 'My brother, return to your house. You will never again see anything you dislike from me.'"

Put up with the harm of a neighbour, even if he is a *dhimmi*. It is related that Sahl ibn 'Abdullah at-Tustari had a *dhimmi* neighbour and there was a leak from his toilet into Sahl's house. Every day Sahl used to put a pot under that leak and collect the seepage from the Magian's toilet and then would throw it away at night so that no one saw it. Sahl continued to do this for a long time until he was dying. He summoned his Magian neighbour and said, "Go into that room and see what is in it." He entered and saw the hole and filth leaking down from it into the pot. He said, "What is this I see?" Sahl answered, "This has been flowing from your house into this room for a long time. I collect it in the day and throw it away at night. If I were not dying and did not fear that the character of others could not bear that, I would not have told you. Do what you think best." The Magian said, "Sahl! Have you been doing this for a long time while I remain in my disbelief? Stretch out your hand. I testify that there is no god but Allah and Muhammad is the Messenger of Allah." Then Sahl died.

We ask Allah to guide us and you to the best character, actions and words, and to make our end good. He is Generous, Compassionate, Merciful.

53. Abusing and insulting other Muslims

Allah Almighty says:

> *"Those who abuse men and women who are believers, when they have not merited it, bear the weight of slander and clear wrongdoing."* (33:58)

> *"You who believe, people should not ridicule others who may be better than themselves; nor should any women ridicule other women who may be better than themselves. And do not find fault with one another or insult one another with derogatory nicknames. How evil it to have a name for evil conduct after coming to faith! Those who do not turn from it are wrongdoers."* (49:11)

> *"Do not spy and do not backbite one another."* (49:12)

The Prophet ﷺ said, "One of the people in the worst position with Allah on the Day of Rising will be the one whom people avoid out of fear of his rudeness." (al-Bukhari and Muslim)

We find another *hadith* saying: "The life, property and honour of a Muslim is forbidden to another Muslim." (Muslim and at-Tirmidhi) The Prophet ﷺ also said, "The Muslim is the Muslim's brother. He must not wrong him, disappoint him, or demean him. It is enough evil for a man to demean his brother Muslim." (Muslim) He also said ﷺ that insulting a Muslim is impiety and killing him is disbelief.

Abu Hurayra ﷺ reported, "Someone said, 'Messenger of Allah, so-and-so prays in the night and fasts in the day but she harms her neighbours with her tongue.' He replied, 'There is no good in her. She will be in the Fire.'" Al-Hakim said that this *hadith* is sound.

Another *hadith* also states: "Remember the good qualities of your dead and expiate their evil deeds." (al-Hakim) The Prophet ﷺ said, "During the Night Journey, I passed by people with copper nails who were lacerating their faces and chests. I asked, 'Who are they, Jibril?' He replied, 'Those who ate people's flesh and attacked their reputation.'" (al-Bukhari and Muslim)

Section cautioning against inciting fights between believers, and between any kind of animals

It is related on sound authority that the Prophet ﷺ said, "Shaytan has despaired of those who pray worshipping him in the Arabian peninsula but he still incites fights between you. So anyone who provokes a dispute between two of the sons of Adam and passes on to one of them anything that will anger the other is a tale-bearer from the party of Shaytan, who are the worst of people." Likewise as the Prophet ﷺ said, "Shall I inform you of the worst of you?" They answered, "Yes, Messenger of Allah. He said, "The worst of you are those carry tales and ruin relations between those who love one another, and who lead the innocent to wrong action." (Ahmad)

It is related on sound authority that the Messenger of Allah ﷺ said, "A tale-bearer will not enter the Garden." (al-Bukhari and Muslim) A tale-bearer is someone who carries tales between people, and particularly between two people in order to harm one of them or alienate his heart from his companion or friend. He says, "So-and-so said this about you and did such-and-such." The only time such a thing is permissible is if there is some real benefit in it, such as warning him of some evil which is happening or to be watchful.

As for instigating fights between animals, beasts, birds and other things, it is unlawful. This applies to cock-fighting, ram fighting, dog fighting and other such things. The Messenger of Allah ﷺ forbade that. Anyone who does it disobeys Allah and His Messenger.

Another aspect of this is alienating a woman's heart from her husband, or a slave from his master, or since it is related that the Messenger of Allah ﷺ said, "Cursed is the one who alienates a woman from her husband or a slave from his master." (Abu Dawud) We seek refuge with Allah from that.

Section encouraging reconciliation between people

Allah Almighty says:

"There is no good in much of their secret talk, except in the case of those who enjoin sadaqa *or what is right, or putting things right between people. Whoever does that, seeking the pleasure of Allah, We will give him an immense wage."* (4:114)

Mujahid said, "This is general for all people, and means that there is no good in the conversations of people unless they are for the good, as indicated by His words: *"except in the case of those who enjoin sadaqa"*. Ibn 'Abbas ﷺ said that "what is right (*ma'ruf*)" means maintaining ties of kinship and obeying Allah. It is said that it is all good actions. *"Putting things right between people"* is something which the Messenger of Allah ﷺ encouraged. He said to Abu Ayyub al-Ansari ﷺ, "Shall I direct you to a *sadaqa* which is better for you than red camels?" He answered, "Yes, Messenger of Allah." He said, "Putting things right between people when they have been set at odds and bringing them together when they are far apart."

Umm Habiba ﷺ related that the Prophet ﷺ said, "The words of the son of Adam are all against him and not for him except those which involve enjoining the right, prohibiting the wrong or remembering Allah." (Ibn Majah and at-Tirmidhi) It is related that a man said to Sufyan, "How severe this *hadith* is!" Sufyan said, "Have you not heard the words of Allah Almighty: *'There is no good in much of their secret talk, except in the case of those who enjoin sadaqa or what is right'*?' This is the same thing. Then the Almighty informs us that such talk only benefits a person who does it to seek what is with Allah. Allah Almighty says: *'Whoever does that, seeking the pleasure of Allah, We will give him an immense wage.'*"

We find in a *hadith*: "He who puts things right between people and hopes for good or speaks good is not considered a liar." Al-Bukhari related this. Umm Kulthum ﷺ said, "I did not hear the Messenger of Allah ﷺ make an allowance for anything that people say except in three instances: in war, putting things right between people, and the words between a man and his wife or a wife and her husband." Abu Hurayra ﷺ related that the Messenger of Allah ﷺ said, "One cannot do anything better than walking to the prayer, putting things right between people, or organising a permissible alliance between Muslims." (al-Isbahani)

The Messenger of Allah ﷺ said, "If someone puts things right between two people, Allah will put his business right and give him the reward for freeing a slave for every word he speaks, and he will return having been forgiven his past wrong actions." (al-Isbahani) All success is by Allah.

O Allah, treat us kindly and give us Your pardon, O Most Merciful of the Merciful.

54. Harming people and being overbearing towards them

Allah Almighty says:

"Those who abuse the believers, men and women, when they have not merited it bear the weight of slander and clear wrong-doing." (33:58)

"Take the believers who follow you under your wing." (26:215)

Abu Hurayra ﷺ related that the Messenger of Allah ﷺ said, "Allah Almighty says, 'I have declared war on anyone who is hostile to a friend of Mine.'" (al-Bukhari) We find in another *hadith* that Abu Sufyan went to Salman, Suhayb and Bilal ﷺ, who were in a group, and they said, "The swords of Allah have not taken their due from the enemy of Allah." Abu Bakr ﷺ said, "Do you say this to the elder and master of Quraysh?" He went to the Prophet ﷺ and told him. He said, "Abu Bakr, perhaps if you made them angry, you have also made your Lord angry." Abu Bakr went to them and asked, "My brothers, have I made you angry?" "No," they replied. "May Allah forgive you, my brother."

Section on the words of the Almighty:

"Restrain yourself patiently with those who call on their Lord morning and evening, desiring His face." (18:28)

This *ayat* affirms the excellence of the poor. The reason for its revelation was that it was the poor who were the first to believe in the Prophet ﷺ. The same was true for every Prophet: the poor were the first to believe in them. So the Messenger of Allah ﷺ used to sit with his poor Companions, such as Suhayb, Bilal and 'Ammar ibn Yasir. The idolators wanted to induce him to drive the poor away because they had heard that one of the signs of the Messengers was that the first of their followers came from among the poor.

Some of the leaders of the idolators came and said, "Muhammad, drive the poor away from you. Our souls are averse to sitting with them. If you drive them away, the noble people and leaders will believe in you." So Allah Almighty revealed: *"Do not chase away those who call on their Lord morning and evening, seeking His Face."* (6:52)

When the idolators despaired of them being driven away, they said, "Muhammad, if you do not drive them away, then give us one day and them another day." So Allah Almighty revealed: *"Restrain yourself patiently with those who call on their Lord morning and evening, desiring His face; and do not turn your eye from them, desiring the attractions of this world."* (18:28)

Then Allah coined a likeness for them of the wealthy and the poor in His words: *"Cite an example for them of two men..."* (18:32) and *"Make a simile for them of the life of this world..."* (18:45) The Messenger of Allah ﷺ used to esteem and honour the poor. When the Messenger of Allah ﷺ emigrated to Madina, they emigrated with him and stayed in the *Suffa* (veranda) of the mosque, praying and supplicating, and they were called the People of the *Suffa*. The poor who emigrated were put with them until they were many in number. They witnessed the goodness Allah has prepared for His friends, seeing it with the light of faith, and their hearts were not attached to anything in existence. They said, "We only worship You, and before You we are humble and prostrate. By You we are guided and seek guidance. We rely on You and trust in You and find delight in Your remembrance. We graze in the meadow of Your love and work and toil for You, never leaving Your door."

Then Allah addressed His Messenger about them, saying: *"Do not chase away those who call on their Lord in the morning."* (6:52) In other words, "Do not drive away people who spend the night remembering their Lord and in the morning remain at His door. Do not drive away people from the mosque, which is their refuge." Allah is their goal and their Master. Hunger is their food and wakefulness while other people sleep is their condiment. Poverty and need are their badge, and humility and modesty their blanket. They have tethered the horses of their resolve at the door of their Master, and turned their faces to striving to enjoy intimate conversation with their Lord.

181

Poverty is both universal and particular. Universal poverty consists in our need for Allah Almighty, and this is the attribute of every creature, believer or unbeliever. It is the meaning of the words of the Almighty: *"Mankind, you are the poor in need of Allah."* (35:15) Particular poverty is the attribute of the *awliya'* of Allah and His lovers. Their hands are empty of this world and their hearts are empty of connection to it, being occupied with Allah and yearning for Him and intimacy with Him, along with devotion and being alone with Allah.

O Allah, let us taste the sweetness of intimate conversation with You and let us travel on the road of Your pleasure so that we may be cut off from everything that will put us far from Your presence. We ask You to make easy for us what You make easy for the people You love, and to forgive us and our parents and all the Muslims!

55. Wearing one's waist-wrapper, robe, clothing and trousers long out of arrogance, pride and boastfulness

Allah Almighty says:

"Do not strut about arrogantly on the earth. Allah does not love anyone who is vain or boastful." (31:18)

The Prophet ※ said, "Every part of the waist-wrapper below the ankles is in the Fire." (al-Bukhari) He ※ also said, "Allah will not look at anyone who wears his waist-wrapper long out of arrogance." (Malik, al-Bukhari, Muslim and others) And he ※ also said, "There are three to whom Allah will not speak on the Day of Rising, nor will He look at them nor purify them, and they will have a painful punishment: one who wears his garment long, one who reminds people of his charity, and one who sells his goods with a false oath." (Muslim) The Prophet ※ said, "Whoever wears his garment long out of arrogance, Allah will not look at him on the Day of Rising." He ※ also said, "Dragging applies to the waist-wrapper and turban. Whoever does any of that out of arrogance, Allah will not look at him on the Day of Rising." (Abu Dawud, an-Nasa'i and Ibn Majah)

The Prophet ※ said, "The waist-wrapper of the believer should reach to the middle of the calves, and there is no harm in what is between there and the ankles. What is lower than the ankles is in the Fire." (an-Nasa'i)

This applies to trousers, robes, gowns, and other garments. We ask Allah for protection. Abu Hurayra ※ said, "A man was praying wearing his waist-wrapper long, and the Messenger of Allah ※ said to him, 'Go and do *wudu'.*' Then he came back and he again said, 'Go and do *wudu'.*' A man asked him, 'Messenger of Allah, why have you ordered him to do *wudu'?*' He was silent and then he said, 'He was praying wearing his waist-wrapper long and Allah does not accept the prayer of anyone who wears his waist-wrapper long.'" (Abu Dawud)

When the Prophet ﷺ said, "On the Day of Rising Allah will not look at anyone who wears his garment long out of arrogance," Abu Bakr ؓ said, "Messenger of Allah, my waist-wrapper hangs down unless I attend to it." The Messenger of Allah ﷺ told him, "You are not a person who does that out of arrogance." (al-Bukhari, Muslim, Abu Dawud and an-Nasa'i)

O Allah, treat us with Your good and excellent kindness by Your mercy, O Most Merciful of the Merciful!

56. Men wearing silk and gold

It is reported in the two *Sahih* collections is that the Messenger of Allah ﷺ said, "Anyone who wears silk in this world will not wear it in the Next World." This is general to soldiers and others by the words of the Prophet ﷺ, "It is unlawful for men of my Community to wear silk and gold." Hudhayfa ibn al-Yaman ﷺ related: "The Messenger of Allah ﷺ forbade us to drink or eat from gold and silver vessels, and to wear or sit on silk and brocade." Al-Bukhari transmitted this.

Anyone who says that it is lawful for men to wear silk is an unbeliever. The Lawgiver ﷺ made a concession for those with the itch or scabies or some other such thing and for fighters when they meet the enemy. As for wearing silk for adornment, it is unlawful for men by the consensus of the Muslims. The same applies when it is mostly silk: it is unlawful.

It is also unlawful for men to wear gold, whether it be a ring, belt or scabbard. It is unlawful to wear it or use it. The Prophet ﷺ saw a gold ring on a man's hand and he removed it and said, "One of you goes to a ember of fire and puts it on his hand." (Muslim)

It is the same with gold embroidery and silk brocade: it is unlawful for men. Scholars disagree about permitting a young boy to wear silk or gold: some people allow it and others forbid it by the generality of the words of the Prophet ﷺ about silk and gold: "These two are unlawful for the males of my Community, but lawful for their women." Boys are included in the prohibition. This is the school of Imam Ahmad.

We ask Allah for success in what He likes and is pleased with. He is Generous, Magnanimous.

57. Absconding by slaves

Muslim related in his *Sahih* that the Messenger of Allah ﷺ said, "When a slave runs away, his prayer is not accepted." Ibn Khuzayma related in his *Sahih* from the *hadith* of Jabir ﷺ that the Messenger of Allah ﷺ said, "There are three whose prayer Allah will not accept and from whom no good action will rise to heaven: a runaway slave until he returns to his master; a woman whose husband is angry with him, until he is pleased with her; and a drunkard until he is sober."

Fadala ibn 'Ubayd says, according to a *marfu'* report: "Do not ask about three: a man who leaves the community and disobeys his ruler, a runaway slave who dies in disobedience, and a woman whose husband is absent and provided her with adequate maintenance but who displayed her beauties in his absence, as the people of the *Jahiliyya* did." (Ibn Hibban)

58. Slaughtering to other than Allah Almighty

This is like when people say, "In the name of *Shaytan*," or an idol or the name of a certain Shaykh. Allah Almighty says:

> "Do not eat anything over which the name of Allah has not been mentioned. To do so is sheer deviance. The shaytans inspire their friends to dispute with you. If you obeyed them you would then be idolators." (6:121)

According to Ibn 'Abbas ﷺ this refers to carrion, animals that have been strangled, and the other categories mentioned in the third *ayat* of *Sura al-Ma'ida*. Al-Kalbi said, "It means that over which the Name of Allah has not been mentioned or what has been slaughtered to other than Allah." 'Ata' said that it declares unlawful those animals which Quraysh and the Arabs slaughtered in the name of idols.

If it be asked how an animal can be allowed by a Muslim when the *tasmiya* (saying the name of Allah) has been omitted, and when this *ayat* contains a clear prohibition against doing so, the answer is that commentators explain that in this *ayat*, "what does not have the name of Allah mentioned over it" refers to carrion: no one applies it to an animal slaughtered by a Muslim who simply omits the *tasmiya*. Various points in the *ayat* indicate that the prohibition refers to carrion. One of those points is the subsequent words: "*To do so is sheer deviance*," and eating an animal slaughtered by a Muslim who has omitted the *tasmiya* is not considered deviance. Another thing is His words, "*The shaytans inspire their friends to dispute with you;*" and the dispute was about carrion, by the consensus of the commentators, not about an animal slaughtered by a Muslim without the *tasmiya*. Another thing is His words "*If you obeyed them, then you would be idolators,*" when idolatry is deeming carrion lawful, not deeming lawful a slaughtered animal over which the name of Allah has not been mentioned.

Abu Mansur reported that Abu Hurayra ﷺ said: "A man asked the Messenger of Allah ﷺ, 'What do you think about a man who slaughters and forgets to mention Allah Almighty?' The Prophet

🏵 said, 'The Name of Allah is on the mouth of every Muslim.'" (at-Tabarani) Abu Mansur also reported from Ibn 'Abbas 🏵 that the Prophet 🏵 said, "His Name is enough; and even if someone forgets to mention it when he slaughters, he should say the Name, remember Allah, and then eat." (ad-Daraqutni)

'Amr ibn Abi 'Amr reported from 'A'isha 🏵 that some people said, "Messenger of Allah, some people bring us meat but we do not know whether the name of Allah has been mentioned over it or not." The Messenger of Allah 🏵 said, "Say the Name over it and eat." (Malik and al-Bukhari)

It has already been mentioned that the Prophet 🏵 said, "Allah curses anyone who slaughters to something other than Allah."

59. Knowingly ascribing oneself falsely to someone other than one's actual father

Sa'd 🙷 related that the Messenger of Allah 🙷 said, "Whoever claims someone other than his true father to be his father, the Garden is forbidden to him." Al-Bukhari related this. Abu Hurayra 🙷 related that the Prophet 🙷 said, "Do not disdain your fathers. Whoever disdains his father is an unbeliever." Al-Bukhari related this. On the same subject we find: "Whoever claims anyone other than his father to be his father, on him is the curse of Allah." Abu Dharr 🙷 said that he heard the Prophet 🙷 say, "Any man who ascribes himself to someone other than his actual father knowingly has committed unbelief; anyone who lays claim to what is not his is not one of us and should take his seat in the Fire; and if anyone charges a man with disbelief or says 'Enemy of Allah' when that is not the case, it comes back on him." Muslim related it.

We ask Allah for pardon and protection and success in what He loves and pleases Him. He is Generous, Magnanimous.

60. Argument, quarrelling and disputation

Allah Almighty says:

> *"Among mankind there is someone whose words about the life of this world excite your admiration, and he calls Allah to witness what is in his heart, while he is in fact the most hostile of adversaries. When he leaves you, he goes about the earth corrupting it, destroying crops and animals. Allah does not like corruption."* (2:204-205)

Part of what is censured here is argument, disputation and quarrelling. Al-Ghazali said, "Disputation means picking apart words to show discrepancies in them with no other desire than to denigrate the speaker and demonstrate your superiority over him. Argument is concerned with explaining legal positions and affirming them. Quarrelling means insistence in words in order to obtain an ample part of wealth or something else, sometimes initiated and sometimes in response."

An-Nawawi said, "Argument can be true or false. Allah Almighty says: *'Contend with the People of the Book only in the kindest way.'* (29:46) The Almighty says: *'Argue with them in the kindest way.'* (16:125) Again, Allah Almighty says: *'No one disputes Allah's signs except those who disbelieve.'* (40:4)" An-Nawawi further said, "If one argues in order to inform others about the truth and to uphold it, it is praiseworthy; if one does so to oppose the truth or argue without knowledge, it is blameworthy." Those are the criteria according to which the texts permitting it or disapproving of it were revealed. One scholar said, "I have not seen anything more likely to remove the *deen*, decrease manliness, or distract one's heart than disputation."

If it be objected that one must argue to get his rights, the answer is as al-Ghazali said: "Know that the censure here is directed against someone who argues using falsehood and without knowledge, like the deputy of a *qadi*, who engages in argument before recognising which side the truth is on, debating without knowledge." Also censured is anyone who goes beyond what is necessary to get what is due to him, and indulges in disputation, lies, abuse, and verbal assault of his adversary. The same applies if one is moved to argue by a simple obstinate desire to overpower his opponent and break him. This is blameworthy.

As for someone who is wronged and supports his argument by way of the *Shari'a* without undue disputation, or excessive insistence, and without sheer obstinacy or abuse, that is not unlawful, but it is better to avoid it if there is any way of doing so, because keeping one's tongue in check when arguing is virtually impossible. Argument provokes rancour and anger in the breast, and when anger erupts each opponent delights in harmng the other and is sad to see him happy, and tends to unleash his tongue on the other's reputation. Anyone who argues is at risk from these disasters. The least harm it brings about is distraction of the heart so that while you are praying your thoughts are preoccupied with proofs and argument, and your state is perturbed. Disputation is the start of evil, and the same applies to argument and quarrelling. So one should not open the door of dispute to himself except in case of real need. In the book of at-Tirmidhi we find that Ibn 'Abbas ؓ related that the Messenger of Allah ﷺ said, "It is enough of a sin for you to continue to be an arguer." It is also reported that 'Ali ؓ said, "Disputation is dangerous."

Section. Abu Hurayra ؓ related that the Messenger of Allah ﷺ said, "Anyone who indulges in disputation without knowledge remains under the wrath of Allah until he stops." (Ibn Abi ad-Dunya) Abu Umama ؓ related that the Prophet ﷺ said, "A people will not be misguided after receiving guidance unless they are given to debate." Then he recited, *"They only say this to you for argument's sake."* (43:58) The Prophet ﷺ said, "What I most fear for you is the slip of the scholar, the argument of the hypocrite about the Qur'an, and this world severing your necks." Ibn 'Umar ؓ related this *hadith*. The Prophet ﷺ said, "Disputation about the Qur'an is unbelief." (Abu Dawud)

Section. It is disliked to use linguistic artifices in argument. A person's intention in his address should be to make the words clear and understood. According to the book of at-Tirmidhi, 'Abdullah ibn 'Amr ibn al-'As ؓ reported that the Messenger of Allah ﷺ

said, "Allah hates an eloquent man who moves his tongue like a cow (in enunciation)." According to at-Tirmidhi this *hadith* is *hasan*. It is also related from Jabir 🌸 that the Messenger of Allah 🌸 said, "Those whom I love the most and who will sit closest to me on the Day of Rising are the best in character. The most hateful of you to me and those who will sit furthest from me on the Day of Rising will be those of many words, those who overpower people with words, and the verbose." They said, "Messenger of Allah, who are they?" He answered, "The arrogant." According to at-Tirmidhi it is a *hasan hadith*.

Know, however, that there is no blame in making the words of *khutba*s and admonitions eloquent. The goal in this is to stir people's hearts to the obedience of Allah Almighty, and eloquent language has a clearly effective role in this; and Allah knows best.

61. Denying spare water to others

Allah Almighty says:

"Say: 'What do you think? If one morning your water disappears into the earth who would bring you running water?'" (67:30)

The Prophet ﷺ said, "Do not deny spare water in order thereby to deny pasture by it." (Agreed upon) He ﷺ also said, "If someone denies excess water and excess pasturage, Allah will deny him His bounty on the Day of Rising." (Ahmad)

The Messenger of Allah ﷺ said, "There are three whom Allah will not speak to or look at or purify on the Day of Rising, and who will have a painful punishment: a man in the desert with spare water who denies it to a traveller, a man who gives his allegiance to a leader but only does so to obtain worldly things – if he is given them, he is faithful and if not, he is not – and a man who sells goods to a man after *'Asr* and swears by Allah that he paid such-and-such for them and is believed though that is not the case." This is transmitted in both *Sahih* collections.

62. Giving short measure and weight

Allah Almighty says:

> "*Woe to the stinters!* (meaning those who give people short measure and and weight) *Those who, when they take a measure from people, exact full measure, but when they give them a measure or weight, hand over less than is due.*" (83:1)

As-Suddi narrated that "When the Messenger of Allah ﷺ came to Madina there was a man there called Abu Juhayna who had two scales – one for giving and one for taking – and so Allah revealed this *ayat*.

Ibn 'Abbas ﷺ reported that the Messenger of Allah ﷺ said, "Five for five." They asked, "Messenger of Allah, what is 'five for five'?" He answered, "A people do not break a contract without Allah giving their enemy power over them. They do not judge by other than what Allah has revealed without poverty spreading among them. Fornication does not appear among people without Allah making the plague descend on them (meaning frequent deaths). They do not skimp in the weight and measure without being denied crops and experiencing famine. They do not deny *zakat* without rain being withheld from them."

A stinter is someone who gives short measure and weight because although he almost always only steals an insignificant amount, to do so is theft, treachery and consumption of the unlawful. Allah has promised "woe" to anyone who does it. Woe (*wayl*) denotes intense punishment. It is also said that it is a valley in Hell such that if all the mountains of this world were put into it, they would melt from the intensity of its heat.

One of the early Muslims said, "I testify that everyone who weighs or measures is in danger of the Fire – except someone who is protected by Allah." Another of them said, "I visited a sick person who was close to death and began to instruct him to say the *shahada*; but his tongue could not articulate it. When he recovered I asked him, 'My brother, when I instructed you to say the *shahada* why could your tongue not articulate it?' He answered, 'My brother, the tongue of the Scale is on my tongue stopping me, from articulating it.' I asked him, 'By Allah, did you use to give short measure?' He answered, 'No, by Allah, but I did not use to check the accuracy of my scales.'" If that is the situation of someone not sufficiently concerned with the accuracy of his scale, what is going to be the state of someone who deliberately gives short weight?

Nafi' related that Ibn 'Umar 🕮 passed by a seller and said, "Fear Allah and give full weight and measure. The stinters will be made to stand until they are up to the middle of their ears in sweat. The same is true of a merchant who pressed his hand on the scale at the moment of selling and releases it when buying."

We ask Allah for pardon and protection from every affliction and trial. He is Magnanimous, Generous.

63. Feeling secure from Allah's devising

Allah Almighty says: *"Until while they were exulting in what they had been given, We suddenly seized them"* (6:44): in other words, Allah's punishment seized them from a direction they were not expecting.

'Uqba ibn 'Amir ﷺ related that the Messenger of Allah ﷺ said, "When you see Allah giving His slave what he wants while he remains disobedient, that means He is drawing him on." Then he recited, *"When they forgot what they had been reminded of, We opened up for them the doors to everything, until while they were exulting in what they has been given, We suddenly seized them and at once they were in despair."* (6:44) (at-Tabarani) Despair here means despair of salvation when death arrives. Ibn 'Abbas ﷺ said that it means despairing of any good.

The Prophet ﷺ often used to say, "O Overturner of hearts, make our hearts firm in Your *deen!*" He was asked, "Messenger of Allah, do you fear for us?" The Messenger of Allah ﷺ said, "All hearts are between two of the fingers of the All-Merciful, and He turns them however He wishes." (at-Tirmidhi)

We find in a sound *hadith* that a man may perform the actions of the people of the Garden until there is only a span between him and it, and then the Decree overtakes him and he does the actions of the people of the Fire and enters it. And in *Sahih al-Bukhari* it is reported from Sahl ibn Sa'd as-Sa'idi ﷺ that the Prophet ﷺ said, "A man may perform the actions of the people of the Fire and yet be one of the people of the Garden. And a man may do the actions of the people of the Garden although he is one of the people of the Fire. Actions have seals."

Allah Almighty recounted in His Mighty Book the story of Bal'am who was stripped of faith after having great knowledge. That was also the case with Barsisa the devout worshipper, who died an unbeliever. He was a man of Egypt who was always in the mosque for the *adhan* and the prayer. He had the radiance of worship and lights of obedience of Allah. One day he went up the minaret, as was his custom, to call the *adhan*. There was a house belonging to a Christian below the minaret. He looked into it and saw the daughter of the owner of the house, who was very beautiful, and he was tempted by her. He abandoned the *adhan* and went down to her. "What do you want?" she asked him, and he answered, "I want you." She said, "I will agree to nothing questionable." He told her, "Then I will marry you." She said to him, "You are a Muslim and my father will not marry me to you." He said, "I will become Christian." She said to him, "If you do that, I will." So he became Christian to marry her, and stayed with them in the house. During that day he went to the roof of the house, fell off it and died. So he neither gained by strong practice of the *deen* nor did he enjoy the girl. We seek refuge with Allah from His devising and from a bad end and a bad conclusion!

Salim reported from 'Abdullah ﷺ that the Messenger of Allah ﷺ often used to swear, "No, by the Overturner of hearts!" Al-Bukhari related this. It means that He moves them quicker than the wind, in various directions: from acceptance to rejection, from desire to antipathy, and between other opposites. In the Qur'an we find: *"Know that Allah intervenes between a man and his heart."* (8:24) Mujahid said, "The meaning is that He comes between a man and his intellect so that he does not even know what his finger is doing." Allah says: *'There is a reminder in that for anyone who has a heart.'"* (50:37) According to at-Tabari this is a statement from Allah Almighty that He has more control over the hearts of His slaves than they do, and that He comes between them and their hearts if He wishes so that man does not know anything except by the will of Allah.

'A'isha ﷺ reported: "The Messenger of Allah ﷺ used often to say, 'O Overturner of hearts, make my heart firm in obeying You !' I said, 'Messenger of Allah, you often make this prayer. Are you afraid of not being so?' He replied, 'How could I feel secure, 'A'isha? The hearts of the slaves are between the fingers of the All-Merciful, who turns them however He wishes. Whenever He wants to turn the heart of His slave, He turns it.'"

Given that guidance is known, going straight is dependent on His will, the end is unknown and your will is not in your control, do not admire your faith, actions, prayer, fasting, or any of your acts of worship. Even if that is included in your earning, it is also part of the creation of your Lord and His favour to you. If you boast about any of that, you are boasting about a gift received from someone else. If He strips you of it, your heart will be emptier of good than the inside of a donkey. How many a meadow full of red flowers becomes dry stubble when the barren wind blows on it! The same applies to someone whose heart is sound and bright in the morning, obeying Allah, and then in the evening sick and dark, disobeying Allah. That is the decree of the Almighty, the Immense. Son of Adam, the pens are recording you, and yet you are heedless and do not realise! Son of Adam, leave the songs and lutes and houses and hearths, and arguing in this abode until you see what is decreed as your destiny!

A caller shall call from before the Throne, "Where is so-and-so? Where is so-and-so?" Anyone who hears that voice trembles. Allah Almighty will tell that person, "You are invited to present yourself before the Creator of the heavens and the earth." So creatures will direct their eyes towards the Throne and that person will stand before Allah Almighty. Allah will give him some of His light to veil him from other creatures and then will ask him, "My slave, did you not know that I could see your actions in the Abode of this world?" He will answer, "Yes, Lord." Allah Almighty will ask, "My slave, did you not hear of My vengeance and punishment of anyone who disobeys Me?" "Yes, Lord," he will say. Allah Almighty will ask, "Did you not hear of My recompense and reward for anyone who obeys Me?" He will reply, "Yes, Lord." Allah Almighty will ask, "My slave, did you disobey Me?" He will reply, "Lord, that was the case." Allah Almighty will ask, "My slave, what do you expect from Me today?" He will say, "O Lord, that You will pardon me." Allah will ask, "My slave, are you certain that I will pardon you?" He will say, "Yes, Lord, because You saw me disobeying and veiled it for me." Allah Almighty will say, "I have forgiven you and pardoned you, and your opinion is correct. Take your book in your right hand. I accept whatever good actions are in it and I forgive you any evil deeds. I am the Magnanimous, the Generous."

64. Despairing of the mercy of Allah and losing hope

Allah Almighty says:

"No one despairs of solace from Allah except people who are unbelievers." (12:87)

"It is He who sends down abundant rain, after they have lost all hope." (42:28)

"Say: 'My slaves, you who have transgressed against your-selves, do not despair of the mercy of Allah." (39:53)

The Prophet ﷺ said, "None of you should die except with a good opinion of Allah." (Muslim)

Our God, were it not for Your love of forgiveness, You would not grant any reprieve to him who disobeys You! Were it not for Your forgiveness and generosity, none would reside in the Garden! O Allah, You pardon and You love pardon, so pardon us! O Allah, look at us with pleasure, confirm us in the register of the people of piety, and preserve us from the register of the people of unrighteousness. O Allah, realise our hopes and make our actions good in all states. Make it easy for us to please You, and and impel us towards good deeds. *"Give us good in this world and good in the Next World, and safeguard us from the punishment of the Fire."* (2:201)

65. Abandoning the Group Prayer and praying alone without a valid excuse

Abdullah ibn Mas'ud ﷺ related that the Prophet ﷺ said about people who failed to attend the prayer, "I wanted to order a man to lead the people in the prayer and then burn down the houses of men who stayed away from the group around them." Muslim related this. He ﷺ also said, "People should stop abandoning the group prayers or Allah will seal their hearts and they will be among the heedless." Muslim related this. The Prophet ﷺ also said, "If someone misses three *Jumu'a*s out of lack of concern, Allah will put a seal on his heart." Abu Dawud and an-Nasa'i transmitted it. He said, "Whoever misses the *Jumu'a* without any excuse or necessity will be recorded among the hypocrites in a register which cannot be effaced or changed." Hafsa ﷺ related that the Messenger of Allah ﷺ said, "Going to *Jumu'a* is mandatory for every male past the age of puberty."

We ask Allah for success in doing what pleases Him and what He likes. He is Magnanimous, Generous.

66. Persistently missing the *Jumu'a* and Group prayers without a valid excuse

Allah Almighty says:

"On the Day when legs are bared and they are called on to prostrate, they will not be able to do so. Their eyes will be downcast, darkened by debasement; for they were called upon to prostrate while they were in full possession of their faculties." (68:42)

It is on the Day of Rising that the abasement of regret will cover those referred to here. They were called upon to prostrate in this world. Ibrahim at-Taymi said, "What is meant is the obligatory prayer with the *adhan* and *iqama*." Sa'id ibn al-Musayyab said, "They hear 'Come to the prayer. Come to success' but do not respond although they are healthy and whole." Ka'b al-Ahbar 🙼 said, "By Allah, this *ayat* was only revealed about those who failed to attend the group prayer; and what threat could be stronger or more far-reaching than this for someone who abandons the group prayer although he is able to attend it?"

As for the *Sunna*, it is confirmed in both *Sahih* collections that the Messenger of Allah 🙼 said, "I seriously considered commanding the prayer and the *iqama* and ordering a man to lead the people in prayer, then going around with some men with bundles of firewood to some people who do not attend the group prayer and burning down their houses on top of them." And he only desisted from burning down their houses for failing to perform an obligatory act as a threat because their offspring and goods were in the houses.

In *Sahih Muslim* it is stated that a blind man came to the Prophet 🙼 and said, "Messenger of Allah. I do not have a guide to lead me to the mosque." He asked the Prophet 🙼 to grant him an allowance to pray in his house, and he gave him an allowance. When he turned, he 🙼 called him and said, "Can you hear the call to the prayer?" He answered, "Yes." He 🙼 said, "Then respond to it."

Abu Dawud related that 'Amr ibn Umm Maktum went to the Prophet ﷺ and said, "Messenger of Allah, there are a lot of vermin and beasts in Madina. I am blind and live in a house which is far away. I have a guide who is not kind to me. Will you give me a dispensation to pray in my house?" He asked, "Can you hear the call?" He said, "Yes." He said, "Then respond. I do not find any dispensation for you."

This was a blind man who complained of the difficulty is going to the mosque without a guide to lead him, and in spite of that the Prophet ﷺ did not allow him to pray in his house; so what can be said about someone healthy who has good sight and no excuse at all for not going? That is why when Ibn 'Abbas ﷺ was asked about a man who fasted in the day and prayed at night but did not pray in a group or join others for the prayer, he said, "If he dies like that, he will be in the Fire." And Abu Hurayra ﷺ said, "It would be better for the ear of a son of Adam to be filled with molten lead than for him to hear the *adhan* and not respond to it."

It is related from Ibn 'Abbas ﷺ that the Messenger of Allah ﷺ said, "If someone hears the call to prayer and no excuse prevents him from responding to it..." Someone asked, "What constitutes an excuse, Messenger of Allah?" He said, "Fear or illness," and continued, "The prayer which he has prayed in [his house] is not accepted from him." Al-Hakim transmitted in *al-Mustadrak* from Ibn 'Abbas ﷺ that the Messenger of Allah ﷺ said, "Three people will be cursed by Allah: someone who leads a people when they dislike him; a woman who spends the night with her husband angry with her; and a man who hears 'Come to prayer. Come to success' but does not respond."

'Ali ibn Abi Talib ﷺ said, "There is no prayer for the neighbour of a mosque except in the mosque." Someone asked, "Who is the neighbour of a mosque?" He answered, "Anyone who can hear the *adhan*." Al-Bukhari related in the *Sahih* that 'Abdullah ibn Mas'ud ﷺ said: "Anyone who wants to meet Allah tomorrow as a Muslim (i.e. on the Day of Rising) should persevere in these five prayers when they are called. Allah prescribed the *sunna*s of guidance for your Prophet and they are *sunna*s of guidance to be followed. If you pray in your houses, as this one who stays behind prays in his house, you have abandoned the *sunna*s of your

Prophet. If you abandon the *sunna*s of your Prophet, you are mis-guided. I can remember when only a known hypocrite or someone who was ill failed to join us. A man used to come supported by two men until he stood in the row or until he reached the mosque for the group prayer."

Ar-Rabi' ibn Khuthaym was paralysed in his left side, and he used to go to the prayer leaning on two men. He was told, "Abu Muhammad, you may pray in your house. You have an excuse!" He said, "It is as you say, but I hear the *mu'adhdhin* say, 'Come to the prayer. Come to success,' and whoever is able to respond to it, even creeping or crawling, should do so." Hatim al-Asamm said, "Once I missed the time of the group prayer and Abu Ishaq al-Bukhari alone consoled me. If a child of mine had died, more than ten thousand men would have consoled me because in the eyes of people an affliction in the *deen* is less serious than an affliction in this world!"

One of the *Salaf* used to say, "No one misses the group prayer except on account of a wrong action he has committed." Ibn 'Umar 🙵 said, "'Umar went out one day to a walled garden and returned after the people had prayed '*Asr*. 'Umar said, 'We belong to Allah and to Him we return! We have missed the '*Asr* prayer in the group. I testify to you that my garden is *sadaqa* for the poor in expiation for what 'Umar has done.'" It was a palm grove.

Allah Almighty says: "*On the Day when legs are bared and they are called on to prostrate, they will not be able to do so. Their eyes will be downcast, darkened by debasement; for they were called on to prostrate when they were in full possession of their faculties.*" (68:42-43) Ka'b al-Ahbar 🙵 said, "This *ayat* was only revealed about those who did not go to the group prayers." Sa'id ibn al-Musayyab, the Imam of the *Tabi'un*, said, "They are people who used to hear, 'Come to prayer. Come to success,' and did not respond although they were healthy and sound."

We find in both *Sahih* collections that the Messenger of Allah 🙵 said, "By Him Who has my soul in His hand, I wanted to order some firewood to be brought, then order the prayer and give the *adhan* for it and then order a man to lead the people, and then I would go to some men who did not attend the prayer in the group and burn their houses down on top of them." We find in the variant of Muslim, also from Abu Hurayra ﷺ: "I wanted to order my servants to gather firewood for me and then go to some people who prayed in their houses without illness and burn them down on top of them." These *hadiths* contain a strong threat against anyone who misses the prayer in a group without excuse. At-Tirmidhi related from Ibn 'Abbas ﷺ that he was asked about a man who fasted in the day and prayed at night but did not pray in the group prayer or the *Jumu'a*. He said, "If this one dies, he will be in the Fire."

Section. The group prayer is an immense matter, as is clear from the *tafsir* of the words of the Almighty: *"We wrote in the Zabur after the Reminder came: 'It is My slaves who are righteous who will inherit the earth.'"* (21:105) This is said to refer to those who pray the five prayers in a group. The Almighty said, *"We record what they send ahead and what they leave behind."* (36:12)

In the *Sahih* it is reported that the Messenger of Allah ﷺ said: "Whoever purifies himself in his house and then walks to the one of the houses of Allah to fulfil one of the obligations of Allah, with one step he takes one of his errors falls away and with the other he is elevated by one degree. When he prays, the angels continue to pray as long as he is in the prayer. They say, 'O Allah, forgive him. O Allah, show mercy to him!' as long as he does not commit harm in it or break *wudu'*." The Prophet ﷺ also said, "Shall I direct you to something by which Allah will efface your errors and raise you in degree?" Those present said, "Yes, Messenger of Allah." He said, "Doing *wudu'* thoroughly when it is difficult, taking many of steps to the mosque, and waiting for the next prayer after the prayer. That is *ribat* (fighting to defend the frontiers of Islam). That is *ribat*." Muslim related this.

67. Causing harm in bequests

Allah Almighty says:

> *"After any bequest you make or any debt, making sure that no one's rights are prejudiced."* (4:12)

That means without causing any harm to your heirs, for instance by leaving a debt by which harm is intended to someone's rightful heirs. Allah forbids that. Allah Almighty says: *"An instruction from Allah; and Allah is All-Knowing, Ever-Forbearing. Those who obey Allah and His Messenger"* regarding inheritance, *"He will admit them into Gardens with rivers flowing under them, remaining in them for ever. That is the Great Victory. As for him who disobeys Allah and His Messenger..."* Mujahid said that this means with regard to the shares of inheritance Allah has allotted. 'Ikrima related from Ibn 'Abbas ﷺ that it means anyone who is not pleased with the division decreed by Allah and exceeds what Allah has said – *"He will admit him to a Fire, to remain in it forever. He will have a humiliating punishment."* (4:12-14)

Abu Hurayra ﷺ reported that the Messenger of Allah ﷺ said, "A man or woman may obey Allah for sixty years and then death comes and they cause harm through bequests they make and so the Fire becomes mandatory for them." Then Abu Hurayra ﷺ recited this *ayat*: *"After any bequest you make or any debt, making sure that no one's rights are prejudiced."* (4:12) Abu Dawud related it. The Prophet ﷺ said, "If someone makes off with the inheritance of an heir, Allah will cut him out of his inheritance of the Garden." The Prophet ﷺ also said, "Allah has given everyone with a right his right, and so there is no bequest to an heir." At-Tirmidhi described this as sound.

68. Deceit and treachery

Allah Almighty says:

"Evil plotting envelops only those who do it." (35:43)

The Prophet ﷺ said, "Deceit and treachery will be in the Fire." (al-Bazzar) The Prophet ﷺ also said, "A swindler, a miser and someone who reminds others of his charity will not enter the Garden."

Allah Almighty says about the hypocrites: *"They think they deceive Allah, but He is deceiving them."* (4:142) Al-Wahidi said, "They will be treated in the same deceptive way they treated others. That is to say they will be given light as the believers are given it; but when they go onto the *Sirat*, their light will go out and they will be left in darkness." The Prophet ﷺ said in a *hadith*, "The people of the Fire are five;" and among them he mentioned a man who deceives you with regard to your wife and wealth, morning and night. (Muslim)

69. Spying on the Muslims and pointing out their weaknesses

According to the *hadith* about Hatib ibn Abi Balta'a ❁ 'Umar ❁ wanted to kill him for what he had done, but the Messenger of Allah ❁ forbade him to kill him since he had been at Badr. If the consequence of someone's spying is weakness for Islam and its people, and it results in killing or capture or looting or anything of the kind, he is someone who "creates corruption in the earth and destroys tillage and offspring" and so it is obligatory to kill him and he deserves that punishment. We ask Allah for pardon and protection. Of necessity it is known that tale-bearing is one of the greatest forbidden things, and the tale-bearing of the spy is worse still.

We seek refuge with Allah from that, and we ask Him for pardon and protection. He is Subtle, Aware, Magnanimous, Generous.

70. Insulting one of the Companions

It is recorded in both *Sahih* collections that the Messenger of Allah ﷺ said that Allah Almighty says, "I have declared war on anyone who is hostile towards a friend of Mine." The Prophet ﷺ said, "Do not abuse my Companions. By the One who has my soul in His hand, if one of you spent the like of Uhud in gold, it would not reach the *mudd* or a half of it of one of them." (al-Bukhari and Muslim) The Prophet ﷺ said, "Allah, Allah! My Companions! Do not make them a target after me. Whoever loves them, loves them by love of me. Whoever hates them hates them by hatred of me. Whoever harms them has harmed me. Whoever harms me has harmed Allah. Whoever harms Allah is about to be seized." At-Tirmidhi transmitted it. This *hadith* and those like it contain clarification of the state of the one who makes the Companions a target after the Messenger of Allah ﷺ or curses them or forges lies about them or censures them or rejects them or is disdainful of them.

The words of the Prophet ﷺ, "Allah, Allah" are an expression of caution and warning, as when a warner says, "The Fire! The Fire!", meaning "beware of the Fire." His words, "Do not make them a target after me" mean "Do not make them a target of attack and abuse, as when one says, 'So-and-so is a target of abuse'." He said, "Whoever loves them, loves them by love of me. Whoever hates them hates them by hatred for me." This is because love for the Companions is on account of the fact that they accompanied the Messenger of Allah ﷺ and helped him, believed in him, boasted of him, and assisted him with their lives and property. Whoever loves them loves the Prophet ﷺ, and so love for the Companions of the Prophet ﷺ is a mark of love for him ﷺ and hating them is a mark of hatred of the Prophet ﷺ, as stated in a sound *hadith*: "Love of the Ansar is part of faith, and hatred of them is part of hypocrisy." That is only on account of their precedence and striving against the enemies of Allah in the company of the Messenger of Allah ﷺ.

The same applies to love of 'Ali ﷺ being part of faith and hatred for him being part of hypocrisy. The virtues of the

Companions ﷺ are known to anyone who reflects on their states, their lives and their record both during the life of the Messenger of Allah ﷺ and after his death, on account of their precedence in faith, striving against the unbelievers, propagating the *deen*, making Islam victorious, making the word of Allah and His Messenger uppermost, and teaching the obligations and *sunna*s he taught. If it were not for them nothing of what has reached us of every aspect of the *deen* would have done so; we would not have known a single *sunna* or obligation; and we would not have known anything about the *hadith* or *sira*.

Anyone who attacks them or abuses them has left the *deen* and split from the religion of the Muslims, because attack only arises from believing evil of them, concealing rancour towards them and dislike of what Allah Almighty mentions in His book in praise of them and of the praise of the Messenger of Allah ﷺ for them and their virtues, excellence and love. Attacking the means is tantamount to attacking the root cause, and disdain for the transmitter is disdain for what he transmitted. That is clear to anyone who reflects and is safe from hypocrisy, dualism and atheism in his belief. Enough for you are the reports and traditions about that, such as the words of the Prophet ﷺ, "Allah chose me and chose companions for me, and from them He gave me assistants, helpers and in-laws. If anyone abuses them, on him is the curse of Allah, the angels and all mankind. Allah will not accept any recompense from him on the Day of Resurrection."

Anas ibn Malik ﷺ reported, "Some of the Companions of the Messenger of Allah ﷺ said, 'We are insulted.' The Messenger of Allah ﷺ said, 'If someone insults my Companions, the curse of Allah, the angels and all mankind are on them.'" Anas ﷺ also related that the Messenger of Allah ﷺ said, "Allah chose me and chose companions for me, and from them He gave me assistants, helpers and in-laws. People will come after me who criticise them and deprecate them. Do not eat or drink with them or intermarry with them, do not pray over them, and do not pray with them."

Ibn Mas'ud ﷺ reported that the Messenger of Allah ﷺ said, "When my Companions are mentioned, hold back. When the stars are mentioned, hold back. When fate is mentioned, hold back." Holding back is a sign of faith and submission to the command of Allah. The same is true of stars. If someone believes that they have an effect outside of the will of Allah Almighty, he is an idolator. The same applies to anyone who criticises the Companions of the Messenger of Allah ﷺ at all or seeks out their faults or mentions a fault and ascribes it to them: he is a hypocrite. It is obligatory for a Muslim to love Allah and love His Messenger and love what has he has brought, love those who carried out his commands, and love those who took on his guidance and acted by his *sunna*; to love his family and Companions, wives, servants and slaves, and love those who love him and hate those who hate him – because the strongest handhold of faith is love in Allah and hatred in Allah.

Ayyub as-Sakhtiyani ﷺ said, "Whoever loves Abu Bakr, it is he who erected the minaret of the *deen*. Whoever loves 'Umar, it is he who made the way clear. Whoever loves 'Uthman, he was illuminated by the light of Allah. Whoever loves 'Ali, he took hold of the firmest handhold. Whoever says good about the Companions of the Messenger of Allah ﷺ is free of hypocrisy."

Section. As for the virtues and excellent qualities of the Companions, they are too many to mention. Scholars of the *Sunna* agree on the excellence of the ten Companions for whom it has been attested that they will be in the Garden. The best of the ten are Abu Bakr, 'Umar ibn al-Khattab, Uthman ibn 'Affan, and then 'Ali ibn Abi Talib ﷺ. Only a foul, innovating hypocrite doubts that. The Prophet ﷺ stated in a *hadith* reported by al-'Irbad ibn Sariya: "You must keep to my *sunna* and the *sunna* of the rightly-guided caliphs after me. Hold onto it with your teeth. Beware of innovated things." The rightly-guided caliphs are Abu Bakr, 'Umar, Uthman, and 'Ali ﷺ.

Allah revealed *ayat*s in the Qur'an about the virtues of Abu Bakr ﷺ: *"Those of you possessing affluence and ample wealth should not make oaths that they will not give to their relatives and the very poor."* (24:22) There is no disagreement that this is about him, and so he is described as having *fadl* (affluence). Allah Almighty calls him *"The second of two in the Cave."* (9:40) There is no disagreement about Abu Bakr being that companion and having been given the good news of tranquillity and being the second of two. As 'Umar

🕮 said about him, "Who could be better than the second of two when Allah is their third?" *"He who brings the truth and those who confirm it: those are the godfearing."* (39:33) Ja'far as-Sadiq said, "There is no disagreement that the one who brought the truth was the Prophet 🕮 and the one who confirmed it was Abu Bakr 🕮. What virtue could be greater than that? May Allah be pleased with all of them."

Glossary

Abu Jahl: One of the important men of Quraysh who was violently opposed to Islam.

adhan: the call to prayer.

Amir al-Mu'minin: "the Commander of the Believers," the title of the Caliph.

Ansar: the "Helpers", the people of Madina who welcomed and aided the Prophet ﷺ.

'Arafa: a plain fifteen miles to the east of Makka which is visited as part of *hajj*.

'araq: the arak tree, twigs of which are used to make *siwak* sticks for cleaning the teeth.

'Asr: the afternoon prayer.

awliya': plural of *wali*.

ayat: a verse of the Qur'an.

Badr: a place near the coast, about 95 miles to the south of Madina, where the Battle of Badr took place.

barzakh: the interspatial life in the grave between death in this world and resurrection on the Day of Rising.

Baqi': the main cemetery in Madina.

Basin: *al-Hawd*, the watering-place of the Prophet ﷺ in the Next World, whose drink will refresh those who have crossed the Bridge over the Fire before they enter the Garden.

Chosroes: the Greek form of Khusraw, the title of the Persian Sassanid emperor.

deen: the life-transaction between the Creator and created.

Dhat as-Salasil: a military expedition which took place a month after the Battle of Mu'ta in 8 AH led by 'Amr ibn al-'As.

dhimmi: a non-Muslim living under the protection of Muslim rule.

Dhu al-Qa'da: the eleventh month of the Muslim calendar.

Fajr: the dawn prayer.

faqih, plural *fuqaha'*: a man learned in knowledge of *fiqh* who by virtue of his knowledge can give a legal judgement.

fuqaha': see *faqih*.

ghusl: major ablution of the whole body with water, required to regain purity after menstruation, bleeding after childbirth and sexual intercourse.

hadd: see *hudud*.

hadith: reported speech of the Prophet ﷺ.

hajj: the annual pilgrimage to Makka and ots environs which is one of the five Pillars of Islam.

Haman: the chief minister of the Pharaoh in the time of Musa.

haram: unlawful in the *Shari'a*.

Harut and Marut: two angels sent to test the people of Babylon by teaching sorcery.

Hijra: emigration, especially that of the Prophet ﷺ and his Companions from Makka to Madina.

hudud: plural of *hadd*, Allah's boundary limits for the lawful and unlawful. The *hadd* punishments are specific fixed penalties laid down by Allah for specified crimes.

Iblis: the personal name of the Devil. He is also called Shaytan.

imam: Muslim religious or political leader.

iqama: the call which announces that the obligatory prayer is about to begin.

'Isha': the night prayer.

isnad: the chain of transmission of a *hadith* from individual to individual.

Jahiliyya: the Time of Ignorance before the coming of Islam.

janaba: major ritual impurity incurred by sexual intercourse, sexual discharge, menstruation, childbirth.

al-jarh wa at-ta'dil: the science of critiquing a narrator's position as a narrator.

jihad: struggle, particularly fighting for the cause of Allah to establish and defend Islam.

jinn: inhabitants of the created universe, made of smokeless fire, who are normally invisible.

jizya: a protection tax payable by non-Muslims living under Muslim rule as a tribute to the Muslim ruler.

Jumu'a: the day of gathering, Friday, and particularly the *Jumu'a* prayer, which is performed instead of *Zuhr* by those who attend it.

Ka'ba: the cube-shaped building at the centre of the Haram in Makka, originally built by the Prophet Ibrahim.

Khaybar: a Jewish settlement to the north of Madina which was besieged and captured by the Muslims in the seventh year after the *Hijra* because of the continual treachery of its inhabitants.

kharaj: taxes imposed on revenue from land or the work of slaves.

khutba: a speech, and in particular a sermon given by the Imam before the *Jumu'a* prayer and after the two *'Id* prayers.

Mada'in: the site of the cities of Seleucia and Ctesiphon for a time the capital of the Sasanid rulers of Persia, also referred to as Seleucia-Ctesiphon.

Maghrib: the sunset prayer.

mahram: a relative of the opposite gender with whom marriage is forbidden.

marfu': "elevated", a narration from the Prophet ﷺ related by a Companion but without the last link in the chain of transmission, as in "The Messenger of Allah said..."

Mina: a valley five miles from Makka on the road to 'Arafa where the three *jamarat* (pillars stoned by the pilgrims on *hajj*) stand and animals are sacrificed.

mu'adhdhin: someone who calls the *adhan* or call to prayer.

Muhajirun: Companions of the Messenger of Allah who accepted Islam in Makka and made *hijra* to Madina.

Murji'iyya: A theological school of thought who adherents held that it is faith and not actions which are ultimately important. They also have a political position which suspends judgement on the final destiny of a person guilty of major sins.

Musnad: a collection of *hadith*s arranged according to the first authority in their *isnad*.

nabidh: a drink made by soaking grapes, raisins, or other ingredients in water without allowing them to the ferment to the point of becoming intoxicating.

Najran: a province in the southern part of Arabia.

Qadariyya: a sect who believed that people have complete power (*qadar*) over their actions and hence free will.

qadi: a judge, qualified to judge all matters in accordance with the Shari'a and to dispense and enforce legal punishments.

Qarun: one of the tribe of Israel in Egypt at the time of Musa. He possessed enormous wealth and was arrogant, and so Allah made the earth swallow him up.

qibla: the direction faced in the prayer: towards the Ka'ba in Makka.

Quraysh: one of the great tribes of Arabia. The Prophet Muhammad ﷺ belonged to this tribe, which had great moral and financial power both before and after Islam came. Someone from this tribe is called a Qurayshi.

Qurayza: one of the Jewish tribes in Madina.

rak'at: a unit of the prayer consisting of a sequence of standing, bowing, prostration and sitting.

Ramadan: the month of fasting, the ninth in the Muslim lunar calendar.

ribat: defence of the frontiers of territory held by Muslims.

ruku': bowing, particularly the bowing position in the prayer.

sadaqa: charitable giving for the Cause of Allah.

Salaf: the early generations of Muslims.

Saqar: "Scorching Heat," part of Hell.

shahada: bearing witness, particularly witnessing that there is no god but Allah and that Muhammad ﷺ is the Messenger of Allah.

Shari'a: The legal modality of a people, based on the Revelation given to or followed by their Prophet. The final *Shari'a* is that of Islam.

shaytan: a devil, particularly Iblis.

shirk: the unforgiveable wrong action of worshipping something or someone other than Allah or associating something or someone as a partner with Him.

sira: 'conduct, behaviour, way of acting', hence a biography, particularly the biography of the Prophet ﷺ.

siwak: a stick of the arak tree used to clean the teeth.

Subh: the dawn prayer.

sujud: prostration.

Sunna: the customary practice of a person or group of people. It has come to refer almost exclusively to the practice of the Messenger of Allah ﷺ.

Sunan: plural of *sunna.*

Tabi'un: the second generation of the early Muslims, who did not meet the Prophet Muhammad ﷺ but learned the *Deen* of Islam from his Companions.

takbir: saying '*Allahu Akbar*', "Allah is greater".

taqwa: awe or fear of Allah, which inspires a person to be on guard against wrong action and eager for actions which please Him.

Tasmiya: saying "*Bismillah*," "In the Name of Allah".

tayammum: purification for prayer with clean dust, earth, or stone, when either water for *ghusl* or *wudu'* is unavailable or its use would be detrimental to health.

Tihama: a narrow coastal region of Arabia on the Red Sea.

Ubayy ibn Khalaf: a contemporary enemy of Muhammad who was killed in the Battle of Uhud.

Uhud: a mountain just outside Madina, where five years after the Hijra the Muslims lost a battle against the Makkan idolaters. Many great Companions, and in particular Hamza, the uncle of the Prophet, were killed in this battle.

Wadi al-Qura: a place between Syria and Madina.

wali: someone who is a "friend" of Allah: that is, who possesses the qualities that make someone especially beloved to Him.

wittol: a man who knows of and yet tolerates his wife's infidelity.

wudu': the lesser ritual washing to be pure for the prayer.

Zabaniyya: the angels of Hellfire.

zakat: an annual tax on wealth and property, one of the five Pillars of Islam.

Zamzam: the well in the Haram of Makka.

zindiq: a term used to describe a heretic whose teaching is a danger to the state. Originally under the Persian Sasanids it meant a freethinker or atheist.

Zuhr: the midday prayer.

Index

'Abd al-Malik ibn Marwan 71-72
'Abd ar-Rahman ibn 'Awf 157
'Abd ar-Rahman ibn Jarir 83
'Abd ar-Rahman ibn Mahdi 162
'Abd ar-Rahman ibn Samura 87
'Abdullah ibn 'Amr ibn al-'As 16, 68, 80, 113, 115, 159, 191
'Abdullah ibn Abi ad-Dunya 95
'Abdullah ibn al-Mubarak 16, 103
'Abdullah ibn Salam 91
'Abdullah ibn Shaqiq 15
'Abdullah ibn Sharik 119
'Abdullah ibn Unays 92
Abu al-'Aliya 96
Abu Ayyub al-Ansari 95, 178
Abu Bakr 11, 48, 52, 85, 104, 134, 180, 184, 210
Abu Bakr al-Athram 76, 118
Abu Bakr ibn Abi Maryam 33
Abu Burda 156, 159
Abu Dharr 26, 52, 87, 189
Abu Hurayra 6, 19, 20, 24, 31, 38, 46, 49, 53, 59, 62, 64, 66, 67, 76, 79, 80, 90, 103, 106, 108, 111, 113, 115, 122, 137, 156, 169, 170, 171, 172, 174, 175, 176, 178, 180, 183, 187, 189, 191, 202, 203, 205
Abu Juhayna 194
Abu Lahab 139, 142
Abu Lubaba 128
Abu Mansur 187
Abu Mas'ud 169
Abu Musa al-Ash'ari 20, 68, 69, 71, 110, 156, 161
Abu Sa'id al-Khudri 50, 53, 67, 156
Abu Sa'id as-Sa'luki 46
Abu Salama 163
Abu Sinan 26
Abu Sufyan 180
Abu Talha 161-162
Abu Umama 86, 92, 113, 123, 126, 173, 191

Abyssinia 91
'Adi ibn Hatim 6
Ahmad 16, 47, 71, 80, 103, 119
'A'isha 82, 111, 147, 150, 151, 154, 155, 158, 188, 197
'Ali ibn Abi Talib 12, 15, 48, 75, 111, 124, 134, 147, 150, 155, 171, 191, 202, 208, 210
'Ali ibn al-Husayn 38, 138-139
'Alqama ibn Mirthadd 158
al-A'mash 82
'Ammar 34, 180
'Amr ibn Abi 'Amra 188
'Amr ibn al-'As 106
'Amr ibn Hazm 149
'Amr ibn al-Muhajir 62
'Amr ibn Murra 33
Anas ibn Malik 42, 52, 55, 102, 157, 168, 209
Ash'ath, al- 86
Asiya 151
al-Asma'i 149
'Ata' 41, 148, 187, 166
'Atiyya 84
'Awn ibn 'Abdullah 15
al-Awza'i 84, 114, 157
Ayyub 151
Ayyub as-Sakhtiyani 15, 16, 52, 112, 210
backgammon 74, 75, 76
al-Badri 20
Bajala ibn 'Ada 11
Bal'am 196
Bara', al- 44
Barsisa 196
Bilal 33-34, 180
Bilal ibn al-Harith 110
Burayda 87, 111
chess 74, 75, 76
ad-Dahhak 144, 166
Dawud 55
Dhat as-Salasil 106

Fadala ibn 'Ubayd 83, 186
Fatima 83, 150, 159
al-Fudayl ibn 'Iyad 7, 70, 111, 124
al-Ghazali 137, 142, 190
hadd (hudud) 4, 70-71, 77, 84, 141
Hafs ibn Maysara 87
Hafsa 151, 200
Hakim ibn Hizam 169
al-Hasan 12, 52, 58, 156
al-Hasan ibn Dhakwan 47
Hasan al-Basri 21, 84, 115, 119, 123, 126, 149
Hashish 70-71
Hatim al-Asamm 203
Hatim ibn Abi Balta'a 207
Hayyan ibn Husayn 155
Hilal ibn al-'Ala' 126
Hisham ibn 'Abd al-Malik 95-96
Hisham ibn Hassan 131
Hudhayfa ibn al-Yaman 21, 185
Husayn ibn Mihsan 149
al-Husayn 12
Ibn 'Abbas 4, 15, 18, 21, 24, 29, 30, 31, 45, 46, 59, 66, 68, 75, 84, 85, 102, 103, 106, 118, 119, 121, 125, 128, 131, 133, 144, 146, 147. 148. 154, 162, 166, 167, 160, 178, 187, 188, 191, 194, 196, 202, 204
Ibn Hazm 15
Ibn al-Jawzi 54, 58, 59, 131, 146, 166
Ibn Mas'ud 11, 15, 24, 41, 51, 52. 86, 93, 96, 108, 109, 113, 118, 125, 129, 156, 159, 168, 172, 200, 202, 209
Ibn al-Mundhir 118
Ibn Rahawayh 16, 75
Ibn Shihab 82
Ibn Sirin 130
Ibn 'Umar 22, 30, 31, 64, 66, 67, 68, 74, 75, 82, 87, 97, 103, 115, 117, 118, 131, 132, 154, 158, 169, 172, 174, 191, 195
Ibn Umm Maktum 151, 202
Ibn Ziyad 96
Ibrahim ibn Adham 172

Ibrahim an-Nakha'i 15, 16, 76, 119
Ibrahim at-Taymi 201
'Ikrima 96, 154, 295
'Imran ibn Husayn 140
'Isa 48
Isma'il ibn Sa'id 119
Jabir ibn 'Abdullah 67, 91, 100, 148, 186, 192
Ja'far as-Sadiq 211
Jundub 11, 106
al-Juzjani 118
Ka'b al-Ahbar 31, 201
Ka'b ibn 'Ujra 62, 104
al-Kalbi 128, 130, 187
Karkara 80
Khalid ibn al-Walid 48
Khalid ibn Yarmak 92
al-Khattabi 9, 12, 16, 123, 155
Khaybar 80
al-Layth ibn Sa'd 119
Lut 45, 48, 141
Makhul 41, 96, 112
Malik 16, 84, 119
Malik ibn al-Mundhir 112
Masruq 113
al-Mawardi 166
Mi'raj *see Night Journey*
Mu'adh ibn Jabal 62, 77, 90, 93, 111, 132, 151
Mu'awiya 10
Mu'awiya ibn Iyas 161
Muhammad ibn Ka'b 75
Muhammad ibn al-Mubarak 124
Muhammad ibn Wasi' 111, 112
Muhammad ibn Yusuf al-Faryabi 26
Mujahid 76, 84, 125, 148, 169, 178, 197, 205
Muqatal ibn Hayyan 144, 167
Musa 18, 33, 42, 63, 97, 166, 167
nabidh 69
Nafi' 115, 195
an-Nawawi 75, 160, 190
Night Journey 33, 108, 176
Qabisa 147

Qadariyya 131-132
Qarun 14, 166-167
Qatada 50, 123, 146, 166
ar-Rabi' ibn Anas 125
ar-Rabi' ibn Khuthaym 203
ar-Rafi'i 119
Rifa'a ibn Yazid 80
Sa'd ibn Abi Waqqas 13, 157, 189
Sa'd ibn 'Ubada 157
Sa'id ibn Jubayr 29, 132
Sa'id ibn al-Musayyab 13, 84, 96,
119, 201, 203
Sahl ibn 'Abdullah 175
Sahl ibn Sa'd 196
Salama ibn al-Akwa' 63
Salih al-Murri 163-165
Salim 196
Salman al-Farisi 21, 170
Samura ibn Jundub 41
ash-Sha'bi 125, 148, 163
ash-Shafi'i 16, 74, 84, 119, 158, 162
Shaqi ibn Mati' 121
Shurayh (Qadi) 95, 112, 163
as-Suddi 53, 96, 194
Suffa 181
Sufyan ath-Thawri 57, 75, 96, 103,
112, 119, 178
Suhayb 34, 180, 180
Talha ibn 'Ubaydullah 111
Tawus 95
Thabit ad-Dahhak 107
Thawban 163
'Ubada ibn as-Samit 20
'Umar ibn 'Abd al-'Aziz 112, 138
'Umar ibn al-Khattab 11, 15, 20, 29,
51, 62, 85, 104, 118, 123, 131, 134,
150, 151-152,157, 159, 203, 207, 210
Umm 'Atiyya 156
Umm Habiba 178
Umm Kulthum 178
Umm Salama 69,163
Umm Sulaym 161
'Uqba ibn 'Amir 77, 118. 196
Usama ibn Zayd 82, 158, 160, 169

'Uthman ibn 'Affan 118, 134, 210
Wahb ibn al-Ward 103
Wahb ibn Munabbih 11, 33, 91, 112
al-Wahidi 84, 100, 106, 125, 128,
146, 148, 206
Waki' ibn al-Jarrah 75
al-Walibi 84, 146
al-Walid ibn 'Uqba 136
Wathila ibn al-Asqa' 76
wittol 43,116
Yahya ibn Abi Kathir 136
Yusuf ibn Asbat 103
az-Zajjaj 144
zakat, 22-27, 79, 90, 94, 141, 194
Zamzam 38
Zayd ibn Arqam 104
Zayd ibn Khalid 80,146
az-Zubayr ibn 'Abd al-Muttalib 115